TINKER, TAILOR, SOLDIER, ARTIST

The Story of Ron Baker - A Child of the Black Country

Written by Ann Gallo

Illustrated by Ron Baker

To. John Hughes

With Best Wishes.   Ron Baker,
March 2002

Sedgley History Society

First Impression November 2001

ISBN 0 904015 64 5

Produced by Waterloo Design & Print PLC incorporating
Reliance Printing Works, Birmingham Street, Halesowen,
West Midlands B63 3HW.

CONTENTS

FOREWORD

RON Baker seems to be part of the very fabric of Sedgley. He is well known by a wide variety of people throughout an extensive area and for a variety of different reasons. Some will know him for his skills as a bespoke ladies and gentlemen's tailor, and others for his almost compulsive desire to record the streets, scenes and buildings of the area's past through his skill as an artist. His two Pictorial histories of Sedgley are already highly collectable, though there is an even greater value in their contribution towards the archival record of Sedgley's past. His involvement as Treasurer of The Sedgley Local History Society from its beginning in 1984, has added another dimension to his service to the area. Now, at last, he presents his own complete story. A history of a childhood beginning in Woodsetton at the end of the First World War to the present day, encompassing his craft training, his own wartime military service, and all that has happened to him since, in a life lived to the full. It has been my privilege to know Ron from the day he first measured me for a suit at "Quality Clothes" to his friendship at the Local History Society, and particularly in our shared interests in Local History where we have been able to provide information for each other. He has greatly helped me both in his advice and search for material amongst his many friends, for my own books, and I have enjoyed to the full those opportunities we have created for sharing some of each other's enthusiasms.

Trevor Genge.

"THE MORE THINGS CHANGE . . . ."

INTRODUCTION

THIS is a story of an ordinary boy, born to an ordinary family, in an ordinary home in the heart of the Black Country in the early part of the twentieth century . It tells of the hardship that he endured and the hurdles he surmounted, the disappointments he overcame and the efforts he made to achieve his goal and to make a success of his life.

His childhood was spent in the rigorous twenties, and despite his intelligence, studious nature and artistic leanings, the lack of money was to hamper his endeavours and thwart his latent ambition. Firstly, he was denied a grammar school education and later he was to be prevented from taking up a professional apprenticeship because of the absence of the necessary funds.

Although he never became the architect he wanted to be, he has left behind, for the people of the Black Country, a legacy. This legacy is their history - a reminder of how they were and how they came to be what they are. His pictures of their streets and buildings will remain, when so much of the reality has been removed by progress.

The buildings may have changed and the landscape may be different but the people of the district do not alter. They remain as diverse and full of character as in his youth. Hence - the more things change, the more they stay the same.

RON'S TALE

FIRST YEARS
(1918 - 1932)

"YOU was lucky, ducks," she said as she scrubbed her hands over the bowl. "I wish they was all that easy."

The baby cried as if to testify to its existance and another child joined in from outside the door, having been denied the presence of his mother for far too long. Kenneth was two and felt that he was missing all the fun.

The room was lit by an oil-lamp and the bed almost filled the tiny room into which the new child had been born. The rest of the house was small too - just one more bedroom upstairs and the living room downstairs. There was no gas or electricity, and water was obtained from a tap in the back "Brew-House", next to the earth closet.

The new lad, soon to be named Arthur Ronald, was born on the eve of Armistice day - 10th November 1918, a time of new hope to so many more than just little Ron's parents.

The home into which Ron had been born was typical of the Black Country. A coal fire provided the heating and cooking in a black-leaded cast iron grate with an oven to one side. The pots too were cast iron and a spit hung over the top of the fire. A Dutch oven was placed in front of the fire and used to cook bacon, sausage, eggs and fried bread in the fat which dripped into it from the spit. A large stew-pot containing a selection of vegetables and perhaps a pig's trotter or a rabbit could often be found within the oven late at night as the fire was dying down, and there it would stay slowly cooking until the next day. The fire, remade in the morning, would then be used to toast a chunk of bread using a long-handled brass fork. If the bread should happen to drop in the ashes it would get a quick flick of Mom's apron and a bit of a blow and was then stuck back on the fork - nothing went to waste in this house. "A bit of ash never killed anyone," she'd say.

The house was typical of the area - no better and no worse. All showed signs of the hard life the occupants lived and the struggles they experienced in keeping the wolf from the door. But Ron grew up in a happy home with friendly, helpful neighbours and his infancy was not a time of great discomfort.

By the time Ron was old enough to go to school, a third son had been born and, as Gordon was just a few weeks old when the new school year started, Ken, now all of seven years old, took his little brother to the West Coseley Church of England Infants School, attached to St. Chad's church. Their parents thought the seven- year-old quite capable of taking his younger brother on the mile-long walk to school and back again every day in all weathers. The journey consisted of a short walk along Vicarage Road, turning left past the Vicarage itself through a large gateway and along a dirt road that led to the church. The young lads then went through another closed gateway past the Mill and Millhouse, past a small collection of cottages and across another road before reaching the Church schools. In fact the boys made this journey four times a day as there was no provision for eating a mid-day meal in school and they would have to return home after morning lessons to eat a quick meal before returning for the afternoon lessons.

This daily trudge continued back and forth for three years until Ron was eight when he moved up to Mount Pleasant junior school and another half mile was added to his journey in each direction. The year was 1926 just one year before the new Birmingham road was opened.

Ron would remember with great affection those formative years in his infant and junior schools and not surprisingly could recall that the Misses Salt, Pepper and Snead soon became Miss Salt, Miss Pepper and Miss Sneeze.

These school days passed happily enough and at the age of ten he was moved up to the senior school. Now he was in his element as he began to learn the skills which were to control his life and work. His practical skills in art and woodwork were very apparent from the outset and his teacher was none too gentle in instilling in the youngsters the need for careful handling of the tools.

If the plane was inadvertantly placed on its base the master would come up behind the offending boy, spank the lad's bottom with the flat of his hand and shout "Don't leave it on its bottom."

Or if a piece of timber was seen to be gripped too tightly in the vice he would pinch the bottom of the miscreant and yell "Don't pinch the wood in the vice."

Painful lessons, but mistakes were seldom repeated!

Ron was a diligent child and was always in the top group throughout his education. By the age of twelve he could draw a map of the world and mark on it all the rivers, capital cities and mountains. He often gained top marks in both art and geography and one of his first successes in the field of art was in a public competition. A local firm called Claco-Grates had advertised in all the local schools to illustrate a tile to fit in with their grate designs. Young Ron won with his design and watercolour and was awarded the mighty sum of five shillings as his prize. Having never had more than sixpence in his whole life this was riches indeed, and he bought his first real fountain pen and a bottle of ink from Woolworths in Dudley market-place to celebrate his new found wealth.

His confidence in his studies grew apace and whenever the teacher asked the class a question you could be sure Ron's hand would be the first to shoot up. At times his teacher, Mr Greensill, could be heard to say, with just a little exasperation "Oh, not you again Baker."

But his studious nature had been noticed and he was selected to take extra private tuition in order to prepare him, with two or three other boys, for a special examination to get a free place into Dudley Grammar School. The examination was to take place at Bilston Girl's High School on a Saturday morning and, as Ron's parents showed no interest in taking him, the determined youngster decided to go it alone. The fact that it was nearly three miles away and the bus only ran every hour and he had missed it, did not deter the young chap. He just set out to walk, up to his knees in snow! He knew the way to Ladymoor as his Aunt lived there and when he arrived at the large pool he chanced to meet up with some people who were on their way to Bilston, and they accompanied him the rest of the journey. He found the school and the examination hall where the pupils had already started the test. The time allocated was two hours, so, not knowing how much time he had lost, he sat himself down in his alloted desk and began his task.

All this effort had made him hungry so when he had completed the examination and all the children were allowed to leave, Ron went into Bilston Market to buy himself something to eat and drink. He then retraced his steps home, intent on regaling his parents with tales of his eventful day. But his Mother was too busy to listen and his Father did not seem all that interested. Poor Ron had to store up his excitement and await the outcome of his efforts on his own. He was just eleven years old and in 1929 he was offered a place at Dudley Boys' Grammar school.

All the school fees would be paid for by the local authority, but his uniform and satchel would have to be bought by his parents. They must have discussed this, as, just as Ron was getting used to the idea of his success and what it would mean, they called him to them and informed him that he would not be able to accept the place.

"We have three of you to bring up," his Dad said "We just can't afford it."

At this moment Ron really knew what it meant to be 'working-class' and resolved to improve his lot by sheer hard graft.

The dream was ended. All he had to look forward to was leaving school at fourteen, getting a job and making some money to bring into the house.

Apart from this disappointment, Ron's schooldays were to be a happy time, and in the five years he spent at Mount Pleasant he never had a day off school. He had to plead with his Mother on several occasions for her not to keep him away for family outings, such were his feelings for his studies. At the end of his time there he received a certificate for excellent attendance from the local education authority.

Despite his obvious liking for school he, like any other lad, looked forward to the holidays and the odd half day which would be granted on special occasions.

One such event took place when he had just started at the senior school in 1927. The Prince of Wales came to open the Wolverhampton to Birmingham New Road at Coseley.

The excitable children assembled, class by class, marching along in lines to stand on the pit clay banks (which later, in 1935, were to become Coseley Jubilee Park), and waved their Union Jacks. They watched the Prince arrive in an open-topped car and walk over to cut the ribbon. Along with the rest of the crowd, they cheered - as much for the occasion as for the fact that they had the afternoon off when it was all over!

The year before this opening had seen much different scenes along this stretch of countryside. It was the time of the Great Strike of 1926 and few of the people around had money coming in to heat their homes or to feed their families. A digger was used to cut the gorge through the high ground near what is now the King Arthur Public House, and a coal seam was discovered just yards beneath the surface. The news spread like wild-fire and, as soon as the workmen had left for the night, all the villagers descended on the area, with spades, shovels, buckets and any other useful utensils they could lay their hands on, to dig out the coal.

Next morning, when the workmen returned, the whole area was a total mess and the engineers had to send all the available carts to the local steel works at Coseley to collect large clinkers to shore up the sides of the gulley to prevent it from falling in.

These stones can still be seen in the sides of the banks today, a reminder of the hard times experienced by the people of the Black Country. But, when finished, this major new road made a big impression on people's lives and altered their landscape as much as their mode of travel. It was a broad, straight road when it was first made and had wide grass verges down which many people still rode on horse-back. Many years later, these were to be reduced when the road was made dual-carriageway.

The local milkman, Clem Wheeler, was a small farmer, who kept his few cows in sheds behind his house in Vicarage Road.

Before the New Road was built, Clem would drive his cattle down a small lane by the brook which led to the meadows where they grazed. Once the road was under construction there was a problem. The cattle could not cross the workings, and a tunnel had to be dug under the road, just wide enough for the cows to pass in single-file. It's still there today, but the meadows have long gone, having given way to an industrial estate.

As a young lad Ron would sometimes be given the job of going out into the street to wait for Clem on his milk-round. Ron would stand, with jug in hand, until Clem appeared with his horse and trap bearing the churns full of fresh milk. Beside the large churn was a small pail with two metal jugs hanging from it. These were half and one-pint measures. Clem would fill the pail with milk from the churn and carry it with the measuring jugs to each house on his round. Then he would use the jugs to deliver the required amount of milk into each customer's own milk-jug.

"A quart today." Ron would say, as his Mom had given him the big jug, and Clem would fill his pint measure from the foaming creamy liquid, then carefully pour it into the container. A second measure was added as Ron gripped his precious load tightly, then a wink from Clem as he dipped his measure in the pail a third time and gave the lad a drop extra. "Just for luck", he'd say.

Once the road was completed, Coseley Council decided to plant flowering cherry trees along both sides of it from their boundary at Parkfield Road at one end, to the Dudley boundary by the Castle grounds at the other. Each tree had a metal fence around it and bore a plaque with the name of a Coseley soldier who had been killed in the First World War.

Ron, aged 7 years being ducked into the village brook by his mom.

Ron tormenting the curate of St. Chads, West Coseley, 1925.

Many were the times that Ron would wander down the grass verge, on the way back from school, reading the inscriptions on each plaque bearing the name and regiment of one local hero. He could recognise many of these names as being repeated in the names of childen in his school, "perhaps those men were their relatives; fathers or uncles", he thought as he passed them by each day.

Another consequence of the new road was the amount of housing which had to be demolished along its path. Many of Ron's school pals who lived in Ebenezer Street and Bond Street saw their homes fall to make way for it. One family, called Smout, were told that they were to lose their home, but it was reprieved and from being a quiet terrace house with a private garden it became a noisy home with its tiny back-yard over looking a major thorough-fare, and across the road from Ebenezer chapel.

When Ron was eight years old, he and his brother Ken and their Uncle Ben sang in the choir at St Chad's, and after church the Vicar, Father Rose, would allow them to play croquet on the vicarage lawn. This was soon brought to a halt as the land was needed for the road and the lawn was reduced to one quarter of its original size.

At first, after the road was opened, there were very few cars travelling along it, but one memorable sight was a coach and horses which came by occasionally carrying fee-paying passengers between Shrewsbury and Birmingham. Upon approaching Coseley the coachman would sound his horn and people would come out of their houses to wave and cheer as it passed by.

Ron was never to have the luxury of this form of travel but, during the twenties, he would travel on the bone-shaking solid wheeled 'charabanc'. The annual choir outing - the highlight of the year, was in Ted Barnett's coach. It had a canvas top and rows of seats which stretched from one side of the coach to the other, and with a small door between each row. The solid wheels made for a very bumpy ride along some of the rough lanes over which the coach often drove. The journey was never very long, however, usually no more than to the Shrewsbury Flower Show. This was a favourite of Ron, with his already developing artistic eye. He particularly liked the excitement of the rousing music played by the Military Band which performed on these occasions and he would also enjoy a boat trip on the river if his meagre pocket money could stretch to it.

When Mr Barnett finally changed his coach to one with a fixed top and the fancy new pneumatic tyres (or 'blow-up' tyres as the lads liked to call them) things changed considerably and longer journeys could be undertaken in relative comfort.

As a child, Ron longed to go to the sea-side, but the family circumstances denied him this simple pleasure until one memorable day in 1930 when he was almost twelve years old.

Ron, Ken, Mom and Hilda (Mom's best friend) walked to Deepfields Station to catch a Special Excursion steam train to Liverpool, Lime Street station which Ron knew to be somewhere way up north and across the river from their true destination, which was New Brighton. At Lime Street, the boys were wide-eyed at the sight of the stationmaster bedecked in his dark frock-coat and a tall hat on his head as he oversaw all the comings and goings of the busy station. It was a magical day and the memories had to keep him going for many years and it was to be some time before he would see the sea again.

Ron savoured every moment of this wonderful treat. Each new experience added to the excitement; the smell of the train, the clatter of the metal tracks, the noise of the busy platforms as they alighted were all noted with wide-eyed innocence. But more was to come. From the station the little group made their way to the docks and the ferry-boat which was to carry them over the Mersey to New Brighton.

Ron and Ken grasped the rails which ran down the side of the ferry-boat and watched the other traffic along the river. All of this was such a novelty to the pair of brothers that they kept pulling at the other's sleeve and pointing out each new vessel in case the other had missed it .

"Hey look, our Ken! That smokey black one. It ain't arf dirty." declared Ron .

Then a shiny ferry steamer, similar to the one they were on passed going back to Liverpool and the lads waved frantically, to be rewarded for their efforts by some returned waves from the passengers who, in jovial holiday mood were also watching the activity on the busy river.

The happy little band disembarked at their destination and a short walk brought them to the sandy beach. Mom and 'Aunt' Hilda lugged their shopping bags full of sandwiches and 'pop', a slice or two of cake and an apple for each of them. Ron and Ken settled down to the serious business of sand-castle building. They had seen a tower on the head-land and Ron, with his usual meticulous eye for detail, set out to make a copy of it with the damp sand.

When this was accomplished they found a pool containing wonderful creatures which they cautiously extracted from the water with a piece of drift-wood and inspected in minute detail before dropping them back with a satisfying 'plop', and giggled together as they watched the small crab or shrimp scuttle away again.

Then to the fairground with its own special sounds and smells. A ride on the galloping-horses and a slide down the helter-skelter and the boys' day of fun was complete.

They trudged weary but happy back to the ferry to retrace their steps home, their young heads full of all the new sights of the day.

And back to reality!

In the early '20s, the majority of the basic fresh foods were delivered to the doorstep by travelling tradesmen. Milk was of course delivered every day. Green-grocery was available twice a week on Tuesday and Friday and, in addition, on Friday, there would also be supplies of fresh fish and rabbits. When he arrived at the end of each lane, Mr Nicklin, perched on his cart pulled by a dappled horse called George, would yell through cupped hands to let the people know he was around. The youngsters loved to stand alongside the cart whilst their Mother made her purchases. What they really wanted to see was Mr Nicklin's party trick when a rabbit was bought. It was chosen in its fur, but before it was handed over, he would skin the animal with deft slits around the feet and head with a sharp knife, then some clever slight of hand and the rabbit lay stripped and ready for the pot.

Another essential commodity, especially during the winter months, was paraffin. This arrived on another interesting van, stacked with jangling pots, pans, brushes and other household hardwear. The paraffin tank was at the back of the van with the tap opening over the tailgate for easy delivery into the customer's own can. This vendor was Mr White and Ron looked forward to his fortnightly visits.

One particularly intriguing traveller the lads liked to see in their area was the knife sharpener on his specially adapted bicycle. As he slowly passed down the alley, giving his own distinctive call to herald his approach, the woman would bring out the knives or scissors to be sharpened, or the men would bring their shears, and the chap would leap off his bike, flip it over so that it stood on the handle-bars and saddle, and a grinding wheel would be visible. This was connected to the back wheel in such a way that, when the pedal was wound quickly, the grinding wheel spun round and could be used to sharpen the tools. The children loved to watch the sparks fly and were occasionally allowed to help in turning the pedal, their eager faces flushed and eyes bright with the effort.

Once a month, an old lady called Morgan came, pushing a three wheeled wicker barrow piled high with various drapery and linen items.

She was very slow in her progress through the streets as she was blind in one eye.

Another favourite traveller of the local children at that time was the 'jam-jar man'. He had an adapted cart which had been converted into a round-about. The payment for a ride was one empty jam jar. This man had a bit of competition from another man who gave the youngsters a goldfish for two jars. This took a bit of organising, as a third jar containing water was also needed to collect your goldfish. The children were often disappointed at how quickly their new aquisition died as they knew nothing about feeding them and the fish seldom lasted more than a few days.

Coal was delivered by lorry and a ton of the stuff was tipped into the roadway at the nearest point to the house. Ron's Mum would take two coal buckets out to the glistening stack and first choose some of the biggest pieces to carry back down the entry and build a retaining dam so that when she took the bucketsful of smaller lumps they would be held in place. It took a long time to complete the task of carrying all this coal and when it was finished Ron and Ken would be given the job of sweeping up the last tiny pieces and the dust left in the road, leaving it all clean again. Then the path and entry were washed down with pails of water and swept carefully to remove all the grime that had accumulated to ensure it was not carried into their or the neighbour's houses.

The most important daily commodity was also delivered to the home by horse-drawn van and Ron would marvel at the huge shire-horse which would plod along stopping and starting at regular intervals, as its load gradually diminished over its journey. This was the bread van and its progress was slow as it stopped so often to deliver the goods it carried; crusty loaves, small rolls and sometimes sticky currant buns would be popped into Mom's basket for a special teatime treat.

A 'jack-of-all-trades' was also a welcome sight when jobs around the house needed doing. Tools were dear to buy and Ron's father, like most other men, had few of his own. The house was rented anyway, so the family were reliant upon the landlord paying for any repairs that were needed. The travelling repairmen most often seen, were brothers from Tipton, who would travel around the area with a push-cart containing all their essential materials; roof-slates, sand, cement, some lengths of spouting and a few tools were stacked on or around the ladders on the back of the cart.

Ron particularly liked to watch Mr Bates at work. He was the painter and decorator and Ron would sit and watch him work for hours when he was wood-graining a front door. The shapes and swirls which developed fascinated the lad and he knew that this would be something he would like to do in the future. Ron was intrigued to see how Mr Bates managed his intricate work with a finger missing. He had had an accident years previously which had left him hampered but still a capable and sort-after artisan.

The local blacksmith actually lived in the same street as Ron and his family. He could produce anything in metal and on occasion could be seen shoeing the tradesmen's horses. Here too Ron learned his love of design as he saw the products of this man's craft develop.

Although the proper name of the village was Woodsetton, one area of it took on a new name when public transport began to run through the village. The local public house was called 'The Swan' and, as the bus approached this stop, the conductor would call out "Anyone for The Swan?" and so it became known as Swan Village.

The pubs were naturally a pivotal part of village life during Ron's childhood years. Fathers would send their young sons to their local with a screw-topped bottle so that they could have a drink of beer with their meal after a hard day's work. Ron would take his Dad's bottle and hand it to Mrs Holden, who would fill it up, then carefully put a gummed sticker over the stopper to ensure that the full measure arrived back home without the lad taking a swig of the tantalising contents.

At the back of the pub was a crown bowling green where Ron's Dad played. Mrs Holden's nephew would take Ron onto the green when no-one was using it. They would borrow some woods out of the shed and amuse themselves pretending to be grown-ups, and not the twelve year olds that they really were.

There was also an 'off-licence' in a side street called Regent Street. This place brewed its own beers and had its own clients with a taste for its products.

The only other pub in the village was The Summer House, next to the chapel. This was run by Mr Reynolds and his wife. They had arrived in the village with their two sons and the wife's unmarried sister, Elsie. The boys were Lawson and his brother, Reg, who became a special friend of Ron.

Mr Reynolds became a local councillor and the Tory party members would hold their meetings in the clubroom at the back of the pub. Ron was playing games in the front dining room with Reg while one such meeting was taking place, when his Dad came in and told him to take the white enamal bucket round to the off-licence in the next street to collect some beer for the meeting. Ron thought this very strange as

St. Chads Church, West Coseley and the mill and mill-house.

Ron's birth house with him sitting in front of the fire place.

20

they were sitting in a public house, but assumed that even publicans felt like a change once in a while.

In the late twenties Mr Reynolds, who as well as keeping the Summer House with his wife, also worked at the Coseley steelworks. He was cycling to work one morning when he was knocked down and killed by a lorry as they were both crossing the narrow hump-backed bridge at Deepfields.

Mr Reynolds had served in the 1914-18 war and had been decorated for his actions. He was granted a military funeral, which was a great honour and an unusual event in the small village. Apart from the personal significance to Ron, as this was his best friend's father, the pomp of the occasion was to move him too. The coffin was placed on a gun-carriage and a Union Jack draped over it. The carriage was then drawn by four horses to the church and afterwards to the cemetry.

Ron's parents had lived at 17 Sedgley Street, Woodsetton since 1916 and had seen many changes as their family grew. Joseph Baker and Lilian had many friends but one particular woman remained Lilian's close friend and confidante. The house, as has been said, was rented, but Joe was not to appreciate the significance of their landlord and his family until he moved into his first home with Lilian, his new wife. Their landlord was Tom Smith, who also owned the grocery store at the end of the row. Tom had a son, also called Tom, and a daughter called Hilda.

Hilda and Lilian had been great friends at school but had lost touch until, by chance, Joe had found this place to rent and make his home. The women were delighted to re-establish their old friendship and from then on the lives of the Bakers and the Smiths became entwined.

Young Tom was a good sportsman and played for Woodsetton Rovers. He would cycle to work at Perry's in Bradley and one Sunday took Ron on his cross-bar to see the place where he worked. Ron was only nine and had never seen inside a factory. He was amazed at the vast space and the enormous size of the machinery and the metal rolls which Tom said came from Germany.

Tom got married in 1928 and Ron lost touch with him.

Hilda never married however but spent many hours with Lilian's family and became 'Aunty Hilda' to the boys and often accompanied them on family outings. Her Mother was taken ill at a relatively young age and it fell to Hilda to take over her position at the family shoe shop at Princess End. During school holidays or on saturdays, Hilda would sometimes take Ron with her to the shop. They would have to walk to FiveWays Tipton to catch a tram to the High Street. Ron could fill his time looking through the other premises near the shoe shop.

Nearby was a haulage contractor which was particularly fascinating to Ron. He loved to watch a transformation which took place in the back of the premises especially during the summer months. He would watch as the workmen unbolted the container from the rear of one of the large lorries, remove it, then drive the vehicle further into the yard to the garage, where up above, suspended on beams was a strange shell which was then lowered onto the base. When it was bolted in place, the lorry had miraculously been transformed into a charabanc.

Rows of seats stretched from side to side and a canvas hood rolled up at the back to be used in case it rained. Ron never wearied of watching this clever manoevre.

As well as accompanying Hilda to work, Ron would also keep her Mother company in her nice warm living room. The Smith's home was much bigger and more opulent than that of the Bakers, so this was hardly an imposition to him. Hilda was a Sunday-school teacher, and often had stacks of children's books which she had bought as prizes. There were also piles of goods for the grocery shop lining the hallway. Very few of them were in cardboard boxes but were wrapped around in thick white paper with coloured advertisements on the side. These sheets were never burnt, but salvaged for Ron to draw on and he would use the children's books and this paper, happily passing the time away copying the figures from the colourful illustrations which he found. The cowboys and indians were a special favourite of his.

The Smith's house was large and imposing with a shop at the front, under which was a cellar reached by stone steps. A spacious sitting room was behind the shop, separated from it by a glass door. Another door from the sitting room opened out onto the verandah and a third to the upper floor. The sitting room had a low open fire and an elaborate black marble clock chimed regularly. Alcoves on either side of the fireplace housed two large cupboards and a set of drawers which held the household linen. Against one wall was a stately shiny black piano which had two brass candlesticks which could lie flat against the piano or swing out at right-angles when they were used to illuminate the sheet-music. A large dinner table dominated the centre of the room and four chairs stood neatly around it, with two more placed against the wall. A single-drop treadle sewing machine stood near the window under which was Mr Smith's large easy chair.

The spacious verandah housed a variety of large evergreen pot plants on a table under the window and a collection of smaller pots lined up along the wall facing the side entry door. This side door would at times be used by customers who needed something from the shop outside opening hours. The kitchen led off from the verandah and, as their situation permitted and their social standing required, the Smith's had a servant. She was a girl by the name of May Cartwright who lived in Regent Street and was kept busy in the Smith's house, in the kitchen, washing, cooking and baking as well as cleaning the house and keeping the fires made-up in cold weather. The kitchen was the hub of the home and, even in this house, there was still no bathroom and bathing also took place here.

The eldest Baker brother helped out in the shop part-time until he reached the age of fourteen, when he left school to take up permanent employment at Price's bed and cycle shop in Sedgley. It was now Ron's turn to help out in the grocery shop which he did quite willingly most Saturdays for the princely sum of sixpence. His first job each morning was to take down the shutters which was quite a task for such a small boy, still only twelve years old. There were eight pieces in all, and, although only just over a foot wide, they were nearly six feet high. Ron was told that he must never try to do this if it was windy as they could be blown into the windows and glass was very expensive to replace. When the shutters were neatly stacked in sequence Ron would then go down to the cool cellar to fetch the dairy produce which had been stored there overnight to keep fresh. Milk could by this time be bought from shops. The milk crate contained two dozen bottles and Ron could just manage to manoevre it up to the shop by hoisting it up the stone steps one at a time counting each one as he did so - all fourteen of them. Then back he would go for butter, cheese and maybe a boiled ham or a piece of bacon.

Throughout the day, it was Ron's job to check to see which goods needed replacing and to fill in the gaps on the shelves. All the extra stock was kept in the old bakery behind the house so it was quite a trek to go and fetch an odd item if anything was missing and customers didn't always have time to wait for it to be brought back.

The shop itself was 'A' shaped. It was entered down two stone steps on the left of which was a display window containing examples of the goods to be found within the shop. Shelves inside the shop and down the walls were stacked with large glass jars containing a variety of colourful items, including the children's favourite sweets. Care had to be taken to ensure that the tops were screwed on tightly so that the contents did not go soft.

Mr Smith had his own special position where he could invariably be seen sharpening one of his long knives on the steel in readiness for slicing the bacon or ham on his counter. This section of the shop was separated from the rest of the counter by a partition to the side of which was a container for the remnants of the bacon or mis-shaped chunks of ham which had been discarded as not being of top quality. Towards the end of the week, when money was running out for some of the poorest families, they would come in and ask for a 'penn'uth' of the bacon-bits to help to feed their family. These, together with the few vegetables which many families grew in their back gardens, made a tasty and nutritious meal. The other cold meat found on this counter was corned-beef, which came in large slightly tapering tins. The tins were always opened by Mr Smith who had a strong tin-opener with a handle in the shape of a bull's head. The wider end of the can was cut off, the can turned upside down over the counter and a gentle knock on the base caused the solid contents to slide out. The deep pink block of meat, speckled with flecks of creamy coloured fat was then lain on its side ready for slicing. The can itself was squashed flat, firstly so that it took up less space, but also so that the jagged edges posed less of a danger to those handling the rubbish.

Further down the counter where it joined the main serving area was the large weighing scales. To one side were the weights, some brass and some cast iron. These were checked every so often by the Weights and Measures office in Roseville.

Some items on sale required the customer to bring their own container in order to carry them home. One such item was pickles. The jar or jug was placed on the scales and weighed first, then the brass weight, corresponding to the amount of the goods required was added to the scale and then the food (often pickled onions or red cabbage) was added to the jar until the scales balanced out again. Ron liked to watch this process.

A large cold slab housed the margerine, butter and cheese. The butter always arrived in wooden tubs and was weighed onto greaseproof paper on the scalepan before being patted into shape and wrapping up. The cheese arrived wrapped in cotton scrim, which was carefully peeled off, then a fine piece of wire was wound round it and pulled tightly using the wooden handles at each end of the wire. This cut the whole cheese in half and the process was repeated to obtain smaller and smaller portions and the use of the wire meant that the cheese cut through smoothly without breaking up. Next to this was a sizeable tin containing broken biscuits. One of Ron's jobs was to sort these out occasionally and weigh them out into bags. Further along still the bread-bins could be found, under the small counter. Bread was now delivered to the shops early each day, always fresh and crusty, and each morning the young children would be sent to fetch the day's supply for the family. You could be sure that by the time the loaf reached home a corner had been nibbled off.

Hanging from the inner corner ceiling was a large scale-pan which was used to measure the quantities of dry ingredients bought in bigger sacks; ten, twenty or even forty pound amounts. These goods were malt, barley, hops and food for the poultry and pigeons that many families kept in their back-yards. Sometimes Mr Smith would use a quiet moment to weigh out these commodities into sacks, label them and place them against the counter in readiness. Sugar, too, was weighed out from a large sack. This was always sold in special bags made of thick blue paper.

In the Twenties and early Thirties, most items were sold loose and people also relied on the village shop for medicines, pills and potions to cure common ailments and even toothache, as they couldn't afford to go to the Doctor or the Dentist unless it was a genuine emergency.

A cane chair was situated by the main counter to be used by the older customers. They could put their shopping basket on the counter and give their list to whoever was serving at the time. Each item would be assembled from around the shop while the elderly customer sat and chatted. Very few people paid for the goods as they went along during the week, but Mr Smith would keep a careful record in his ledger and then enter the amount into the customers own small account book. Each one would then settle up at the end of the week when their husband had been paid. When, as it sometimes happened, the man had had a short week, only a portion of the bill could be paid and the full amount was repaid when the situation improved.

Salt was sold from large blocks supplied to the shop by Wattons travelling salt people. Ron would watch all the transactions carefully and on one occasion heard Mr Smith ask the price of the block. The reply was "One shilling."

"It was only eleven pence last week!" exclaimed Mr Smith.

"OK. You can have it for that then" was the response.

Ron then watched as Mr Watton went back to his van, take his saw and slice a piece off the block so Mr Smith was, unknowingly, only getting eleven pence worth anyway. The losers were of course the customers, as Mr Smith would take his own saw and meticulously cut it into twelve slices and then each into half again to give twenty-four chunks, each of which sold for one penny.

Another job which Ron liked to do was to serve the children their sweets. This was usually on Saturday morning after they had received

Ken (aged 5) and Ron (aged 3).

their meagre pocket money. Toffee came in slabs, each flavour in a different box; cream, palm, nut, treacle - each child had his or her own favourite. There was a special small set of brass scales to weigh the toffee and a little hammer to break it into pieces. Inevitably tiny fragments of the toffee flew off across the counter as Ron hit the block and when he had finished serving, he would scoop the bits back into the box. Every so often, when the block was finished, the container would be cleaned out, the fragments collected up and Ron would be given them as a treat.

Ron, being a healthy young lad, rarely had to make use of any of the patent medicines which were to found in the shop, but one weakness did cause him considerable discomfort. He had very poor teeth as a child and many a time he would be crying in pain with a warm pillow to his face, lying in front of the fire to alleviate his agony. His Dad would go across to the pub to fetch a tot of whisky for Ron to put on the hollow tooth to ease his pain. A visit to the dentist at that time was not something that anyone relished.

Ron's younger brother, Gordon, was not so fortunate with his health, however, as when he was only four years old he contracted rheumatic fever. The family had just recovered from the death of Grandad Jeavons who had been living with them for about three years. Gordon had been the apple of his eye and his blond curly head made him stand out beside the old man's massive frame. The double shock of the young boy's dreadful illness after the loss of Lilian's father was almost too much for her to bear and she had to watch as he became thin and emaciated as the disease took its toll. The frail skeletal body was stronger than they had imagined, as he pulled through with the help of his family's love and care. The effects of the illness were to remain with him, however, as he was declared medically unfit to serve in the Second World War years later as a result of it.

Apart from school and helping in the shop, Ron and his family did what most other people did in those days - created their own entertainment.

Bank holidays meant time together, going to a local beauty spot such as Penn Common or Kinver Edge. The Common was not too far and they would go laden down with all the day's necessities; drinks, sandwiches, games-equipment and rugs to sit on. Buses might take them part of the way but then they would have to share out the load and continue on foot.

Locals on the Common would be happy to take advantage of the occasion and would set out tables and chairs and had baked cakes and prepared tea and sandwiches to cater for the influx of visitors. Also on these days, the ice-cream man was there to supply a really special sweet treat. He carried his goods on a motor-cycle, which, instead of a normal side-car, had an adapted box containing two drums of ice-cream packed around with the ice. When both drums were empty, the vendor, Mr Pioli, had to return to Owen Street in Tipton to replenish his stock.

Nearer to home for Ron was Dudley Castle which was always open at holiday-times and a fete was held on special occasions. In November there would be a fire-work display and the explosions would light up the ruins causing the younger spectators to squeal with glee.

They did not all need the public display as many families celebrated Bonfire Night in their own back gardens. Ron's friend, Jack Flavell lived in a back-to-back terraced house with a large communal garden behind it. At the beginning of October Jack, Ron and their mates would start to collect the poor quality coal called 'bats', which were to be found at the disused open-cast mine holes. They were quite heavy and the boys used a make-shift trolley, made of strips of wood and a set of old pram-wheels to carry their booty home. These 'bats' would be carried two or three at a time back to the garden, and then just before Bonfire Night they would be built into a circular fire about three feet high. Gaps were left between the slabs to allow air to circulate and also to allow potatoes to be cooked in the fire. Anyone was allowed to attend the party provided they brought a firework with them!

The fire sometimes lasted twenty-four hours and the children's clothes reeked of smoke when they had finished their fun.

If the Baker family wanted a day out they could set off very early in the morning, walk to Five Ways Tipton and catch a tram to Dudley Station. They would change there and get on another which passed through the town on towards Brierley Hill, through Wordsley and arrived at Stourbridge Bus Station. There the family would alight and find a single-decker tram which passed via Stourton through the countryside until it arrived at their intended destination of Kinver. The journey took the best part of two hours and although it was in reality not many miles from home, the children felt that it was another world. They would climb through the trees to the top of Kinver Edge and play among the gorse and heather and run freely on the open common ground. The boys always took a bat and ball with them and would encourage other youngsters they met to join in their games.

From the Edge they could look out and see for miles. Dudley church spire and Gornal Windmill stood out on the skyline, and when they wanted a rest the brothers would sit on the grass, gaze out at the view and eat their picnic. If they were lucky their Mum would treat them to a ha'penny ice-cream cornet in the village shop as they made their way back to the tram.

The way down the hill took the family past the Sandstone rock houses. They were inhabited in the twenties by three families and caused a great deal of interest to the visitors.

When they arrived back at the tram station there would invariably be long queues of people waiting to go home. Each tram could only carry forty-eight people, so the boys would occupy themselves on the swings nearby or on the slot machines in the row of huts beside the station fence while they waited for their parents to reach the head of the queue.

Whole day trips like this would be very few and far between and more usual treats were likely to be picnics on the Wren's Nest or at Bluebell Park or maybe West Park in Wolverhampton.

From a very early age Ron enjoyed the excitement of the cinema. At first he would tag along with Ken to watch the silent movies, either cowboys and indians or comedies. The cinema was in Providence Row and was privately owned by Pages. For one penny the children endured hard wooden benches set on bare wooden floors. The machinery was not very efficient and would often break down, whereupon the boys would stamp their feet on the bare boards until Mr Page came out and demanded silence. On the way to the little cinema was an orchard containing pear trees. The pears were really too hard to be edible but the lady of the house would sell the lads a capful for halfpence and they would take these with them to the filmshow. They would nibble the hard fruit as best they could and then use the rest as ammunition to bombard the screen whenever the projector broke down.

As they grew older and silent films gave way to the 'talkies' the boys would go to the Regent cinema in Tipton, where the seats were softer and tipped up. It also now cost two pence so visits were strictly rationed. Ron had good reason to remember seeing his first 'talkie' with Al Jolson singing 'Sonny Boy' with his face all blacked up. The day was memorable in another less pleasant way as he had been promised the treat after a visit to the dentist which was nearby.

A favourite early summer-time entertainment was the annual arrival of Pat Collins' Fair. It came to Tipton each May for a week and was eagerly awaited by Ron and his mates. As they approached the fairground, they could see the bright lights shining upwards into the sky, and hear the steam-organ playing all the well known tunes to encourage the people to draw near. There were very few gas street lights in the locality so, when the people turned into the fairground it was like walking onto a theatre stage and they were immediately a part of the fun and hurly-burly. At the centre of the fair was the most exciting ride, and if they could only afford one, it had to be this one. This was the galloping horses. After their ride they would be quite happy to stand and watch the other side shows and rides. Some entertainment was in closed tents, but the lads would creep round the back of the tents and peer through the cracks in the canvas.

At the boxing booth, the promotor would challenge any man to take on the fair's champion for a bout of three rounds. If the contender won he got three pounds and if he went the full three rounds and was still standing he was allowed a collection. This meant a hat was sent round the booth and people dropped coins into it.

An exhibition of nature's oddities was always to be found at these fairs. Animals with two heads and those with an extra leg along-side the bearded lady, the tallest, smallest and the fattest man also attracted the crowds.

There was a coconut shy and a tall pole with a bell on the top which was used by the men to test their strength. A mallet was used to hit a platform at the base of the pole, this sent a piece of metal up the pole. If the man was strong enough the metal reached the top and hit the bell. The boys never wasted their money on this as they saw those much stronger than themselves fail. Tests of skill rather than strength were more to Ron's liking and if pocket-money permitted, he would have a go at the rifle shooting. There were two stalls for this; the first used a small feathered dart and the aim was to hit the bull's-eye on a target, the second used lead pellets and the target was a row of moving ducks which continually moved across a wooden fence. If the boys had any money left as they made their way home, they would buy a hot potato to fill their young stomachs and warm their hands. Ron was nearly fourteen before he was allowed to go to the fair without his parents.

There was little by way of entertainment on a Sunday, but many people attended church and used the opportunity to catch up with the local gossip and meet up with friends after the service. Ron sang in the choir and attended choir practice each Friday evening; he never laid claim to any great musical ability, but sitting in the choir-stalls gave him the opportunity to study the beautiful carvings and the ornate architecture of the building, an interest indicative of his innate artistic leanings.

During the time he spent in the choir, his Uncle Ben sat behind him in the choir-stalls. Ben was a tenor, and would sometimes put his own words to the hymns, to pass messages to his nephew and was a source of amusement of the younger choristers.

'O come let us adore him,
The Vicar's watching you oo'

or

'We three kings of Orient are,
You Mom and Dad are not very far'

Ron was glad when he was asked to go to pump the bellows so that he would not have to conceal his giggles. There was a long lever behind the organ and hanging from the airbox above was a long piece of cord fitted with a lead weight. As the box was filled with air the position of the weight indicated the amount of air in the box. Ron should have kept his eye on the marker and pumped the lever when the box was running low. However Ron was much more interested in what he could see out of the window and would often have to be reminded to do his job so his services were not required for long.

The church had a single bell which was rung before each service. Ron was allowed to do this on one or two occasions, but he always did it in fear and trepidation. If the rope was pulled too hard, the heavy bell would turn upside down and a steeple-jack had to be employed to right it again.

1928 brought another new innovation into the Baker house-hold. Mum bought a gramophone! It had to be wound up and needed a special needle before the records could be played. Each record had to be placed on the machine one at a time, but for a family who had very few luxuries, this acquisition caused great excitement. At first the family only had three records, two of which were 'Bye Bye Blackbird' and 'In a Monastry Garden'. As the family had neither a radio nor a piano, it was quite strange for them to hear music being played in the house.

During the summer school holidays nothing could keep Ron indoors, and the only time he came home was to go to bed.

He would leave home first thing in the morning with a few sandwiches and a bottle of cold tea, spending the day in the open air, on the Wren's Nest, climbing trees, looking for bird's nests, hunting for blackberries, wild strawberries or crab-apples.

In those days, boys collected bird's eggs but were told by their school teacher that they must never do this unless they left three eggs behind.

The boys would keep their collections in a small cardboard box lined with sawdust to protect the eggs. When one of them had two eggs of the same type they would barter amongst those who did not possess one. A particular favourite with the boys was the skylark, but these were very hard to find as the bird hid her nest well. Ron would lie for hours

Ron's School Class, Mount Pleasant, 1930.

Ron in the brook near the Toll House, Woodsetton which was rebuilt in the Black Country Museum.

watching the mother circling in the sky and waiting for her to land. He would carefully note where she came down in the long grass, and later would hunt for the nest, but could never find it. It was years later that he discovered that the skylark always came down a distance from her nest and scurried through the grass to her nest to prevent its discovery. Ron never added a skylark's egg to his collection.

These same fields were a source of fodder for Mr Wheeler's cows during the winter months. In September, two men would come with their scythes and cut it down by hand. After a couple of days Ron and his mates would help to turn the grass as it dried into hay. Later it was put onto a farm-cart using a pitch fork to throw it on. Mr Wheeler did not allow the boys to use the pitch-fork until they were thirteen years old, but until then they could help in other ways, even playing in the hay and throwing it around helped the drying process. The hay was taken to a spot near the cowsheds, where the hayrick was built, the top being thatched, so that it looked like a shed with a sloping roof.

The open clay banks were a colourful sight from Spring-time onwards, with a mass of wild flowers. Wild marguerites, or 'Dog- Daisies', tall and impressive were interspersed with coltsfoot, buttercups and daisies, and wild roses also flourished.

Ron and his mates would begin the first week of the long summer holiday by building their camp. During the coal-strike of 1926 the fields around the village had been dug up to reveal the coal which lay just below the surface. The area, as a result, looked more like a deserted battlefield than green pastures, but it created an interesting place for the boys' games. They would choose one of the hollow dug out spots, covering over the space with leafy branches to make their 'den'. Then they would find a large round rusty tin to make into their camp-fire. Holes were poked into the sides and bottom of the tin, with a metal spike to allow air to get through. A length of wire was made into a handle and attached to the top of the tin. Small pieces of coal were readily available, as were twigs and bits of waste-paper. The young boys did not have access to matches, however, but had soon learned to make a small fire without them. Ron would collect little bits of dry straw and use the bottom of an old glass bottle as a magnifying glass to direct the sun's rays onto the dried strands or onto a piece of paper until it burst into flames. The boys would then use this to light their fire in the tin. By careful arrangement of the wood and coal and by swinging the tin by its handle, in a circle at arms' length, over their head, they created a draught which soon gave a good fire. This could then be used to cook small potatoes or chestnuts.

Ron also made himself a cache for the summer. Close to the den, so that it would be easy to find again, he dug out a square of turf. He dug the soil out to a depth of six to eight inches, making a nice, neat little box. Here he could hide his secret possessions and, when it was covered over with an old piece of roof-tile and the piece of turf, it was undetectable. One of Ron's secret treasures which was stored there was a penknife which he didn't want his parents to know he possessed.

The Wren's Nest was an exciting place for children, but it was not without its dangers. Beneath the hills were deep caverns which were left over from the limestone workings of the late 19th and early 20th century. They had been named the 'Seven Sisters' due to there being seven large openings to the system. It was the ambition of every young lad to be able to brag to his friends that he had descended to the very bottom of the caverns. The first time Ron attempted this feat, he was only ten and he was accompanied by his elder brother Ken. As the cavern was pitch-black, they prepared a light using an old tin can. They stuffed it with rags, which they soaked in paraffin oil. They then replaced the lid, in which they had pierced a hole, and pulled a bit of the rag through the hole to be used as a wick. When they reached the entrance to the cave they lit the rag and scrambled down the long slope of stones and gravel, eventually reaching the lowest point, minus skin to their knees and elbows. A short walk brought them to the underground canal, which had been built in the early part of the 19th century to carry the limestone from the workings to the lime kilns at Tipton Road. There were no tow-paths through the caves and the men lay on their backs on the top of the boat and, using their legs against the roof of the cave, projected the boat along. Although the mining had stopped by the time Ron first ventured down, he had heard the explosions, usually at midday, during his pre-school years, when the mines were still being worked. A stone building called the Powder-House stood on the nearby Mons Hill. It had no windows and a strong steel door, and was used to store the explosives used for the mining.

Mons Hill itself was a fascinating place as it contained an abundance of fossil remains. Ron became particularly interested in these as he approached his teenage years and would spend many hours, chipping at the limestone rock looking for the remains of sea-fossils. Although he found thousands of different shell remains, he was never lucky enough to find the prized Trilobite, or 'Dudley Bug' as it was known locally.

The Wren's Nest was an enchanting place to Ron during his childhood. On it grew many types of tree and in the Autumn the narrow paths would be strewn with beech nuts and 'conkers'. A farm stood on the top of the hill and cows wandered in the fields.

Mushrooms could be found at the edge of the woods and fresh water-cress in the clear stream that rippled down to the Cuckoo Pond. Ron would collect the free treats as he made his way home and the family would have them for tea.

The large pool was known as the Donkey Pool and it never ran dry. It was edged with reeds and bullrushes and the lads loved to bring their makeshift rods and catch the 'jack bannocks' or tiddlers that swam there. Another large pool that was found nearby between the claybanks was the Horse Pool. This was very deep and was formed as a result of the clay pits that had occupied the area. No-one seemed to make use of much of this land at the time but Ron learned that it belonged to the Earl of Dudley.

Although the area saw most activity during the summer months, the large pool was also a place where people went to skate during the winter time when the ice formed thickly on the pool.

A brook led from Hurst Hill and joined with another from Parkes' Hall, together flowing through the village and on through Tipton. On hot summer days the young children spent hours making a dam to hold back the water until it was deep enough for them to paddle in. Another great game was to try to jump across the brook without falling in or getting their feet wet. The first time Ron attempted this he was only eight years old and he misjudged the leap entirely and fell backwards landing on his bottom in the muddy water. He had to go home to tell his Mother what had happened.

"Show me!" she demanded, and marched off to the water's edge with Ron scurrying along behind her trying to keep up.

"There, just there" he said pointing to the slip marks his heels had made. Whereupon his mother took him by the scruff of the neck and dunked him in the water, soaking him from head to foot. She plonked him back on his feet, then turned round and flounced back to her kitchen. It was some time before Ron went near the brook again.

Water has always proved to be a source of fascination to young children and, then as now, they were given the same warnings about keeping away from the pools and the canal, and the dangers of both. But they wanted to learn to swim, and, although Tipton baths had opened, it cost three whole pence to get in, and you could get into the cinema three times for that, so Ron did what many others did and tried the pool first, and then the canal. He soon discovered that the pool was not deep enough as his feet kept touching the muddy bottom. He then ventured further to the part of the canal across the waste-ground near to the Iron-works. As the boys had to ensure that their parents did not discover their disobedience, they always swam in the nude. Their clothes were carefully piled in a dry place on the bank, as each of them knew they would get a spanking if they were caught out. They soon found that the water at this particular spot was especially warm and later were to establish the reason. The canal water was used to cool down the furnaces and was then returned to the canal at this point.

Ron never did get the hang of swimming as a child and only mastered the skill years later when he started work.

Most of the children's games were less messy than their watery antics however. 'Tip-Cat' required two pieces of stick, one about five inches long and pointed at each end and the other a couple of feet long and much sturdier. A fair bit of space was needed so that a starting line was marked as well as a target circle about fifty yards away. The small piece of wood was placed on the line and struck with the long stick so that it leapt up into the air and while is was still off the ground it had to be hit again in the direction of the circle. The process was repeated where it landed and the number of strikes needed to reach the circle was counted. Each child in the group had their turn and the winner was the one with the least number of strikes. This game could not be played in the street because of the danger of breaking windows with the flying 'cat', so the clay-banks were usually used.

Footballs were seldom used by children at that time, but a suitable alternative was a makeshift ball made out of a pig's bladder obtained from Mr Hill, the butcher. He had a good return for providing the 'games-equipment', because the boys would gladly help in herding the cattle and sheep from the goods depot at Deepfields Railway Station and drive them home to the slaughter house behind his shop. Occasionally a cow would break away when it arrived at the narrow entry to the side of the shop (perhaps sensing its destiny!) and it was then that the children would be needed to round the animal up. Pigs were usually reared locally and those who kept pigs would rear two, one for themselves and one for the butcher. A 'swill- bin' would be kept so that neighbours could contribute their kitchen waste towards the fattening process. The children soon learned when it was time for the pig to be killed and they would then be given the cleaned, fresh pig's bladder which they blew up by mouth and tied with string to make their ball.

Another homemade toy which was made new each spring was a kite. Each boy had his own design and Ron was no exception. He took two thin pieces of wooden rod, one longer than the other, and lashed them together in the form of a cross. He then cut a piece of supple willow and fastened that across the top of the cross. He made a gooey flour paste and glued sheets of newspaper onto the frame. A long piece of string was attached to the bottom of the kite and small pieces of folded paper attached at intervals to make the 'tail'. A penny then bought a ball of fine sugar string, which was tied to the centre of the kite, and it was ready for action and gave hours of entertainment.

The lads would collect cigarette cards for another harmless game. One card was placed against a wall at an angle and another card was flicked at it from a prescribed distance, attempting to displace it. If the card fell, the player kept it, if not, his opponent took it, and it was then his turn with another card. The boys would sometimes wait outside shops selling tobacco and ask those purchasing the more expensive cigarettes for the cards in the packet. The cards were originally put in the packets as strengthening, to stop the contents from being damaged, but as interest grew in the pictures themselves, they became quite collectable and not all those asked wanted to part with them.

Marbles were also collected when pocket money allowed, and most children at that time had a good selection of the colourful glass toys. Various games were devised with these, but all tested the dexterity of the players and were all played in single sex groups.

Boys would very rarely play the sort of games which the girls played, such as skipping and hop-scotch, but the younger boys and girls did both play with a top and whip. It was usually played on the tarmaced roadway as the cracks in the pavement made it difficult to keep the top spinning.

The village street was dimly lit by two gas lamps, one at each end. Every evening as it was getting dusk, the local council lamp-lighter would go round with his long hooked pole and his short pointed ladder. He used his pole to light the lamp and the ladder was needed if the lantern had to be cleaned or the mantle needed to be changed. If he had to climb up, the ladder rested on the arms of the lamp-post. This post too provided a source of play for the youngsters. They would struggle to shin up the shiney metal stem to reach the out-stretched arms, here they would swing, letting out blood-curdling yells as they did so, in true 'Tarzan' fashion. A look-out was needed before they embarked on this activity, as it was frowned upon by the village 'Bobby' - P. C. Castle, stationed at Roseville police station.

Ron did not spend all his spare time playing games as he was always on the look-out among the neighbours for errands to run to augment his meagre pocket-money. One lady who lived just a few doors away, could always find him a little errand to perform, such as fetching paraffin from Mr Whitehouse. Ron would take the large glass bottle to his house,

Pages Cinema.

A distant view of Swan Village, drawn from Donkey Pool.

enter through the front door (which was always open) and go through onto the front room. A forty-four gallon drum of the oil was in one corner of the room. Mr Whitehouse was blind but this did not hamper him in his work. He would take the bottle off the boy and place a funnel into the neck, pick up a metal pint can, and placing his thumb on the top of the can begin pumping the oil out of the drum into the container. When the liquid reached his thumb he knew that he had a full measure, and transfered the contents to the bottle while he held the funnel with his other hand.

Another task which Ron was asked to perform was to fetch a hundred-weight of best coal from Hughes's coal-yard. It was usually Mrs Hughes who would serve the customers in the yard as her husband would be out on his rounds with the horse and cart or collecting fresh supplies from the coal barges at Coseley or Tipton coal wharf. It was quite a sight seeing these barges being unloaded. Two men, stripped to their waist, would stand in the bottom of the boat and, with the help of large coal shovels, pitch it, bit by bit, onto the canal bank. When it was all unloaded, it then had to be transfered to special enclosures at the back of the wharf. While all this was happening, the horse which had pulled the barge was resting and feeding in a nearby field in preparation for his return journey to the pit. In the twenties there were two local working pits, each very small and employing only two or three miners. Neither of them was deep and the coal was hoisted up a slope by a horse walking round a wooden wheel attached to a pulley system. This enabled the iron trucks on the rails to be pulled from the shallow mine quite easily with the wire cables.

Ron and a friend decided to investigate the workings of the smaller of the mines, one week-end when the men weren't working. Although it was not very deep, the dark damp atmosphere soon got the better of the lads and drove them out. Ron never attempted it again.

If the coal was bought from the pit-head it could be obtained at a cheaper price and, as it was of poorer quality than that from the deeper seams at nearby Baggeridge, it was cheaper than that too.

During the late nineteenth century there had been many open-cast mines around Coseley, Sedgley and Woodsetton, but by the twenties most had been exhausted and all that remained were large deep pools to show where they had been. The sides of these pools were often very slippy due to the clay and were difficult to get out of. One hot summer, when Ron was a child, some children swimming in the Sedgley Hill pool got into difficulties and drowned. Ron was to remember this tragic year for another reason. A school-friend of his, aged ten, Herbert

Whitehouse was killed one dark November evening on the Birmingham road on the way home from school. A group of boys were running and playing along the pathway beside the road oblivious to any danger. Very little traffic used the roads at that time anyway and the bus only came once an hour, so it was an extremely unfortunate coincidence that, when Herbert dashed out into the road, a single decker bus happened to be passing, and the poor lad was killed instantly. These two incidents, at such a tender age, made Ron and his friends much more aware of the consequences of their actions.

Towards the end of the 1920s there was a major event in the village, when the local authority decided that it was time to install a modern sewage system. The old earth closets were replaced by water closets and this involved a great deal of upheaval as the paths and roadways were dug up and pipes laid.

The main deep trenches in the roads were partly dug by excavator and partly by hand. A steam-roller with a steel spike attached to the front was used to break up the surface. As the trench was dug, and the soil and clay removed, the underlying coal could also be seen. Once again, as at the time of the new road building, the local inhabitants took their buckets and shovels to collect the fuel when the workmen were out of the way. Extra soil had to be brought from the old pit banks by horse and cart to fill in the space left.

This new innovation meant that everyone had flushing water toilets, but an added bonus was that there were noticeably less flies collected on the fly papers which hung in the house, and less illness. However the toilets were still outside, so it still meant a trek out in the cold in all weathers.

At this time, there was a factory nearby called Beans which made car. At various times these could be seen being tested up the steep Sedgley Hill. They would be in a very basic form, consisting of a chassis, four wheels and the engine, the body being a basic wooden box to protect the driver. These bases would eventually be driven to Dudley where the bodies were assembled and the cars finished off.

Ron found that a quantity of tokens from the works canteen had been dumped on the waste tip by the Fox-yards Pub, and he and his friends spent many hours grubbing them out and later used them to barter or swap collectables with. At face value they were worth one, three or six-pence and were stamped with the Beans Industry name, having been produced originally as dinner tokens for the employers.

There were only two or three cars owned by the villagers at this time, so the sight of one was quite an event. Mr Ewell, the coal and steel merchant from Tipton not only had a car, but also a chauffeur. He was Mr Bullock, and he lived just outside the village in a small cottage surrounded by fowl-pens. During the day, the poultry would roam free to forage where they pleased. They also were known to lay their eggs amongst the grass and shrubs on the clay banks. One day, while playing on the banks Ron came across a clutch of six eggs. Gathering them up into his arms, he ran home to take his precious find to his Mother. He stumbled and broke half of them but managed to keep three intact. The next day, being Sunday when the family often had boiled eggs for breakfast, Ron's Mum duly used the eggs. Ron sat at the table, egg-cup ready, toast soldiers buttered and waiting and his egg was placed in the cup. He eagerly tapped the top of the egg only to be greeted by a foul stench and the sight of a tiny yellow beak and a closed eyelid beneath. Poor young Ron was horrified and it was to put him off looking for eggs for the rest of his childhood.

Also in the area of the tip lived a family of gypsies. They had built themselves a shack out of materials discarded on the tip and used the clear water from the brook for drinking, cooking and cleaning. A fire was usually burning nearby and a big black pot hung above it. The man and his son worked in one of the local foundries, but the woman, who everyone knew as Georgina, stayed close to their camp. She was occasionally seen in the village shop but discouraged any kind of conversation by her gruff attitude and her swarthy appearance. Her general demeanour was quite sufficient to prevent the young lads from venturing too close to their camp.

Although Ron lived a comfortable life as a child, his behaviour showed that he was well aware that money was necessary for some of life's little extras. He particularly looked forward to his weekly visit to his grandmother's house, where other members of the family would be assembled. Uncle Ben, who still lived at home with 'Nan' and worked as a bricklayer, gave Ron one penny, Aunt Lily, who was a tailoress, also gave him a penny, but Aunty Mary who worked at Palethorpe's sausage factory, only gave him a ha'penny as she said that was all she could afford.

His grandparent's house was larger than Ron's own home and had a parlour which was only used on very special occasions and was strictly out of bounds to the children. The big living room had a shiny black-leaded grate surrounded by equally bright horse-brasses. These had a special purpose as Ron's Grandfather was a haulier for Cannon Works in Coseley and on particular occasions he would use the brasses to decorate his horse and cart for parades.

The rest of the house was also an exciting place for the young brothers. The dresser in the kitchen contained a collection of blue and white pottery and a jug of beer was always to be seen on the grate on cold winter mornings, its aroma wafting around the kitchen. Nan brewed her own beer and baked her own bread so that her kitchen was always a warm and inviting place to be.

As the boys became old enough, they made this weekly journey on their own, Mum staying at home to prepare the Sunday lunch and Dad spending the time downing a few pints in his local. They all assembled promptly at one for the usual Sunday Roast followed by a creamed rice pudding. Then, regular as clockwork, Dad would take himself off to bed, not waking until the family had left the house for the evening church service, when he would make his way back to the pub for a few more drinks with his mates. He wouldn't get home until the brothers were fast asleep in bed so they saw very little of their father on Sundays.

Ron's Mother had very little recreation as much of her day was spent on household chores. Her day started at five when she went down to the kitchen to make up the fire. She would then return to bed for another couple of hours of fitful sleep while the fire got going. This was probably the most important job of the day, as without the fire there would be no cooking and no hot water for washing and cleaning. When the fire was well alight she would get up, get dressed and descend again to the kitchen, put the big black kettle on the fire and begin to make breakfast, first for her husband and then, if it was a school-day, for the children, before getting them ready for the day. While father would get a substantial meal of bacon and sausage to set him up for a heavy day's work, the boys had bread and jam or porridge according to the time of year. The boys would be out of the house by half-past eight to be at school for nine, their father having been gone long before.

Mother would then begin the real work of the day. Monday was always wash-day. This entailed lighting another fire under the boiler in the wash-house. The clothes which had to be boiled were put in the boiler and, when they were done, the water was ladled out into the wooden barrel which stood by the kitchen door and the other clothes were placed a few at a time into it and washed by hand. This meant pummelling them with a wooden maid until they were clean. Everything then had to be thoroughly rinsed and mangled by hand using a heavy wooden contraption. The washing was then hung out to dry. Father expected all signs of the washing to be finished and put away before he returned from work in the evening, so the ironing was done on the kitchen table during the afternoon using two flat-irons heated alternately on the fire.

Ron's Mum, too, did most of the caring for her three boys. She cooked and cleaned of course, but she also cut their hair and mended their shoes. For this task she would go to Woolworths and buy the pieces of leather and studs and then out would come the three-legged shoe 'last', which had two sides for different sized soles and the third was for the heel. She would sit in the kitchen with her little hammer and cobble away until the shoes were repaired and wearable once more, maybe to be used by the next child down if the original owner had out-grown them.

At night when the boys were in bed, out would come her knitting needles and she would fill her time producing socks, vests and jerseys for her growing brood. She was a thrifty woman and nothing went to waste. When the foot of the socks became too worn to darn anymore she would unpick the foot section, pick up the stitches and re-knit a new foot onto the leg. Lilian also crocheted, embroidered and made podged rugs. These rugs were made on a base of a thick jute sugar sack which Mr Smith provided. Old discarded cloth was cut into strips about four inches long and one inch wide. This task could be undertaken in any odd moment during the day, and the bits kept in an old pillowcase until there were enough of them to start the job and the sack base was obtained. The 'podger' was then used to pull the strip through the loose weave sacking. A podger was not unlike a large crochet hook, and it was poked through a piece of the base which had been pinched between the finger and thumb of one hand. The strip of cloth was then folded in half, and the folded loop caught around the hook of the podger and pulled back through the sacking. Keeping the cloth on the hook the loose ends of the strip were then wrapped around the end of the podger which was then drawn back through the loop forming a knot against the base. This process was repeated with different coloured pieces of cloth, each piece attached close to the next one, making a colourful and hard-wearing hearth-rug unique to that family. When a rug was complete the family would place the clean new one in pride of place in front of the fire and ritually relegate the old dirtier one to the back door-step.

Some women (her own mother-in-law included) brewed beer at home, but Lilian did not, although she did make flavoured 'pop' for the family. Many a time the contents of the stoppered bottles, which she stored in the outside wash-house, fermented and blew the tops off, spilling most of their contents over the floor.

Friday night was bath night. Dad would be in the pub and it was left to Mum as usual to lug the heavy kettles full of water into the kitchen. Two kettles were placed on the fire to boil then the tin bath was carried in from the back brew-house and placed in front of the fire. Two more

Ron with his two brothers Ken and Gordon in his back yard, 1931.

View of Ron's cottage taken from Farmers Bank.

kettles full of cold water were poured into the bath and the contents of one of the boiling kettles added to it. Gordon, the youngest would be the first to be washed followed by Ron and then Ken. More hot water was added to the tub, from the kettle bubbling on the fire, as the water cooled down. Each child was then dressed in clean under-wear and given their weekly dose of medication. One spoon of syrup of figs and another of cod-liver oil and malt extract was delivered to the three open mouths, followed periodically by a blood tonic.

Lilian treated all the boys' minor ailments. Knees got quite a battering as they were exposed under the short trousers which the lads wore, and they were constantly falling down. Grazed knees were treated with Mum's special bread poultice. It was made with boiling water and bound over the wound with strips of old sheet. When it was removed a few days later, the gravel would have embedded itself in the poultice and the wound would be clean and dry, with no sign of infection.

Lilian had not had an easy life. She was born Lilian Lottie Jeavons in 1895 in Earl Street Coseley. Her mother came from Princess End Tipton and her father and his brother were butchers and tallow (candle) manufacturers. Lilian's mother had had a good education, being sent to study at the Dudley Girl's High School. She was a fine pianist and skater, but when Lilian was only eight years old she went to live with her grandparents as her parent's marriage had broken down. Her mother had become an alcoholic and had failed to care for her properly, so her grandparents took over the responsibility for her upbringing when her father (William or 'Bill as he was known) took her with him to live at his parent's home.

Lilian's Grandmother was Betsy Jeavons and she owned four ale houses; 'The Old Bush' and 'The Swan', both in Bradley, 'The Gospel Oak' in Tipton and 'The Rose and Crown' in Providence Row, West Coseley. The licence for 'The Old Bush' was also in her name as she was the educated one, her husband being unable to read or write. However, he would get up at six o'clock to catch the early morning trade. The workers coming off the night shift would call in for a pint (and some bread and cheese provided free on the bar). A slate was left behind the bar and Great Grandad Jeavons would make marks and symbols on it to denote who owed what each morning. His wife then had to translate this and enter it into a ledger and the customers settled up on pay-day.

Betsy was a woman of substance, owning a row of terraced houses in Tunnel Street, Coseley. Once a week she would take Lilian with her to collect the rent from the thirty-two houses. The rent was between one-shilling-and-ninepence and two shillings at that time. On Sundays she would dress up in all her Victorian finery and Great Grandad would drive her in a horse-drawn 'Governess' trap to Christ Church Coseley.

Lilian continued in this life-style until she was fourteen when her Grandparents died and she went to live with her Aunt Lily Bott at The Rose and Crown in Coseley.

Betsy's estate was by tradition to be divided between the sons of the family and Lily would have got nothing. Bill (being the eldest) declared that he would not settle the estate until his other three brothers agreed to split it equally with their sister. This they did and Lily got her fifth part. Lilian was then safely housed with her Aunt, and Bill felt justified in leaving her and sailing off to America. The year was now 1909 and in five short years he had spent most of his inheritance and returned to England in 1914 when the Great War started and joined the Cavalry. Lilian was now nineteen years old.

Joseph Baker was a year older than Lilian when the war started, and after a short spell of military service he was brought back into 'civvy street' to work on the production of ammunitions. It was during this time that their paths crossed and their friendship led to marriage in 1915.

Their second son, Ron, was born just as the war ended.

Joseph's father, Harry, had been born in 1866 in Upper Gornal to a family of builders. He had a brother Joseph and three sisters, Sarah Jane, Julie and Mary. Young Joseph, named after his uncle, would visit his Gran, who lived in a small cottage in a row called Botany or Botany Bay. Joseph was, years later, to regale Ron with stories of 'the old days' and of the life his own Grandmother lived. Even at the end of the nineteenth century she was making nails in a small nail-shop in the back-garden, besides baking bread, brewing beer, keeping pigs and poultry in addition to bringing up her family, consisting of three boys and two girls. The eldest son worked as a guard on the railway, Ben was a bricklayer and one daughter became a tailoress, the other worked in a factory.

While all the Baker men were hard working, it was normal for the women to take on all the work in the house and the overall care of the children.

It was with these backgrounds and with these expectations that Lilian and Joseph approached their own marriage.

Whilst Lilian filled her time with the house and the children, her husband, Joe, did what most other men at that time did. He worked hard and spent his leisure time in the local or with his beloved pigeons. In the summer-time he also enjoyed a game of crown green bowls on the green behind the pub.

As the space at his own house was limited, his pigeons were kept at his father's home. The birds were entered for races, sometimes from as far as two hundred miles away. Each would have a personal marker attached to its leg. The bird would be put into a carrying basket to be transported to the start of the race by lorry. All the pigeons would be released and Joe would wait by the pigeon-loft for return of his own bird. The marker was removed from the bird as soon as it got home and put into a special clock which recorded the time of its arrival back. The marker was then taken to the judges at the Summer House pub. A prize was given to the owner of the first bird home and there was keen competition among the pigeon fanciers.

The men seemed to be willing to compete in some strange ways, as there was also an event run by the pub whereby each entrant bought a small clay pipe and a quantity of shag-tobacco. At the end of the week, the pipe was returned to the pub and the stem of each one was carefully cut through exposing the nicotine stain through the middle. A prize was awarded to the person who had produced the deepest stain.

Luckily, Ron had more sense than to believe that his father's way of living was always the best, although he always had great respect for both his parents. He was an observant young man and took in all that he saw, not only in terms of buildings and nature, but also the people with whom he came in contact.

Mr Hartland was one such person. He lived nearby and reminded Ron of Father Christmas with his long white beard and friendly chuckle. He was a pianist and organist, playing the organ in the local chapel on Sundays and providing the background music to the silent films on the piano in the cinema the rest of the time.

The local curate intrigued Ron because of his size. He was a tall man and always seemed to be in a hurry moving quickly in his billowing cassock, with his giant strides, often with a couple of choir boys in tow, hanging on to his flowing vestments to keep up.

Then there was tiny Mr Dickie Hilton, a retired bank manager who never seemed to get off his high-framed bicycle, and Mr Pickrell, the tailor, who had a workshop behind his corner shop and spent all his free time either on local council projects or working for the chapel.

Bill-Pop-Posh was the nickname given to another of the village charactors who was slightly backward and was often accompanied by a dwarf called 'Little Albert' from Roseville. Neither of them was employed for most of the time, but they would wander around the village dropping into first one pub and then another in the hope that someone would buy them a drink. At Christmas the small man would get a job in pantomime and occasionally his tall companion made a few pence transfering a delivery of coal into the coal-sheds.

Another village character was a night-watchman who worked for the local council. Whenever there was work being done on the roads and holes were being dug, along would come Harry to erect his hut. The procedure was always the same; first the hut then the coal brazier was lit, then the warning lanterns put round the hole. By the time he had settled himself down there would be two or three children gathered around him, attracted by the warmth of the fire and in the knowledge that pretty soon Harry would have his frying pan on the fire and some fragrant bacon cooking. He always popped a couple of pieces of bread to cook in the bacon fat while he ate his bacon, and if the kids were very lucky, he would break a piece off to give them a morsel. Somehow it always tasted better than what they ate at home.

There was very little money for luxuries as the boys grew up so birthday parties were a rarity and Ron seldom met girls on a social basis at all. He was therefore to remember one event for a long time when these two happy phenomena coincided. He was at the age when the existance of girls was just beginning to mean something, when he was invited to Ron Smart's thirteenth birthday party.

Ron, too was thirteen years old and the party consisted of another six boys and four girls all of about the same age. After a very enjoyable tea of cakes and trifle, Mrs Smart withdrew to allow the youngsters to play games and have some fun. One young girl present was Beryl, whose sister was married to Tom Smith whose parents ran the grocery shop where Ron worked on a part-time basis. As Beryl had often visited her sister's 'in-laws' Ron and she had become good friends but had never met socially until now. There was obviously a mutual attraction and they were able to take advantage of the games played at the party to test it out.

One of the lads would go out into the hall while the girls were each given a number. When he came back in he had to choose a number from one to four, the girl with that number then went into the hall for a kiss. Then the boys were given a number and the process was repeated in reverse. When it was Ron's turn to choose and he returned to the room, he noticed that Beryl's ringlets which had been dangling down her back, had been rearranged so that one now hung forward over her shoulder. On an impulse Ron chose number one, and was delighted to find his hunch was correct. Out he went for his kiss with Beryl! Later they were to become good friends and she later confessed that her trick with her hair had been deliberate.

Thus Ron's childhood passed, with him absorbing all he could of life's experiences, until he became fourteen years old in 1932. During his last years in school he had become very interested in architecture and design and had set his heart on becoming apprenticed to a local architect. He would sit day-dreaming on the steps of the Swan pub and study the buildings across the street. There was the facade of the Mount Tabor chapel with its War Memorial Cross in the forecourt. Next to this was the Summer House Inn, a row of terraced houses each with its own entry, and the village corner shop with colourful enamel advertisements covering the walls. Bournville cocoa, Colman's mustard, Stephenson's ink and poultry food were all to be found there. The intricate patterns in the church stained glass windows also intrigued Ron and he yearned to be able to produce something of substance himself.

But these were the slump years, and his parents could not afford to pay the fee to allow him to achieve his dream. In December 1932 aged fourteen years and six weeks old he was obliged to leave school and find a job, to help to support the family.

LEARNING HIS TRADE
(1933 - 1939)

"WE just can't afford it". This was the second time in Ron's young life that his dreams had been shattered by these words. The year was 1933 and there was a slump. There were difficulties in all areas of trade in Britain and nowhere more so than here in the Black Country. No-one had money to spare, and it had to be earned wherever the opportunity presented itself. Ron's hopes of becoming an architect had to be discarded and his Aunt Lily managed to find an opening for him at her own place of work at the Town Mills clothing factory in Dudley.

An interview was arranged for him with Mr Fryer, the manager of the cutting room. The gentleman seemed genuinely interested in what the lad had to say for himself and Ron was eventually told to report for work the following Monday at eight o'clock. He soon learned that he would be working from 8a.m until 6p.m. with an hour for lunch from Monday to Friday and from 8 'til noon on Saturdays, a total of forty-nine hours for the princely wage of five shillings and ninepence. This would rise to seven shillings and sixpence when he had completed six months with the firm.

The best clothes that Ron possessed were his school uniform short trousers, shirt and jumper, and this is how he presented himself for work at the appointed hour. The first job he was given was to run errands between the cutting room and the rest of the factory. Before each day finished, his task was to sweep between the rows of cutting tables and collect up all the fragments of cloth and bag them up to be returned to the manufacturers to be reconstituted and made into cheaper material.

Ron felt very conspicuous in his shorts and begged his mother for a proper suit with long trousers. She told him that he would have to wait until he had worked three weeks before he could afford the cost, which was twelve shillings and sixpence, even if bought cost-price from the firm. He knew that it would take some time for it to be ready, but he was duly measured up for his suit in the ordering department and then impatiently set to work and wait for its completion. He thought he was so grown-up when it arrived, but in reality was still quite a small fourteen year old.

Naturally, the youngster was given the most menial jobs at first. He would be sent into the town to fetch the boss's 'Du Maurier' cigarettes from Preedies, and to his home a mile away to deliver lengths of wooden board to be used as fire-wood. These boards had been used as strengthening down the centre of the rolls of materials and, instead of throwing them away, the thrifty Mr Fryer would have Ron load them onto a handcart and push them up the Oakham Hill to his home. Very few people owned cars at that time and certainly Mr Fryer could not have afforded one, but it would have been demeaning for him to be seen transporting these boards home himself.

When Ron had been working at the factory for about three months, he was allowed to unload the lift which brought the rolls of cloth up to the cutting room from the basement, three floors below. It was an open lift, dating back to Victorian times when the factory had been built as a corn mill. Each floor had gates across the lift entrance, but the only other protection for those working the lift, was an iron bar across the front to stop them falling down the lift-shaft. The lift was controlled by ropes and personel were not allowed to ride on it, it was only used to transport goods between the floors.

The day that Ron was asked to assist in emptying the load, the bar had been removed temporarily to allow the men to work unhindered and it had been stood up on end at the side of the lift.As Ron stood waiting to take the end of one of the rolls of cloth, the hefty bar rolled sideways and fell, clouting the lad on the side of his head, raising a lump the size of an egg. Mr Fryer was so worried that Ron had been allowed to be so near the lift in the first place, that he sent him home with instructions not to return until his head had healed. It took two days for him to recover!

Town Mills was quite a large establishment, employing about five hundred women and one hundred men. The upper floor was the cutting area, consisting of six rows of large tables lit from above, on dark winter days, by single bulbs hanging from flex, and natural light from windows running the full length of the room down both sides. There was a sprinkler system above the tables which was used in case of fire, and served by a huge water tank that was situated in a tower which dominated both the building and the surrounding area.

The rooms below the cutting area were all full of row upon row of sewing machines, all worked by women.

As a new trainee, especially in his first few weeks, Ron came in for a fair bit of banter from these women. He was obliged to pass through their work area on his way to the different departments and on one occasion, during a break, he noticed how quiet everything had become. He realised that all the women were looking in his direction, and this made him even more self-conscious than usual. His foreboding grew as two of the older women quickly grabbed him, pulled down his shorts and squirted his private parts with machine oil. The poor lad was mortified and ran as fast as he could, with his pants round his ankles and his face red and glowing to clean himself up and resume his work with as much dignity as he could muster. He was later to discover that this was the usual initiation ceremony for all new apprentices!

Every floor where the machinists worked was divided up into rooms, each of which was designated to producing one particular item; trousers in one area, waistcoats in another, jackets in a third. The different qualities of products were also produced in segregated areas, with different managers in charge of each department. Mr Barden oversaw the large trouser room, 'The Vest Room' where the waistcoats were made was a smaller room and was managed by Mr Dick Fellows, the top quality jacket room by Mr Edwards and the cheaper jacket room by Mr Copestake.

The pressing room was on the ground floor and was always full of steam from the large Hoffman presses which were on the go continually. A huge warehouse was situated nearby and stored row upon row of ready-made suits all awaiting despatch to the respective customers. At the end of this building was the department which dealt with the requests from private outfitters for special orders taken over the previous week. These individual orders were dealt with by Mr T. V. Vincent Snr in the cutting room. He worked out the quantity of fabric required and sent down to the fabric store for the exact amount, and the order was followed through its stages of production on an individual basis to ensure that it met the highest standards. Each garment was then carefully packed in a stout cardboard box, wrapped in strong brown paper and tied securely with string, before being weighed, meticulously addressed and the necessary postage being applied to the parcel. At five o'clock precisely, a horse drawn wagon would arrive at the despatch department door to collect the day's mail and transport it in wicker baskets to the main Wolverhampton Street Post Office. Larger consignments to the big cities were put collectively into large baskets and transported, again by horse-drawn wagon, to Dudley goods railway station.

The only other large department was the APTO room which contained shirts, socks, underwear, rainwear and general oufitting. The buyers would visit this area after visiting the main warehouse and finishing their ordering there, and would replenish the stocks for their shops.

The final, small but important department was the office section, where the Managing Director and his secretary had their offices and the wages department was situated. The Managing Director when Ron started working for Town Mills was a Mr B. C English, but neither Ron nor many of his fellow workers ever had occasion to see or speak to him.

Thus Ron began his working life. His day started much as it had in his school-days with a journey by foot and tram, leaving home at a quarter past seven to arrive at the work's gates just before eight to 'clock-on' at the entrance to his own department at the beginning of each day. Each person's card had a personal number and recorded the hours each had worked by punching it in the 'time clock' at the beginning and end of each day. The card was then used by the wages clerk to calculate what each worker was owed and the money was brought to them at their workplace each Friday afternoon.

There was a fifteen minute break at half-past ten and, at one o'clock, an hour's break for lunch. Those who lived near enough made a dash for the door as soon as they could but those, like Ron, who lived too far away, brought sandwiches and a drink, and would sit at one of the cutting tables to have their lunch. If time and the weather permitted, Ron and others of the younger employers would wander round the town to pass the rest of their dinner-break and get a breath of air before the afternoon session. In the summer, the lads would take their lunch boxes and have a picnic in the court-yard of Dudley Castle, where many like-minded workers would congregate and socialise and pass a pleasant hour. It was here that Ron first began to meet girls in a non-working environment, and he quite liked the experience!

Ron tried to save his pennies as and when he could, and would walk home when the weather allowed, traipsing across the Priory Estate and along the Birmingham New Road arriving home at half-past six.

After his six months trial period was complete and he had attained the steady wage of seven shillings and sixpence, he was giving his mother five shillings for his keep, saving one shilling and living on the bit that was left. By the time his fifteenth birthday had arrived, he had amassed the grand total of twenty-five shillings, which he put down as a deposit on a Hercules bicycle at Mr Nicholl's cycle shop in Clifton Street, Hurst Hill. The cost of the bike was three pounds, nineteen shillings and sixpence and Ron paid the rest off at five shillings a month, but, as he saved on bus fares and time, he felt very well off. He cycled to work each day and was able to leave his prized possession with those belonging to many of the rest of the workforce, under cover in the large yard at the back of the factory. Now he really felt that he was one of them.

As he approached the end of his first year, Ron had high hopes that he might be promoted up the career ladder, from runner to trimmer, but, as the market was still very precarious, the firm could not afford a new apprentice and the ambitious fifteen year old had to bide his time and continue in his menial role with as much patience as he could muster.

The next year passed by and, at the start of 1935, a new lad was taken on to do Ron's task and he in turn was promoted. He now worked at the top end of a cutting table, taking each piece of cloth that the cutter had produced, laying them on the lining fabric and cutting out the linings for each piece, making allowance for the turnings. He had to ensure that each piece had its correct lining and stiffening canvas for pockets and collar, before it was passed on to the next stage of the process. All the relevant pieces were rolled up, tied with a strip of cloth and its order-form attached to it before being sent down to the sewing room. At first, Ron was too short to stand and work at the table comfortably and had to be provided with a wooden box to raise him up. The next year saw a growth spurt in the teenager and he was happy to dispense with the makeshift platform.

The cutters had to provide their own cutting shears, which, considering the type of work they were doing, had to be of top quality. Ron's first shears were thirteen and a half inches long and were made by Wilkinson of Sheffield. They cost twelve and sixpence, which was paid for at the rate of sixpence a week out of his already meagre wages, but Ron felt that it was worth it, as he now had his foot on the ladder.

Now that Ron had got over the huge disappointment of not being able to follow his chosen profession, he put his heart and soul into his present occupation and decided to get himself the necessary qualifications to climb higher in the field of tailoring. In September 1935, he enrolled at the night school in Stafford Street, Dudley, to learn all he could about the tailoring trade. As it was a volentary course, he had to pay the registration fee and it cost him seven and sixpence for the first year, up to City and Guilds intermediate level, and then twelve and sixpence for the next two years up to the final Diploma. The course required two nights study each week from September to Easter, but Ron relished every minute of it and truly felt that it was both time and money well spent as it would open the door to so much more in the future.

He would recall, many years later, those basic important but practical lessons in the first year of the course; the use of the sewing machine, and the open-ended thimble were all new to him and he absorbed these skills easily and avidly. Despite his diligence at school, he was always to look back and refer to this period of his life as 'The learning years.'

His enthusiasm and hard work were soon to be rewarded as in 1936 now at the grand age of seventeen, he was made up to 'Under-cutter' to a 'Special cutter' who was fully qualified and from whom Ron could learn all the tricks of the trade. The two worked together, the senior man marking out the length of suiting for the younger one to cut out with shears and match up all the flaps, welts, bands etc so that the machinists knew how to join all the pieces together.

It was at this time too that the Dudley and Staffordshire Technical College opened and the City and Guilds course moved to this new and spendid building. It was situated on land alongside the Broadway, beneath the Castle and overlooking the historic Priory ruins in the Priory Hall grounds.

The college had a refectory for the students to get a light meal before their evening lectures. This was very convenient as many of them, like Ron, came straight from work and had no time to get home for a meal before attending the college. There was a student common-room where the students would congregate before their classes began, and one of them would play the tunes of the day on the piano which had been provided for their entertainment.

Ron's course consisted now of a theory lecture on Tuesday evenings and a practical session on Thursdays. He learned all about the yarns that were used in the clothing industry; the various synthetic fibres which were beginning to be incorporated into the fabrics, as well as the old and well known wools from the different species of sheep around the British Isles. He learned the difference in the wool produced by the cross-bred sheep from Wales and Scotland to those bred on the wild moorlands. He soon realised how different yarns were used for different garments, depending on the strength and texture of the original fibres. He saw that these animals brought up on the rugged terrain produced much harsher and hard-wearing cloth than the fine, long-threaded Botany wools which were imported from Australia, where the sheep roamed freely on the open grasslands. He learned about the way the silk-worm produced its coccoon and man used its fibres, the way cashmere was gathered and cotton was harvested. He learned about the

Alpacca goats and their life on the mountain ranges. He studied each fibre under the microscope and began to recognise each by its feel and different characteristics and soon realised why each was used for the various garments. He was taught too about the different weaves which gave the fabrics their varied natures and this led on in the final year to study the different carpet weaves and their production.

The practical session taught the student how to design and draw out the pattern for a garment on large sheets of brown paper. This pattern-cutting lasted throughout the three year course, and Ron gained his first class certificate at the end of the second year in 'City and Guilds Bespoke and Wholesale Clothing.' The last two sessions of the course continued with further practical experience alongside lectures in the history of fashion and on the human figure and some deformations and how to adjust the design for deformed spines and awkward figures. They were also taught about ladies corsetry and how to design a costume or suit in the modern style.

All basic design was based on what was considered to be the average man or woman of the time. The average man was five feet eight inches tall, weighed one-hundred-and-forty pounds, had a chest measurement of thirty-eight inches, a waist measurement of thirty-four inches and hips of forty inches. He took a six-and-seven-eighths hat, fifteen-and-a-half inch collar and gloves and shoes were size eight. An average woman was taken to be five-feet-four, one hundred-and-ten pounds, thirty -six, twenty-six, thirty-eight, with size five shoe.

There were many differences to the style of tailoring for men and women as the men's suits had a considerable amount of heavy canvas work inside to build up the shape of the male form while the female style of the thirties was softer and draped and did not use so much of the strengthening materials.

The final year, too, taught Ron the essentials of factory management, handling staff and the workforce. He had given up many evenings of socialising and pleasure during his growth into manhood, but he emerged from the course a mature and knowledgable young man and the proud possessor of a 'First Class Diploma in Ladies and Gents Wholesale Tailoring.' He was not quite twenty years old as he gained his qualification and was promoted to the conveniently vacant position of Pattern Cutter and Assistant Clothing Designer. Ron now had his own office and he continued working in that position until the outbreak of the Second World War in 1939, which was to be just over a year away.

Many others of the workforce would turn up for work, only to be told that there was no work for them that day, but Ron was never to hear that his services were not needed, nor experience having to queue up at the Labour Exchange to sign on for unemployment pay. At night-school he had been taught all the basic skills to earn his living for the rest of his life. The most important thing, then, was to stay in employment, for one firm if possible, until retirement at the age of sixty-five.

Ron became friendly at this time with one of the firm's Managers, who gave him some advice, which he was to remember and act upon later in life. The man was a Jew by the name of Mr Goody and he had a contract to work for the Mill for three or four years. Ron met one of his daughters and had occasion to get into conversation with her father, after bringing her home one evening, and what he told Ron was this:-

"I like to see young lads like you get on," he said, "but here is a tip I would like you to know. Now you are a qualified special bestoke cutter, do not stay too long with this firm, but move on to another firm. If you stay with Town Mills all your life you will be in the same place and in the same position as you are now when you reach sixty-five. We Jews move continually from one tailoring firm to another, staying only three to five years before moving on."

He continued, with Ron hanging on his every word and trying to absorb his logic, "When you start a new position, you are introduced as 'Mr Baker, the new pattern cutter and designer.' The firm are very keen to learn all about the firm you have left and the knowledge you have acquired while there, and they are willing to pay you a good salary to glean this information. After a couple of years, with your new firm, you will become 'Mr Ron Baker' and a couple more years just 'Ron', then simply 'the fellow that works in the Pattern office. Move on now, lad, and improve your position."

New positions were not easy to come by and as Ron had only just been given this promotion, he settled into it, storing up his acquired wisdom for future reference.

Ron had been a bit of a slow starter socially and it wasn't until he was eighteen, in nineteen-thirty-six, that he gained some confidence and began to take an interest in the opposite sex. He began to take a pride in his appearance and decided to sharpen up his image.

The first thing that went was his old-fashioned bicycle that had been his pride and joy. In came a modern racer, with drop-handle bars, cable-brakes and three-speed gears. To create the image, Ron made himself a pair of check plus-fours, an 'Alpaca' cycling jacket and a check cap. He bought himself a pair of leather cycling shoes and long tartan stockings complete with tassled garters and off he would go thinking himself the 'cat's-whiskers'.

Ron at his pattern cutting table, Town Mills, Dudley, 1938.

View of Town Mills, Dudley where Ron learnt his trade.

He came down to earth again on returning to his tiny family home however, and he would carefully store his bike in the brew house and open the door to the cramped kitchen with its oil-lamps and smokey fire. But changes were afoot there too and before long, gas was laid on to the houses so that cooking and lighting was now accomplished so much more easily. Cookers were made locally in Coseley at the Cannon factory where, coincidentally, Ron's father had started work many years previously at the age of thirteen.

Mom's life was revolutionised as, although the fire was still needed for warmth, she did not need it stoked up all day to ensure that she always had a kettle boiling for washing and cleaning, or even for a cup of tea, and meals could be prepared so much more easily without having to crouch over the fire.

Changes were happening all around in nineteen-thirty-six, as the new Clifton Cinema opened in Sedgley, modern in design and comfortable - a marvellous boost to the youngsters social life - and one that Ron took full advantage of, with his recently aquired flush of adolescent hormones!

It was during this year, too, that Ron first experienced 'going abroad'. He had to go with his elder brother Ken and it was only the Isle of Man but, with the brothers' limited out-look, it could just as well have been the moon. The first week in August was the annual work's holiday, when most factories were closed and the workers took time to relax with their families. Ken had booked a holiday in one of the first holiday-camps to be established. This was called Cunninghams Holiday camp and was in Douglas on the Isle of Man.

Ken, Ron, Eddie Pitkeighly and Jim Whitehouse, two of Ken's friends, packed their little cases with the few clothes they had and set off on the Friday evening after finishing work, to go to Tipton station, where they boarded a train for Liverpool-Lime Street. It would have been difficult to find a happier and yet less sophisticated quartet of young men anywhere that evening, as they made their way from the train to the docks, trudging by foot, to save their cash for more exciting pursuits. They boarded the ferry at midnight to arrive at Douglas in the early hours of Saturday morning.

The steam-ferry was packed, as this was the main holiday week for everyone, and people sat huddled on their cases and crowded into every available corner as the boat moved out into the open waters of the Irish sea. Ron soon realised that more and more people were disappearing below deck as the waters became increasingly choppy and the boat began to sway about rather unpleasantly. The excitement of the expedition had helped him to steady the rumblings from his stomach at first, but the feelings eventually got the better of him and he was violently sick. Ken noticed his brother's change in colour and took him down below, where they hoped the movements of the sea would not be so pronounced. Ron was beginning to regret Ken's bright idea of a holiday 'abroad' long before the boat tied up on the quayside at Douglas, and he was feeling very dejected when they did at last disembark.

Youthful high spirits were soon re-established once Ron found his feet on a surface which remained still, and the four youths happily hoisted up their bags and set off to walk down the long jetty and then another mile or so to the camp.

Their first impression was of row upon row of small identical wooden huts, which were quaintly called 'chalets'. They were allocated a four berth chalet and settled into it, each dropping his case onto one of the narrow beds in the room. It was now almost midday and lunch-time and the lads had had nothing to eat for what seemed like an eternity, so they were eager to make their way to the large building which had been pointed out to them as being the dining-room. Here they were waited on by a series of young girls dressed in blue uniforms, whom the lads eyed up surreptitiously each time they passed near their table.

The rest of the first day of their holiday passed pleasantly enough, the young men were happy to be free of the shackles of normal home life and work. They explored the camp-site and in the evening saw a show in the entertainment hut, before retiring to their beds exhausted, having missed the previous night's sleep as they journeyed to their holiday destination.

There was plenty of fun and games arranged during the week, as well as swimming and sight-seeing around the island. One day they took a small local steam train to Laxey to see a large water wheel driven by a stream and on other occasions they would board the horse-drawn tram to the end of the pier. Ron enjoyed seeing the huge shire horses which reminded him of those he had seen around the streets during his childhood, delivering supplies to their home.

The week passed quickly and soon they were packing their cases and retracing their steps to the ferry to board the boat to return home. Ron embarked rather timorously remembering his unpleasant experience of the previous week. He need not have worried, however, as the weather was good and the sea was calm and few people were ill on the return voyage. He was glad that he had a happier memory to file away to complete his first big holiday away from home.

The only other holiday he had during his teenage years was not to turn out to be very pleasant. Soon after he had bought his new racer, he and his best friend Reg decided that they would go on a camping holiday. The weather was fine and dry and the forecast seemed promising. They borrowed a small tent and all the basic necessities; pans, kettle, ground-sheet and blankets, and cycled off into the country.

After cycling about twenty miles they found a field near the river at Bewdley, where they could see five or six tents already pitched. They found the farmhouse and asked if they too could pitch their tent in the field. They were told the price for the week and they went down to the site, found themselves a nice spot and set about making themselves comfortable. They had brought sandwiches for their first night, so only needed to make a small fire to brew a cup of tea. This being accomplished they made up their sleeping bags with the blankets they had brought with them and snuggled down for the night. During the night there was a terrific storm and the water came in to the tent from all directions, through the flaps, under the covers, the boys were soaking. Somehow they managed to survive the night huddled up, crouching on the ground sheet which was all but floating away itself.

The next day Ron and Reg could not even find enough dry wood to light a small fire as the rain came down incessantly. They stuck it out for one more night, before giving up in disgust and packing up their sodden belongings and making a very uncomfortable journey home.

Ron's Mum was surprised to see him back so soon but the look on his face and the state of his clothes said it all.

"Never again" said Ron, and he meant it! He only used his bike for local trips and to get to work from that day on.

Ron and Reg remained firm friends, they agreed on most things and just seemed to click. As with most people of their age, then as now, the way they dressed was very important and these two lads had similar taste in clothes, and would often buy the same style of jackets, shoes and hats. In those days every young fellow wore a hat, and Dunn's in Dudley was the place to go to get the most up-to-date selection. Ron was passing by one day and noticed a new style which took his fancy. It was a type of trilby, but more rounded at the top and was called a 'pork-pie' hat. It had a band around it, and stuck in that was a colourful feather. He went into the shop, carefully selected the one that suited him best and bought it. When Reg saw it he wanted one too, and off he went to make his purchase. This happened the other way too, as when Ron saw Reg's new brogue shoes on another occasion, he had to have some of those as well, complete with leather tassels at the end of the laces, and thick crepe soles. Worn with his patterned socks and plus-fours Ron made quite a picture.

Ron and Reg spent most of their free time together, particularly at the weekends, when they would get dressed up and parade up and down Dudley main street from the Castle gate to Top Church along with other like-minded youngsters looking for likely lasses to chat-up. These parades came to be known as 'monkey-runs' and it was a harmless way for young people to meet and make friends. The young men would amble down one side of the street and the girls down the other, until someone caught the other's eye, and the males would move over to the opposite side of the street to continue walking alongside the females and engage them in conversation. If the interest developed, all well and good, if not they moved on and no-one got hurt. Later in the day the young men would visit the Hippodrome in Dudley to see a film, maybe taking a couple of the girls they had met during the day. The lads were very careful to find out where the girls lived before making any offer to walk them home, for, if it was Tipton or even as far away as Netherton, it would mean a long journey back after they had returned the girls to their door. The boys made sure that they really liked the girls before they committed themselves to this extra journey home!

During the early years that Ron had taken an interest in the opposite sex, he became fascinated by a pair of identical twins from Woodsetton. They were called Beryl and Freda and were a little younger than Ron. They did almost everything together, dressed alike and had the same interests. Ron managed to date Beryl and had taken her out a few times to the cinema and for strolls around the area. He went to pick her up at seven o'clock one evening and together they strolled around the Mon's Hill and Wren's Nest area and Ron made sure that they were heading home in good time for Beryl to be delivered to her doorstep before the ten o'clock deadline, with a little time in hand for a kiss and a cuddle before they had to part.

They snuggled up in the nearby alleyway and Ron was astonished at the response he received to his usual kisses.

"Your kissing technique has improved" he remarked to the girl in his arms.

She chuckled as Ron held her closer, and suddenly the penny dropped.

"You're Freda!" he exclaimed.

"Yes" came the whispered response.

Beryl had been feeling under the weather and had asked her twin to stand in for her, to prevent Ron's interest from waning.

The laugh may have been on Ron that evening, but the romance only lasted a short time before his eye was taken by another lass and Beryl was left to find herself another suitor.

Another venue for the 'monkey run' was Tipton High Street, stretching from the railway crossing to the canal bridge, at the Sedgley end. Having sidled up and down on a Saturday afternoon Ron and Reg would then treat themselves to a thre'penny bag of fish and chips to share on the way home, or in the summer, an ice-cream from Pioli's.

The third, and most popular 'monkey run' with the pair, was Sedgley Bull Ring. This had a number of advantages for the scheming adolescent duo. Firstly, it was near Swan Village where they both lived, secondly the girls who walked there also lived in the Hurst Hill or Upper Gornal area and thirdly there were some interesting alley-ways and lanes for a late-night romantic stroll home!

If Ron and Reg were lucky enough to meet up with girls from Hurst Hill, they would choose to walk them home using the main road, through the Gorge, or through Whites Lane. The second had added advantages, as it was dark and narrow, having been built originally for coaches, and at the lower end there were two recesses cut in the stone walls. These had been made to allow for pedestrians to step into as the coach passed by, but the lads found them very convenient now to sidestep into with an attractive girl for a kiss and a cuddle on the way home. The girls must always be home by ten o'clock in those days and the fathers would be waiting on the doorstep if they were late. No young man would wish to attract the wrath of an irate father by bringing his daughter home after the prescribed hour.

When the evening was over, and the girls had been safely delivered home, Ron and Reg could then wend their way back to their own homes, along the main road, if it was a dark night, or taking a short-cut across a dirt track, through the waste land, if it was a moonlit night. This track took them back onto the main road at Four-Lanes End and there was a solitary street light to guide their passage home.

Ron would arrive back home by half-past ten and have to creep quietly indoors, as the rest of the family would, by this time, be tucked up in their beds. The door would have been left unlocked and the slightest noise would alert Mum who would call down "Is that you, our Ron?"

When Ron had acknowledged his presence, his Mum would remind him, as always, to lock up before coming up to bed.

The fire would be nearly out, but the kettle would still be on the hob, quite hot enough for Ron to make himself a cup of cocoa, before going on up. To get into his side of the bed by the wall, Ron had to scramble over the long-suffering Ken who had been happily asleep, before his younger brother made his clumsy entrance.

The previous year, the Coseley council had taken the decision to transform some of the land, made derelict by the open cast mining, into a park which could be used and enjoyed by everyone. The site chosen for this enterprise was land on the north side of St Chad's Church between the private road called Oak Street and Mason Street, and the Birmingham New Road. Ron took a great deal of interest in this project and saw, for the first time in his life something ugly and wasted being transformed into something beautiful and of value to the local inhabitants.

When completed, the park had trees, flower-beds, pathways and a band-stand and the whole area was surrounded by fences and was the pride of all the locals. It was officially opened in 1936 and named Coseley Jubilee Park. From then on, after church, everyone would meander around the park and enjoy the beautiful surroundings; a little oasis in their murky lives of work and toil.

The park became a centre for annual local entertainments. The carnival, fairs and sports could take place in the park and it brought new life to what had been a dead and dreary location. The youngsters now had a new venue for their meetings, and summer evenings would be spent strolling around the park with friends, and although it did not have the boating lakes, as Tipton Victoria Park or Wolverhampton West Park did, it had the advantage of being nearer home for Ron and his friends, so cost them nothing in transport.

Another activity which was very popular with the youth of the day was billiards or snooker, and halls full of snooker tables could be found in several local venues. Ron liked to tag along with his friend, but there was one aspect of these places which he always found distasteful. While Ron's brother and his father both smoked, Ron never had and strongly disliked the halls which were always clouded in thick smoke, no matter what time of the day you entered them. The Labour and Conservative clubs both had tables but only members were allowed to play on them. The hall most often used by Ron and Reg was above Burton's tailor shop on the corner of Castle street and Hall street in Dudley, which was a very narrow shopping alley at that time.

Ron had many amorous encounters at this time, none of which led to lasting relationships however. On one particular Saturday morning he had arranged to meet a girl at the factory gates, as she finished work. He took her to the Criterion cinema to the matinee of the current film show. The film finished at about five o'clock and, being a young gentleman, he offered to take her home. As he had only just met her, he knew very little about her and her home turned out to be in the direction of Netherton. The lass, who was only seventeen herself, informed Ron that they could walk along the canal bank and through the Netherton tunnel to save a long walk along the main road. They set off and Ron was very uncomfortable to see that the dark tunnel was used by numerous courting couples who had congregated there and were kissing and cuddling up against the tunnel wall. He escorted his lady-friend to her door, and decided to take the long way home to avoid the embarrassing spectacle. Unfortunately, it poured with rain on his return journey, and he arrived home at eight o'clock, wet, miserable and hungry, resolving to limit his advances to girls who lived nearer to home!

When Reg was seventeen, his mother bought him a small, second hand car. It was a 1932 M.G. Morris, made in Oxford, purchased from Copes' showroom in the Dudley High Street. They sold motor cycles, three wheeled Morgans and small M.G. cars and this one cost about thirty five pounds. It had a canvas roof which could be removed and stored under the front seats in good weather. The Morris Minor engine had dual carburetters and the gear change was through a gate shift and the driver needed to double declutch with every gear change.

The acquisition of the car revolutionised the boys' social lives as so few people of any age possessed such luxuries, they had certainly moved up in the world.

There was only one petrol station in Sedgley - the High Holborn Garage, and it sold three types of fuel. R.O.P. (Russian Oil Products) cost one shilling and a penny, Shell cost one and tuppence and Benzole cost one and thre'pence. Unfortunately Reg's car needed the dearest as it suited the engine best.

Reg and Ron decided that the car had to have a name, and between them, they came up with the name "Maestro." Within a week, Ron had painted the name on the side of the bonnet and the lads were off on their new exploits.

During the next two years, the vehicle took the young men to many new and exciting places and they felt they had moved into an elite group in the district, along-side the one or two other fortunate young men who also owned motor cars. Teddy Holden, whose mother owned the Park Inn, had a small sports car, as did Dick Hilton, the bank manager's lad, but that was about all.

Occasionally Reg and Ron would drive to Nottingham to visit a relative of Reg's and would drop in at the race track at Donnington

Boys style plates of the 1920's as worn by boys of the middle class.

Park to watch the motor races. Reg's tiny vehicle would be dwarfed by its neighbours as it parked along side the open-topped Bentleys and Rolls Royces, but the lads didn't care, they felt equal to any man as they sat and enjoyed the excitement. The occupants of the large limousines would bring out their picnic tables and folding chairs, their huge hampers and their bottles of champagne and sit in front of the car facing the track while they ate their delicacies and sipped their wine. Ron and Reg would pull out their old blanket and throw it on the grass and then unpack their sandwiches from a brown paper bag and tuck in, without a care in the world.

The racing cars were open topped and the actions of the drivers could be clearly visible as they drove by. The hand break was on the side of the vehicle, and a lever beside the steering wheel could be clearly seen being pumped when the driver needed to increase the oil-pressure to the engine. After the race the young men enjoyed a visit to the pits to see these machines at close quarters.

After one race meeting, when they were returning home it started to rain very heavily and Reg put his foot down to try to get home before darkness fell completely. Their speed caught the attention of the police on the road between Burton and Lichfield and they were pulled up. The police officer had to speak to Reg through a small side flap beside the window. He wanted to know who the car belonged to, where they had been, where they lived and only let them proceed when he was satisfied with the replies.

The constable's parting shot was "Watch your speed, mate. Don't imagine you are Crasher White" (one of the drivers who they had seen racing at Donnington that afternoon!)

They were glad to get back home that night, rather chastened and damp, but with more happy memories to store away, as they put the car away in the old barn behind the Summer House and returned to their homes.

As Ron was by this time devoting much of his spare time to his work and his college studies, the only time available for socialising was Saturday afternoon and evening and the farthest the lads travelled in the motor was to Penn Common or Highgate Common to meet up with other youths who had travelled there on push-bike, motor bike or one or two in cars to congregate and chat together. As it got towards evening, they would make their way back to Sedgley where they would park in the Red Lion car park to continue their conversations while viewing the girls who walked up and down the High Street. The lads had had their own time on the common away from the girls but were now quite happy to meet up with them again. The girls would sidle over as the evening drew to a close, in the hope of getting a lift home on the back of a motor-bike or, even better in one of the few cars that were there.

Reg was, of course, very popular from the time he got his motor car and, if he found someone he liked, he would whisper to Ron "Do me a favour, pal, hang on here until I've taken her home, then I'll come back and fetch you."

If the girl lived in the same direction as the lads, Reg would drive Ron home first with the girl sitting on Ron's knee in the front of the tiny car, but this didn't often happen. More often than not Ron had other plans for himself and would end up walking home the quiet way, with a girl of his own on his arm.

Ron sometimes was allowed to get behind the wheel of his pal's car himself and this was how he first learned to drive. He was hoping to be able to save up to buy a small car for himself, but the Military service and the Second World War was to put an end to that dream for the time being.

Another of Ron and Reg's friends was a young man called Les Nicholls. His father ran a cycle shop in Clifton Street and Les had an electricity business with his brother, Ron. Les also ran a separate part-time business on the side, charging accumulators which were used to run the modern wirelesses. Although many homes now boasted piped gas, very few had mains electricity to run their sets. Les would call round to each customer, once a week and collect the old accumulator and replace it with a recharged one. He would then take all the used ones back to his shop and put them on charge ready for the following week. For this service, he collected sixpence each.

In 1938 Les bought the latest new French Citroen and he would collect Ron and Reg when he had finished his work on a long summer evening, and the three young men would drive off to Rhyl, arriving often as late as half-past seven. They would travel through Shrewsbury to Wrexham, Llangollen, winding precariously around the Horse-shoe Pass and arriving eventually at the promenade and the sea-front. They would spend a couple of hours along the arcades watching the holiday makers and the fun along the sands, before buying a bag of fish and chips a piece and returning to the car to arrive home by midnight.

These were the carefree days, but clouds were beginning to gather over the lives of all the young men as talk of trouble in Europe increased.

Ron's progress through his apprenticeship passed very successfully with him being called upon to assist in the design and production of patterns for more modern styles of garments. They would look at the basic style features such as the lapel width, pocket shape and jacket vents, and try to design subtle differences which would improve and modernise the garments. They would then make up the pattern for the cutters to use, call the factory manager into the design office to hear his views on the modifications before getting the design made up into a wearable garment which could be placed on a standard dummy. If any changes were needed they could be effected at this stage before the garment was finished off and then modelled by one of the factory lads who was of a standard size.

It was then that all the managers would meet together to inspect the new product before Ron was given the go-ahead to make up sets of patterns for the cutters to use. Special stiff brown paper was used and Ron first made the full set of pieces for the basic thirty-eight inch chest size and then scale each piece up, or down, to the next size as he had learned to do at college. The work took several weeks to complete and Ron was meticulous and painstaking in its execution and when completed each set comprised patterns for sizes thirty-four to forty-six chest, in regular, long, short, 'portly' and 'corpulent'. Each set of pattern pieces was punched with a hole so that it could be strung together and the cutter could collect the set he required as the orders came in.

The cutters kept their own record of each garment they had cut out and the material they had used, because they were paid, not only on the number of suits they cut out, but also on the difficulty of the work done. If a check or a pin-stripe material was used, it required a greater amount of skill that cutting a plain fabric, because of all the careful matching of seams, lapels, pocket-flaps and so on that was involved, so they were paid at a higher rate.

On occasions a difficult order would come in which required a special pattern to be produced. Ron would then be called upon to produce a one-off pattern and invariably to cut it out too. This would happen especially on days when there was very little work for the cutters to do and they had been laid off for the day. It was important that the small amount of work that the firm did get was treated with the greatest care, and luckily Ron had the skill and experience to do both jobs well.

Bulk orders of up to ten suits of the same size were cut out all together using a band saw. The stock cutter would take a piece of white waxed linen and place the pattern for the suit he was cutting onto it. The pattern would have small holes along all the lines for cutting. The pattern would be placed on a pile of cloth up to ten layers thick, and held down by heavy flat irons. The cutter would then brush powdered pipe-clay over the pattern so that it dropped into the holes, leaving a row of dots on the fabric beneath. The pile of cloth was then placed over the band-saw and cut into more manageable pieces. These saws were evil contraptions and would not be allowed in the workplace today, but in the thirties they were in common use and were the cause of many accidents and even mutilations of the cutters.

Jobs were too scarce for the workers to complain about their conditions of work and at times the managers took advatage of this fact. If there was very little work on a particular day, a manager would be sent down to the main gate, promptly at eight to lock the entrance, then, a little while later the boss would go down and line up any late-comers and question each one about the reason for their late arrival. If there was no work to be done, he would send them off home with a warning and of course they didn't get paid that day. At busy times they weren't so strict on time keeping and the main gate was never locked against the workers. Christmas, Easter and Whitsuntide were considered to be busy trading times and the cutting room staff could then be told as late as five o'clock, one hour from normal finishing time, that they were required to work on until seven or even half-past in order to complete an order.

'Tank' Siddaway took advantage of these overtime sessions as he kept a supply of chocolate bars in his large drawer under his cutting table. In the ten minute break which the workers were allowed before they resumed their labours, Mr Siddaway, whose wife ran a small sweet shop in Netherton, would bring out his goody bars and sell them to the hungry workers. The cutting room manager always turned a blind eye to this little bit of business done on the side.

Now that Ron had his Diplomas, he was treated with respect and was given much more responsibility. He would be sent down to different parts of the factory to sort out little problems which occured. This enabled him to see at close range the full range of the manufacturing processes involved in making the garments from start to finish. Most of the time, however, he was in his office producing templates to be used by the cutters to shape the various styles of lapels and collars.

The foreman, Gerry Oakley from Gornal Wood, often went into Ron's office and just stand and watch the young man work. He seemed to be genuinely interested by the way Ron designed the different items, and would often question him on what he was doing and how he came by the different ideas. It was some time later, when Ron had left 'Town Mills', that the naive youth discovered that Gerry had left his office on several occasions to attend a managerial meeting, and there would present what he had just learned as his own ideas. Ron had trusted him and believed him to be an honest and religious person but he still had a lot to learn in the cut throat world of business.

Trouble was now looming in the country and everyone became increasingly aware that there was going to be a confrontation with Germany. The Government decided that all twenty-year-olds would have to register for six months military service. Ron came into this category and all the patterns which he had been working on for the new styles for nineteen-forty had to be put into store. Town Mills factory was told, that in the event of a war, they would be commissioned to make military uniforms.

The supply department of the War Office sent the firm the basic pattern for a battle-dress suit and a great-coat. Ron now had to produce complete sets of patterns for these items, for the cutters to use, if and when the country ever went to war. The size, style and shape of all these garments had to meet the stringent details set down. No imagination was allowed, no variation and definitly no fashionable little extras! A new life was approaching fast for Ron as it gradually dawned on him that he could very soon be wearing one of these uniforms himself. The pleasure that he had felt for his design work had gone for the time being.

The long hot summer days of 1939 gave way to fearful thoughts for Ron and his friends. Holidays, new cars, jaunts out into the country and even career advancement soon became of little importance as it was announced that all twenty-year-olds had to register for six months Military service.

In June, Ron and his contempararies had to attend a school in Smethwick to have a full medical examination to see if they were fit to complete the six month training.

Each young man had to strip bare and parade naked in front of three doctors; one tested their eyesight, another their heart and a third took a sample of urine for analysis. Measurements and physical details were noted and the lads were sent off home again to await the findings.

Three weeks later Ron received results of his medical in the form of a card detailing name, height, weight, age, colour of eyes and hair, blood group and general health grade. As Ron was classed as grade 'A' health, he could be called up at a moment's notice.

Reg was not yet twenty-years-old, so he and another friend of Ron called Fred Brooks decided to enlist in the Terretorial Army in Tipton so they could be prepared for any eventuality.

Ron, with his usual attention to detail, decided to take a course in German at the technical college, during the summer months, knowing that in the event of war he would be one of the first to be called up.

Ron had seen a fair bit of tragedy in his family in the preceding year. During the previous summer, his aunt had died very suddenly while on holiday with her husband, Ben. They had not long been married and Ron had seen how happy they had been, buying and establishing their home together in Netherton. They were both in their late thirties when they married, but Uncle Ben was soon to follow his wife to the grave, as only three months later he, too, had a heart attack after church one night and died when he was visiting his own Mother. The shock of the double tragedy took its toll on her, because, before the year was out, she too died suddenly. The family seemed to be surrounded by tragedy as not long afterwards Ron's Grandfather died and Ron's father had to grieve for his family while waiting to hear when his sons would be called up to fight for their country. It was a devastating time for them all.

By the beginning of September 1939 they learned that they had declared war on Germany and their lives would never be the same again.

Ron received a letter telling him to report to an army camp in Prestatyn, North Wales and he took it straight to the Managing Director of Town Mills.

"Leave it to me, lad." He said, "I will tell them that you are needed for service here".

Ron knew that he was working on military uniforms and was quite satisfied when Mr Gordon Smith, another of the directors, went in to see him some time later, and told him that he was to ignore the letter, and get on with producing the uniform patterns. He worked round the clock to complete the patterns that the cutters needed to make the hundreds and hundreds of uniforms which the firm had been commissioned to produce.

Two weeks later, on a Friday afternoon, Ron was alarmed to see his younger brother Gordon approaching him, waving an official looking registered envelope at him. It had been delivered that morning, and his Mother had realised it must have been important and had sent it over as soon as Gordon got home from school.

Ron opened the envelope with shaking fingers. At the top of the letter was an official Army Crest, beneath that was Ron's name and army number, 236369, which was to be etched on his brain for the next six years. But what was written below made the poor young man freeze to the bone. The letter instructed him to report to the army camp at Prestatyn by twelve noon the following day or he would be treated as a soldier 'absent without leave'.

Ron took the letter directly to his superior Sid Fryer and together they went to the Managing Director, who looked somewhat taken aback.

"You'll have to do what they say, now, lad" he said.

Ron realised at that moment, that the firm had been detaining him there to work for them, without military permission.

He returned to his office where Gordon was still standing, opened his drawer, collected his personal belongings, waved a cheery good-bye to his friends and went to collect his bicycle and left the factory, not knowing when he would see it again.

He sent Gordon back home to tell his Mother he would be back soon and then cycled to Tipton railway station to find the times of trains to get him to the army camp before noon the following day. He was told that the train left at half-past eight to arrive at eleven, so armed with this knowledge, he made his way home to face his poor Mother.

He had a few hours to prepare himself to leave for an uncertain future. He visited his friends to bid them farewell and to one special girl who he had been seeing for some time, Cath Sherwood, in the hope that he would see her again soon.

Like so many of his age, Ron could not envisage what life was going to be like from now on, nor the horrors that he would experience, nor the heart-ache and loneliness he would endure.

It was to be six years before Ron's life returned to normal.

ARMY DAYS
(1939 - 1946)

ON Saturday morning, 16th October 1939, Ron left home in fear and trepidation and made his way on foot to Owen Street railway station to catch the train to the army camp at Prestatyn, North Wales. As the steam train chugged its way north, Ron could not help thinking of the life he was leaving behind and the unknown experiences that lay ahead.

He arrived at his destination before midday and looked around to see if there was somebody from the camp to meet him. No such niceties existed in the new world into which he was entering, and on enquiring at the office, he was given directions to the army camp which was situated about a mile and half away along the main Prestatyn to Rhyl road.

The army camp was, in fact, part of the Cook's Holiday camp, some of which was still occupied by late holiday-makers, intent on making the most of their hard-earned pleasure while they still could and before the war started in Britain itself.

Ron reached the entrance to the camp and reported in to the main office. He was sent along to the dining room to get a meal after his journey and found a mixture of civilian and military personnel already there, enjoying their lunch together. He joined them, noting how peace and war was blending together in these early days of the conflict.

Ron's first task after he had eaten, was to report to the quarter-master's stores to be fitted out with his military uniform and, having worked in the trade, was able to tell the officer the sizes of clothes that he required. He was given a battle-dress suit and an overcoat which Ron felt, at first, was a mile too long, but in the cold of the bitter winter, he was to wish was even longer. Three shirts, three vests, two pairs of long-john under-pants, four pairs of socks, a pullover and a cap, with a Royal Corps Signals badge to wear on it, completed his collection of clothes. He continued to assemble his basic necessities by adding an enamel mug, dish, plate and a set of cutlery, and brushes and cleaning materials for his boots and brass buttons. All these newly acquired and strange possessions were stowed into a kit-bag and Ron was taken to one of the cabins which was to be home to him for the time being.

He was introduced to the other occupant, who was a lad from London. There were two narrow beds in the small hut and a wash basin with hot and cold running water, stood in one corner. There were two blankets on each bed, a pillow, complete with pillow-case, and sheets. Baths were to be found in a separate long wooden hut a short distance away.

"Not too bad" thought Ron as he settled in to his new surroundings, "Not like home, but could be worse".

A week later things changed. The holiday-makers left to return home, and the camp was completely taken over by the Royal Signals Regiment. The beds were stripped of their sheets and pillow-cases, the tables lost their table-cloths, the hot water ceased to flow in the basins and reality struck the young soldiers.

The dining-room became the instruction room, and, as there were no morse code keys, spoons would be used as keys, and they would bash out the signals with these on the bare wooden boards of the tables. During the first week at the camp each new conscript was interviewed by senior officers to decide the most suitable course for each to take. Ron was allocated to be trained as a wireless operator, which included a course of study in electricity and magnetism. However, the first month consisted of army drill-bashing which was designed to improve the fitness of the young men and prepare them for the rigours ahead.

The camp was separated from the sea by large rolling sand-dunes and these were often used for physical training during these first four weeks of preparation, and once a week they would take a fourteen mile route march up into the Welsh hills. No leave was allowed during this initiation period, so they knew little of their surroundings other than what they could see on their training exercises. Each Sunday morning they attended a church service in the Entertainment hall. Unless they were Roman Catholic the young soldiers were assumed to be Church of England and attendance was compulsory. Ron was beginning to understand the rules and discipline of army life.

The soldiers also learned their first facts about weaponry and were trained in the use of army rifles, both as a weapon and as a drill implement.

For the following five months Ron was instructed in the work of a wireless operator, a training which was to take place during one of the coldest winters on record in that part of the country, and during which time Ron made good use of his great-coat, both during the day and at night, when it was used as an extra blanket over his bed. The edge of the sea, along the beach, froze solid at times, and the houses along the promenade had icicles hanging from their gutters for weeks on end, as the bitter weather took a hold on the coastal town.

During the signal training period, the regime became a matter of habit, with the soldiers rising at seven, washing, shaving and dressing before making their way to the dining room for a filling but uninteresting breakfast of a type of porridge, followed by beans, bacon and chunks of bread. The young men would then return to their chalets to clean their boots and prepare for the first roll-call parade of the day.

Ron was in squad 26 which consisted of thirty lads all preparing, like him, to be wireless operators. Following roll-call they would be marched in file to a long wooden hut, where they would spend the day learning the intricacies of their new occupation. They learned about radio maintenance as well as the morse code, and Ron found it strange to translate dots and dashes into the letters of the alphabet. The young minds soon picked up the new skills required to send and receive messages in the codes they had learned and would use the sand dunes to send their messages across the beaches while they practiced their art. They used the sun's rays and mirrors to transmit messages and also used semaphore flags to contact their partners situated at the other end of the beach, who received the message and, hopefully, indicated they had understood.

During this first month, Ron legally became a man, as he had reached his twenty first birthday on 10th November. There was no chance of celebration as he was confined to camp and the event went unmarked as he prepared to play his part in the country's conflict in Europe.

After the first month of training, the young soldiers were given a week-end pass, which allowed them to stay out until 23.59 hours. This ensured that they were back in camp by midnight. If the weather allowed, Ron and a friend would walk the two miles into the town of Rhyl in order to save the bus fare. The new recruits only earned one shilling a day, and had to save where-ever they could. The lads never left the camp until they had eaten the lunch which was provided for them, so that they did not have to buy their meal in the town. Ron had been familiar with the many ways of conserving his meagre resources as a youngster, and this knowledge was to come in useful again now.

As the holiday season had ended and the war-time black-out rules were in place, the town looked drab and uninviting at best, but one bright spot was on a Saturday night when 'The Queens Hotel' held a dance. The soldiers were allowed in for one shilling and they had the chance to meet some of the local Welsh girls. These lasses were glad of the company, as their friends had all been called up too, and were in other camps preparing for war in different ways.

One particular girl that Ron took a shine to, lived in one of the hill villages above the town, and after a pleasant evening dancing, Ron would escort her to the main bus station to catch her bus home, then he would have to walk in black-out darkness the three-quarters of an hour journey back to camp. It was a tedious haul, but the female company was worth it.

Next to the camp was a small collection of huts and other buildings which were used by the public for general entertainments. There was a miniature golf course, a small boating lake and a cafe. The complex was known as "Y Frith". The soldiers could walk along the sand-dunes, when they were not training or on duty, and buy a cup of tea and meet some of the local residents. The older people appreciated talking to the young men and the young lads liked to talk to them as it bridged the gulf between the camp and their home and families.

The six months tuition course passed fairly quickly and at the end of it Ron passed out as a grade B3 wireless operator. The soldiers were given a week's leave and a travel pass to allow them to go home to visit their families. Ron walked purposefully towards the station feeling quite elated and knowing how pleased his family would be to see him. His parents greeted him warmly and were pleased to see how fit and well he looked. Ken had tried to join the army, but as he was a carpenter he had been put into the reserves and was occupied building shelters, in and around Birmingham. Gordon had not passed his medical and was never to be fit enough for military service after his bout of childhood rheumatic fever.

The leave was soon over and Ron returned to his camp to be re-assigned to another posting. The original '26 Squad' was now split up and Ron, with five others of the group, was sent to join the 2nd London Divisional Signals which was camped just outside Cambridge. They were housed under canvas and Ron found it quite strange at first to be sleeping on the hard ground, under the apple trees in an orchard. They were not destined to stay there very long, however, but long enough for Ron to make the aquaintance of a local girl called Peggy Ringwood.

After a matter of weeks they were told that they were on the move again and Ron soon learned that they were to go to a more familiar location as far as he was concerned - to Ribbesford House near Bewdley. Once again they were camped under canvas but, as they were already past the cold winter months, it was not an unpleasant experi-

Mogadishu, Italian Somaliland, East Africa.

Fort Wajir, Northern Kenya.

ence. Ron was now just twenty miles from home and could receive visits from his mother and 'Aunty' Hilda on warm afternoons when they could sit beside the river Severn and forget, for a short time, the reason for Ron's absence from home.

The men made several more moves over the next few months, first to Pensay Court, just five miles from Bewdley, where they slept in out-buildings on wooden floors, then a few weeks later to Herefordshire. They camped under canvas again in Hay in the grounds of a large house near to the village. From there Ron and a few more of the squadron were sent with their wireless communications to a small Welsh village by the name of Gilwern, close to Abergavenny. The facilities were spartan and the soldiers had to take their meals in a small local cafe as they had no cook-house of their own. Once a week they were trans-ported by lorry to a coal mine in the valley, where they had their weekly bath.

This posting was only for a few short weeks, but long enough for Ron to get to know some of the local girls at the Saturday dance. One young lady in particular took Ron's fancy and he was taken home to tea on several occasions, getting to meet her mother and father, (who was an Inspector in the local police force). Ron and his girl-friend would wander the hills when his schedule allowed and enjoy the peace that existed in this tranquil place. A particular favourite walk for the couple was up 'sugar loaf' hill, where they would sit and look down on the village below.

This peaceful interlude was short-lived, however, as the group were recalled to their headquarters in Hay to be sent on manoevres again, this time over an area called 'The Black Mountains.' Again they were under canvas, but this time in a large bell tent with a central pole. The soldiers slept around the pole with their feet pointing towards the centre. Space was very limited, as were provisions, and rain coats were used as ground sheets and kit-bags, containing their clothes, doubled as pillows. Two blankets were used to best effect; under as a thin mattress and folded double to make as thick a layer as possible for warmth on top.

Each morning they would wake up, still partially clothed, and make their way outside to a long wooden table along which were a number of taps delivering cold water for them to wash and shave. They returned to the cramped tent to get dressed before going to yet another large tent which was where they ate. After breakfast, they would visit the ablutions cubicals which concealed dug out holes in the ground over each of which was placed a makeshift wooden seat, upon which they attempted to squat. Ron was a fastidious young man and he found it difficult to adjust to these primitive conditions at first.

During this period, the country was on alert as a German invasion was expected at any time. One third of the camp had to do guard duty each night, and the soldiers had to parade around the perimeter of the camp for two hours continuously and then had four hours off. They carried rifles but no ammunition and it was doubtful if they could have been much of a deterrent if "Gerry" had attacked the camp anyway. There were no lights, of course, so it was very difficult for the guards to see where they were going as they patrolled the fences and they were cold and tired as their night duty finished, but it had to be business as usual next day; no time off was given to compensate for their lack of sleep.

They were finally moved to a military camp just outside the City of Hereford, where they enjoyed a last few days of socialising in the town before being told that they were being posted abroad. Naturally they were not told the actual destination, but as they drew their overseas kit out of the quartermaster's stores, a pith helmet was found to be a part of their new uniform and they soon realised that their new destination was somewhere hot, and in all probability North Africa. It dawned on the young men that this was now going to be 'the real thing.' This was what they had been training for all these months.

They were granted seven days 'embarkation leave' and a railway pass to get them home. Ron arrived in the village to be greeted by his best pal Reg, who was also on leave from the army. Reg still had his M.G. sports car and together they visited old haunts and tried to recapture those carefree days of the previous summer. The country was under constant air attack, and the families had become accustomed to disappearing into the cellars and air-raid shelters when the sirens sounded. Ron refused to succumb to the threat from the skies and did not take shelter each time the screeching noise began. He stayed defiantly in his home and, seeing this, his family followed suit and together they waited until the 'all clear' was heard again. Ron used his day-time hours to visit family and friends to say good-bye, not knowing when he would see them again and not daring to wonder 'if?'.

The leave was over and Ron returned to camp and began the task of packing all the signalling equipment into wooden packing-cases. The men then had to report to the medical officer on two consecutive days to receive their tropical diseases innoculations. Some of them reacted quite badly to the tetanus and yellow fever injections and Ron's arm swelled up alarmingly after the first one, but he had to continue with the work while nursing his throbbing limb. So the preparations were completed and one Friday evening in October 1940, almost one year after Ron had begun his training, he, and his comrades were marched down to the railway station to board the steam-train which was to carry them on the first stage of their journey. They were taken to Liverpool, Lime Street station where they were assembled in ranks to be marched down to the docks. There they found that the next stage of their journey was to be on a converted cargo ship, which was named S.S. Orbita. It was a twenty-thousand-ton cargo carrier which had been converted as a troopship, and would be home to the men for the next eight weeks.

The men marched up the narrow gang-plank, and assembled on deck to be assigned their living and sleeping quarters. They were taken to a lower deck, and there they saw row upon row of narrow wooden tables, on either sides of which were long wooden benches, and slung from the ceiling were rows of hammocks for the soldiers to sleep in. Each man was allocated his own eating, living and sleeping space and was informed that two men would be assigned each day from each table to fetch the food from the galley. It would be in alphabetical order, and Ron realised that he would be one of the first to perform this task. Sure enough when the rota was posted Baker A.R. No. 2362396 was top of the list along with a lad called Carter.

As dinner was at six o'clock, the pair made sure they knew where they had to go and found that the kitchens were on a lower deck approached by means of a narrow twisting iron staircase. As the time arrived, Baker and Carter duly made their way to collect the food for their table, and joined the queue of men already in line. The food was delivered to the men in large enamel containers which required both hands to carry. They therefore had to manoevre themselves back along the corridor and up the narrow twisting staircase without a free hand to steady themselves. The first night there were grumbles from those waiting behind to ascend the stairs, as the young men struggled with the difficult task. Those waiting for their meal did not realise what difficulties lay ahead for them as they tucked into their first meal aboard ship. The empty containers then had to be returned below when the meal was finished.

Lights-out was at ten o'clock, but first the soldiers had to perform the novel task of making up and then getting into their hammock. The hammock had to be unrolled and the blankets folded into place and then the soldiers had to find a way of getting onto the mobile sling without being tipped out again. There was a great deal of hilarity as first one and then another of the men triumphantly landed in the centre of his hammock, only to find himself, unceremoniously dumped onto the deck a second later. Ron found that there was quite a bit of skill involved in staying in place, but once achieved found it quite comfortable and easy to sleep in the strange contraption.

Before they knew it, they were up again washing, shaving and preparing for the day. They noticed how difficult it was to get a lather for shaving, and were told that what they were using was salt water as all the fresh water had to be conserved for drinking. Special salt-water soap could be bought, as they continued their voyage, which made washing a lot easier.

The ship took two days to complete its preparations for departure, and when it finally pulled out of harbour and down the estuary the soldiers watched the progress from the rails along the ship's side. As they moved out into the Irish Sea, they joined numerous other vessels. They were told that there were over forty ships assembling to sail in convoy into the North Atlantic, escorted by two warships. It took another two days for all the ships to be assembled and at that point they set off together for their unknown destination.

A heavy swell was felt on the third day and Ron noticed that several of the men turned distinctly strange colours and disappeared for a couple of days leaving those with stronger stomachs with extra rations at table, as their places were left empty when mealtimes arrived. The bad weather lasted only two or three days, by which time most of the men had found their sea-legs and were back to normal.

During the day-time many of the lads would spend time up on deck, watching the progress of the flotilla and counting the number of ships around them. The number changed constantly, depending on the weather and the visibility. Some days were sunny and visibility was good, others were foggy and the ship slowed down and few other ships could be seen.

A week after they had set out, on a Sunday morning, they were woken up to the sound of gun-fire from their own destroyers. The convoy was under attack from a German battleship, 'The Scharnhoerst'. The faster vessels broke away to out-run the enemy vessel, leaving the slower ships with their escort to try to evade the gunfire. The destoyers laid down a thick black smokescreen to cover the positions of the slower vessels as they made their get-away. It was a narrow escape for these raw recruits and they were relieved when they were told they were out of range of the enemy ship and one week later, they put into harbour at Freetown, West Africa, to take on fresh supplies of water and food. It was here that they learned that, in order to evade the German gunboats which were working the North Atlantic, their Captain had taken a route in the direction of Newfoundland, and had covered three times the expected distance to get to this port.

Here in Freetown, S.S. Orbita joined others of the convoy in the large harbour. Small boats came alongside and the locals called up to the young men to entice them to buy their produce. The contents of the tiny vessels looked very tempting to those who had been surviving on dry and uninteresting military provisions for so long. Buckets and baskets were lowered over the side on lengths of rope, then fruit and other delicacies were placed in them, before being hauled back up. The soldiers then put English money into the container again to pay for what they had taken.

After a few days in port the ship resumed its journey south and the weather became noticeably warmer. The lads often took their blankets up on deck at night to sleep, as it became intolerably hot in the confines below deck as they neared the equator.

Days were now taken up with army talks and physical exercises, which helped to pass the time. The young men still had plenty of spare time on their hand however and used it to get to know each other. Ron soon disclosed what his profession had been before he had enlisted, and the Non-Commissioned Officers were glad to avail themselves of his skills to sew badges of rank onto tropical uniforms as they prepared for the different climate. Ron was glad of the job as it filled his time and brought some familiarity to the strange surroundings in which he now found himself.

After a full four weeks at sea, the ship rounded the tip of South African, the Cape of Good Hope. Ron could see Cape Town and Table Mountain in the distance. He realised, from the movement of the ship, that this was not to be a port of call, but a couple of days later the ship pulled further in, towards the land and they docked in Port Elizabeth in South Africa. Here, at last, the men were allowed ashore and had their first opportunity to wear their tropical uniform. It was made of cotton and consisted of a tunic, buttoned high to the neck, with four pleated, patch pockets. This was worn with cotton shorts with turn-ups which could be unbuttoned and turned down at night when the mosquitoes started to bite. The mosquitoes were a constant cause of annoyance, not only because of the irritation they caused, but because of the danger from malaria which they spread. Because of the heat, the men also had 'pith helmets' to wear to protect their heads from the sun. The style of this uniform dated back to the Boer War of 1900 and was still as effective in the heat as it had been then.

Ron took the opportunity to investigate the town of Port Elizabeth, and discovered that it was a very clean place, with lots of green parks and gardens, many of which had wooden benches on which one could rest in the shade. He was astonished to see for the first time in his life, the signs of colour discrimination, as on each seat was clearly marked "WHITES ONLY". Having once seen this, he continued to notice the same warning on buses and on public toilets. It was the first time he had come face to face with the effects of Apartheid in Africa and he did not like how it made him feel.

They continued their voyage from there to Durban, where they stayed for four days, being made to feel very welcome by the local white community. A group of the lads were allowed ashore each day and would visit the local 'Toc H' group which supplied them with free tea and cakes, and they were sometimes invited up to the farms where they would be taken from the ship after lunch to spend some time in the open spaces.

The main street of Durban was very wide and stretched for quite a distance. One sight which caught Ron's eye one day, was a large Zulu male, dressed in African garb and feathered hat, running towards him between the shafts of a rickshaw. On the two seats behind the native were two naval ratings. As he ran along, the vehicle achieved quite a fast pace and his hefty body only just balanced the combined weight of the contraption and passengers behind him. Occasionally, the front would tip up slightly, lifting his feet off the ground for several yards, the momentum keeping the forward movement going sufficiently, until his feet made contact with the ground again. This must have made for an exhilerating ride for the ratings, and not a little frightening. Ron did not follow their example and decided to continue his exploration on foot!

Weeks had passed by while they had been at sea and Christmas 1940 had passed too. As they approached the New Year they were still ignorant of their final destination, and they would discuss where they thought they would be taken. It was suggested, by some, that they would probably continue up the East coast of Africa, turning into the Red Sea, through the Suez Canal to arrive in Egypt to join the North Africa Campaign, but after a few more days at sea, they were told to collect all their kit and prepare for disembarkation. The destination was Kilindini, the harbour for Mombasa, Kenya's main port.

Ron calculated that they had been at sea for eight weeks; aboard ship it had seemed longer, onshore much shorter.

Everyone left the ship and the troups were paraded on the dockside, before being marched to the nearby station to board a train marked with the letters K U R, which stood for Kenya and Ugandan Railways.

It was now evening and the seats were flat slatted benches. Each compartment carried a sign which said "To carry ten people." Ron took his seat and tried to make himself comfortable for the night - a pretty impossible task with all his paraphenalia around him in such a small space. Somehow or other they all managed to get through the night and were quite thankful when dawn broke and they were at least able to look out of the windows and see the landscape on either side. They could see zebra, giraffe and herds of deer in their natural surroundings and later were told that they had passed through Tsavo Game Reserve.

The train stopped at Nairobi station for a couple of hours and the men were able to alight and stretch their cramped legs. They were fed huge egg sandwiches by large East African white ladies, and given drinks to slake their thirst.

Back on board for the final leg of their journey, they climbed up through the Ngong Hills and then down and down into the great rift valley below. Now they could see the huge lake, Naivasha, which was near their military camp at Gil-gil, Kenya. The soldiers had been on the cramped train for twenty-four hours when they finally arrived at their destination. They were shown their new quarters, which turned out to be split-bamboo huts with thick wooden beds arranged in lines on the dirt floor and makeshift cupboards being the only other semblance of furniture there. The beds had no mattresses but strips of canvas stretched across the frame for support and the cupboards consisted of a couple of empty wooden petrol-can boxes perched one on top of the other. These boxes were in plentiful supply, as this was the way that petrol was carried for the East African Forces, so they were always available for many uses around the camp.

These petrol boxes and the cans themselves became treasured possessions as they could be used for many purposes, and basic raw materials were scarce in these parts. Each box held six gallon cans of petrol and were known as 'Debes' in Swahili. They were strong and sturdy enough to be used as makeshift furniture; upside down as small stools, and perched sideways one on top of another, as cupboards. The cans themselves, when empty, also had their uses. They were used to fetch water or as cannisters, and when they were no longer able to be of value for that, they were hammered flat and used as 'tiles' to cover the roof of the hut.

Ron and his comrades unloaded their kit and made their way, as instructed to the dining-room, which was another small building, similar

85

Interior of Fort Wajir.

to their own sleeping quarters. They happily tucked into their first fresh meal since leaving the ship, and were glad to make their way after it to their beds, which although they were pretty basic, were more comfortable that the conditions had been on the train.

Ron slept well in this strange place and woke the following morning to embrace whatever lay ahead, with fortitude. Although washing and shaving took place with cold water, at least it was fresh water and produced a satisfactory lather, and in the heat of the surroundings it was not unpleasant to use the cool water anyway. They soon learned that there was a NAAFI (Navy, Army and Airforce Institute) store on the camp, which was open from early morning until late in the evening for them to buy drinks, cigarettes, sweets and other supplies. The men had been unable to draw any army money since leaving Port Elizabeth, so were owed six weeks pay at one shilling per day, plus another sixpence a day as overseas allowance. This was riches indeed, but the only place they could spend it was on the camp, as they weren't allowed to go into Gil-gil.

A further hut was set up as a store for all the signalling equipment and for use for training and lectures. This valuable equipment had to be guarded at night, and two soldiers, Ron being one of them, was allocated to this position. Ron was quite pleased with this move, as it meant that, instead of being in the noisy hut with twenty other men, he was in a quiet room with only one other.

Again night-duty was called for, and because of his guarding of the supplies hut, Ron had this dubious pleasure only once. The poor fellow was scared witless, not because he thought he may be attacked by the natives or stray Germans, but by all the wild animals which he felt were out there in the dark, waiting to pounce. He counted the different sounds as the night progressed, and detected at least a dozen different calls of animals waiting to drag him off into the dark bush and devour him at their leisure!

At the end of their first week in Kenya the men were told that they would provide communications between South African, East African, Gold Coast, Nigerians and Rhodesian brigades. The Division would be 'The 12th East African Division', and the badge to identify it was to be the South African antelope, the kudu. Ron's unit would now become 'The East African Signals'. The 11th African Division had already been formed and was waiting in camp, somewhere in Kenya.

The Signals camp was situated, from 1941 to 1945, on the Karen Estate which had formerly been the home of Baron and Baroness Von Blixen (nee Isak Dineson). It was she who made the Karen Estates famous in her book 'Out Of Africa'. The whole region was farmed by aristocrats and nobility from the English establishment who had failed to fit in, for one reason or another, with the British way of life, back in the homeland. Here in Africa these 'Socialite Settlers' indulged in a lifestyle where their exclusive aim was the pursuit of pleasure. The area encompassing the homes and farms of these people, therefore, came to be known as 'Happy Valley'.

One such man was Josslyn Hay, Earl of Erroll. He was a leading figure in Kenya's colonial community, and was appointed Kenya Military Secretary in 1940. His life was devoted to the cause of seduction. He liked his women married, rich and beautiful and he was ruthless in their pursuit. "To hell with husbands," he would say, and showed no remorse when marriages broke up and lives were shattered as a result of his actions.

In January 1941 Ron, while stationed in Gilgil, read in 'The East African Standard' that the Earl of Erroll had been found dead in his car. Two African dairy workers had found him in his Buick, at the junction of Karen and Ngong roads with a bullet wound to the head.

There were a number of jealous husbands who were considered as likely suspects, but one in particular became the chief suspect, and was arrested for the murder a few weeks later. Earl Erroll had fallen in love with Diana, the young attractive and popular wife of Sir Jock Delves Broughton. It was he who was brought to trial in May of that year. He, too, was a popular figure in the area and the folk flocked to support him each day at his trial. He was found 'not guilty', released and returned home, only to die himself the following year.

No-one was ever convicted of the 'Erroll murder'and the question of who did kill him became a classic mystery with a book (White Mischief) and a film being made recounting the story. It was widely accepted that another of Diana's jealous lovers had killed Lord Erroll.

During the second weekend at the camp, Ron and a group of the soldiers, were invited to go to the Lake Naivaisha Country Club. They were transported to the club-house, which was situated in an exquisite spot by the side of the lake and from where they could watch the bird-life which swam and paraded along its edge. There was a great variety of birds to be seen in these parts, and the young men were told the names and habits of some of them. The ducks, geese, moorhens and guinea-fowl may have been familiar to them, but the more exotic Ground Hornbill, looking for snakes and grasshoppers at the lakeside, the Green Ibis poking their long beaks into the earth searching for ants, and the White Ibis on a stop-over looking for some herd of animals to 'de-tic', were all new to them. They also saw the long-legged Crested Cranes, Maribou Storks and Secretary birds, and Ron stored these images away in his brain to draw at a later date.

The lake was surrounded by glorious flowering bushes and the young men were courteously entertained by the white farm-owners, first within the club-house, watching the wildlife around them and then later after a light lunch, they were invited to swim in the inviting waters of the lake. Ron joined the group who had taken advantage of this offer and was taken out by motor boat to the middle of the lake to a floating platform, which was used to sit on or dive off into the water. Ron continued on, further out into the lake with some of the others, and they used the boat itself to dive off the side and then climb up back in over the side when they needed a rest. After they had been occupied in this way for quite a while Ron found he was becoming too tired to hoist himself up and over the side of the boat and decided that he would climb in from the back. He had not appreciated that the exhaust of the motor jutted out of the back, and caught his leg on it, just below the knee. He realised that it was hot, but the water took the worst of the pain away and he thought no more about it for the moment.

They all returned to camp, and when Ron was preparing for bed he looked down at his now painful leg and saw to his horror that he had a nasty deep burn. He reported to the medical officer next day, after an uncomfortable night, and the doctor, on inspecting the wound, sent him straight to hospital. It was felt that due to the severity of the burn and the possiblility of infection from the lake they needed to take great care.

Ron was taken to a small hospital, just off the Nakuru road. He was allocated a bed and given pyjamas (two sizes too big!) which were a novelty to him as he did not possess any. His burn was treated with gentian violet by the nurses and he was told to rest in bed. This he found easy to do, as he now had clean sheets and pillowcases which he had not had for several months. The next morning, the Doctor came to examine Ron's leg and remarked to the nurses that, "This is a very nasty one", before issuing his instructions for Ron's care.

Ron was confined to bed for a week thinking it more like a luxury hotel than a hospital, and not until the second week was he allowed up and into the grounds for short walks. Native boys would congregate at the main gate and attempt to sell the inmates their wares. One of the young Kikuyu natives had a small piece of wood and a small sharp knife, which he was using to carve an animal.

"How much is that?" asked Ron.

"One samoone" was the reply, (which translated into sixpence.) Ron was intrigued by the skill of the lad, and made sure that before he was discharged from hospital after twelve days, to return to camp, he bought one of these little figures from him.

Within a few days of his discharge from hospital, Ron and his unit were on the move. Six newly converted wireless trucks departed in convoy. Each truck carried five people; a non-commisioned officer, three wireless operators, and an instrument mechanic, who doubled as the driver. The officer sat in the cab with the driver and the wireless operators sat in the rear part of the van together with all the transmission and receiving equipment. A middle section, approached by a side door behind the driver's cab contained all the rations, kit-bags, aerial-poles and a petrol charging engine. This latter item ensured that there was always power in the batteries that supplied the wireless equipment so that they did not cease to function at an inopportune moment. Other, open-backed trucks also accompanied the unit, to provide spares and back-up when it was needed. Finally a water truck and the kitchen truck brought up the rear, and the Commanding Officer and a junior officer led the convoy in a staff car.

The convoy travelled north towards the Italian Somali border, along dirt tracks so dry that the vehicles raised clouds of red dust as they drove along. They approached their first major obstacle at Garrisa, which was situated on the great river Tana which the convoy had to cross in order to continue travelling north. The source of this river was on the Eastern slopes of Mount Kenya, nearly eighteen thousand feet above sea-level with a permanant ice cap on its summit. The river runs across Kenya eventually reaching the Indian Ocean.

The convoy had to camp by the river for the night and then be prepared for a slow tedious ferry crossing the following day. The ferry could only carry one vehicle at a time, so it took most of the morning to get the full complement to the other side. The lads took the opportunity to have a cooling swim in the river as they waited their turn to cross, but, as Ron still had dressings on his leg, he could only stand and watch enviously. This envy lasted only a few moments, however, as first one then another of the soldiers yelled out in pain as they were bitten by something in the water. They all leapt out of the river and inspected their sore spots. It was later that they were to learn from the natives that there were certain fish in the river that would eat anything with which they came in contact and it was quite unsafe to bathe in it. The soldiers had learned this the hard way! As they had only just begun to learn the local language of Swahili, they did not recognise the name they were given for the fish, but they learned enough not to make the same mistake again.

The end of the second day saw the convoy crossing the Somaliland border having passed through a number of native villages, along rough dirt roads and through semi-desert scrub-land. They made camp at Brava, near Marka and next day found a better tarmac road that took them to Mogadishu, the capital of Somaliland.

They made camp on a captured Italian airfield, around which were the remains of numerous damaged planes. The unit was able to avail itself of what facilities there were, and the soldiers quickly made up their beds in one of the empty barracks. The field kitchen was stationed a short distance from the dining hut, and the soldiers had to carry their plates of food from one to the other each mealtime, fending off the swarms of flies which surrounded them each journey. Even though the door of the dining hut and all the windows were protected with mosquito nets, some of the persistant flying beasts still managed to enter, and the young men had to ward them off as they ate their meals. The worst occasions were when they had jam on their bread, when it was an impossibility to eat it without several landing on the sticky surface. The hungry young men had to decide whether to share the repast with the insects or remain hungry. The consequences of the presence of the flies soon became apparent, as Ron came down with a severe case of dysentry and had to have a second spell in hospital, in Mogadishu, before recovering. He was able to see some of the city for the first time, and one building that particularly caught his eye was a large memorial arch, built by the Italians to commemorate their capture of Somaliland.

When Ron was released from hospital three days later, his unit was on the move again, making its way to Southern Ethiopia, to which most of the Italian army had retreated. They followed the course of the river Guibba until they reached the border, where they had to cross the river on the large pontoon bridge which the British army had constructed at Lugh Ferrandi. It took the unit a couple of hours to reach the border, during which time it rained continuously making the going tough and put the trucks in danger of being bogged down. This heavy rain marked the start of the monsoon season, so they could expect very few dry days for some time and needed to reach their destination as speedily as possible. They stopped at Negelli, which had recently been recaptured from the Italians, and once again set up camp.

There was a large wooden building which had been an entertainment hall for the troops, and around it were a number of smaller buildings.

Groups of soldiers each took up their living space in one or other of these smaller huts and Ron noticed that outside his, across a small yard was a wall made up of hundreds and hundreds of empty wine bottles. This, he assumed, had been constructed by the Italians when they had been in residence here.

Work now began, and the radio transmitter was set up in the large community hall. Ron was now working an eight hour shift, sending and receiving coded messages to the different Brigades.

This now became the 12th Division Command Headquarters and here they were to stay for some time as the rain lashed down, the roads became impassable, the river became flooded and it was quite impossible to attempt to cross it. Rations were now in short supply, as the unit was virtually cut off due to the rains, and for a period they were reduced to quarter rations. One dry biscuit and a small tin of corned beef between four young men became their diet for the day. There were no fresh vegetables and the men would go out into the surrounding area, when they were not on duty, to hunt for wild spinach to augment their meagre rations. Eventually the rains stopped and fresh supplies got through and they were back on full rations, but not before the men had begun to feel the effect of their poor diet. Amongst other things, Ron began to suffer very badly from mouth ulcers. The pain was excruciating, and he required medical attention again. This time he was sent to the army dentist who advised him to have his four top incisor teeth out and a plate fitted, with metal clips that fitted around the eye teeth on either side. This, in time, he did, and once more experienced the medical facilities available in times of war.

The battle to gain control of Southern Ethiopia continued and, after thousands of Italians had been captured by the Brigades, the campaign here was over, and the troops moved on north to Addis Ababa, a distance of fifteen hundred miles. All the equipment was reloaded into the trucks, supplies were stacked aboard and they began their journey.

They had to retrace their steps for the first part, crossing the river Giuba again at Lugh Ferrandi, continuing along its banks. This time the roads were easier and in places the dirt surface gave way to stretches of tarmac, but the terrain was still barren and sandy. After a week of driving, the unit reached Belet Uen, the following day Gabredarre and two days later Fort Jijiga (which was to play an important part in the war twelve months later.) They passed the city of Harar, an old walled city in Abyssinia, and the next day crossed the river of Awash which was in the bottom of a deep gorge, and continued into the town of Dire Dawa, where the main railway station was situated and which carried the line from Addis to Djibouti - the main port and capital of French Somaliland. They were now only two days drive from their destination of Addis Ababa, which had become an 'open city' on the 6th April 1941, having been retaken from the Italians.

On their arrival at Addis, the unit set up their communications head-quarters in the main wireless station, in order to begin their work. The truck on which Ron was based was not destined to stay with the rest of the unit, as two days later, the truck with its five occupants was ordered to leave for Dedessa, on the Blue Nile, to establish communications between Addis Ababa and the Sudan. The vehicle was loaded up once more, this time with sufficient rations for four weeks, and they set out westwards towards the Sudan. The roads were in a terrible state, with deep pot-holes, which made for a very uncomfortable ride. It took them two days to reach their military destination and establish camp.

This camp was situated near to a tributary that feeds the fast-flowing Blue Nile which itself joins the great White Nile at Khartoum. The bridge at this point; Dedessa, had been blown up by the Italians during an earlier skirmish.

They had to find a suitable spot on which to park their truck and set up their equipment. After reporting to the brigade headquarters, they found a position about a quarter of a mile away on a small hillock, above the camp, and here the men set up their radio station.

They used their map and compass to find the direct line to Addis, and this allowed them to erect the aerial pole, connect up the radio set and they were all ready. They gave their call-sign and prepared to receive and transmit coded messages immediately. Ron was allocated the first four hours of radio work while the other men set up the tent and camp beds. The tent was only used for sleeping, which was just as well as there was only just room to stand between the beds. At first the men had to cook their own meals too, but later they were invited to take their main meal in the brigade H.Q. cook-house, which at least gave them one cooked meal a day.

The radio had to be manned twenty-four hours a day and the men decided that instead of four-hour shifts during the night, they would each take eight hours every third night to allow two men at a time to get a decent length of sleep occasionally.

Water was collected from a small stream a short distance from the tent, and once a week each man would strip off and walk the short distance for a dip in the cool clear water. This they called 'bath-night'. Ron noticed that each time he entered the water, the monkeys in the trees around the stream would set up a tremendous chattering noise and

An air mail letter illustrated by Ron, and sent to his parents from Kenya, 1945.

Ron's wireless truck and tent situated outside Gondor, Abbyssinia, 1941.

continue in this vein until he emerged and went away again. They obviously did not want these humans invading their territory.

The routine was established for the time the men were in this camp; one man would work, one rest and one free. During one particular free period Ron decided that he needed to do something different. While they were travelling to Dedessa, he had seen an Ethiopian carrying a large fly whisk. It was long, white and feathery and was made from the tail hair of the black and white Colobus monkey. He had managed to procure an Italian rifle and ammunition from one of the infantry soldiers, stationed at the brigade H.Q. He loaded the gun and set off into the deepest part of the forest where he believed these monkeys to be. He did not tell anyone of his intentions but off he went clutching the loaded rifle, not knowing what wild animals he might encounter. He decided that he would not go far from camp, but in the dense forest it was difficut to judge how far he had travelled, when finally he came to a small clearing and was surrounded by the noise of chattering monkeys. He looked up, hoping that they were the type he wanted to find. As his eyes focussed into the branches of the trees, he was delighted to see the distinctive tails of the Colobus monkey trailing down. He took careful aim and fired. He saw the body of the animal fall to the ground nearby, and he ran forward to claim his prize. He used his army knife to cut off its tail and turned to retrace his steps. He hadn't gone more than a dozen yards before he saw ahead of him, advancing menacingly, a school of large baboons. Ron decided that the only way to get by, was to fire a couple of rounds in the air to scatter the group, and this way he managed to clear a path through them. He hurriedly made his way back along the path, as his original bravado was beginning to flag somewhat. He saw a second group of baboons coming in his direction and this time he decided to make a detour instead of approaching them head-on, knowing how dangerous these animals could be if roused. Ron realised that the dead body of the animal he had shot was attracting the other animals and quickly side-stepped the main track and found the narrow game path which led back to his camp around the outside of the forest. As he was making good progess along this path he noticed there ahead of him on the path was a large coiled black snake, one of the deadliest in Africa - the Black Mamba. He stood stock still, rooted to the spot for a moment trying to decide what he should do. He looked across to the grass-land to one side just two hundred yards away, and over to the little hillock another hundred and fifty yards further on, where his truck was parked. Ron decided that he would go through the grass-land to avoid disturbing the snake. The grass was called 'Elephant grass' due to its height, and for part of the way Ron could hardly see over it, but took

95

what he thought to be a straight line in the direction of his truck. However, after a while, when he calculated he should have reached the other side of the grass, he came upon a small tree and climbed up it to get his bearings. He looked around and realised to his annoyance that he had been going round in circles and was just as far away from his destination as when he had started, and only twenty yards from the path. Ron decided that he could spare no more time and had to take the path home, snake or no snake, and quickly made his way back to the camp.

He was met by Sergeant Carrott who demanded to know where the young soldier had been. Ron told his story of the monkey's tail, the baboons and the snake and showed him his 'trophy' as proof. A few choice words followed and then a stern warning, "Do that again, Baker, and I'll have you up on a charge."

During the third week, the sergeant was taken ill with a bout of malaria and had to remain in bed. He was far too ill to work his shift at the radio. Ron had to call for assistance and to ask for a replacement officer. The two remaining radio operators had to split his shifts between them until a Corporal Sherratt arrived to relieve them two days later. The next day Signalman Morris was taken ill with the same fever, but luckily only mildly and was back on his feet in a few days.

The group were ordered back to Addis and on the journey stopped to camp overnight at a place called Nekemte. During the night, Ron came down with a fever and had to continue the journey the following day feeling decidedly unwell. He, too had contracted malaria and was confined to bed for several days until he was fit enough to resume his duties.

It was now the Autumn of 1941, twelve months since Ron and his comrades had set sail from Liverpool, and the Abyssinian campaign was drawing to a close. On 28th October of that year, the complete unit was on the move again. They packed their equipment into the trucks and headed into the mountains to Gondar. Soon after leaving Addis they reached a long tunnel which took them under the mountain range. This was known as 'The Mussolini Pass' and the results of the Italian attempts at blowing up the tunnel could be seen as they reached the other side.

The first town they came to as they continued their journey, was Dessyee, perched on the side of one of the mountains. A little further on was the mountain of Amba Alagi, which at ten thousand feet high, had been one of the most difficult places to capture in the campaign. They passed on through Debra Markos, where the road divided so that if they continued straight on they would have gone to Asmara near the

Red Sea, but they in fact turned to the west and went back towards the Sudan. The following day they arrived at the ancient city of Aksum - a place full of Abyssinian history, and there they stopped for a break. This gave Ron time to explore some of the ruins of the religious buildings, with their tall columns dating back hundreds of years. He made himself a cup of tea amongst the ruins and his artistic eye revelled in what he saw. The town of Aksum contained Pre-Aksumite stone temples dating back to 1500 B.C., and in the centre of the town are funeral stellac monoliths, larger and taller than anything else found on earth. They had been quarried miles away and transported to this place to be carved and then stood on end.

But Ron could not linger here, much as he would have liked to, he had to rejoin his unit after the all-too-short break, and continue through some of the most difficult terrain possible, to their destination of Gondar. Their journey took them through the Great Rift Valley, which extends from Jordan to Mozambique and is fifteen thousand kilometres long. They descended into the large gorge, some thousand feet deep and then cross the river which ran along the bottom of it. They continued on the other side to climb up again towards the Wolchefit pass almost thirteen thousand feet above sea-level, taking narrow roads which wound around in continuous 'S' bends which took their toll on the engines. The convoy had to stop many times as the engines over-heated and radiators boiled and had to be cooled down and refilled at regular intervals, during the ascent.

The signals unit made camp at the top of the pass inside a walled farmhouse yard and were finally allowed to relax for a complete day. The views around were fantastic and most of the other mountain peaks were below their own eye-level now. They could look down into the gorge from which they had climbed and marvel at the sight. It reminded Ron of picture post-cards he had seen as a boy of the Grand Canyon in Colorado.

The unit finally caught up with the brigade H.Q. and Ron's wireless truck was detailed to make contact with the other H.Q's. When contact was made, Signalman Morris was allocated to do the first four hours duty, while Ron and the others set up camp, under some trees for cam-ouflage. During the day they could dress in bush shorts and shirt, as it was very warm, but at night the temperature dropped dramatically and they needed to don battle-dress and overcoats to withstand the night-time cold.

Ron had bought a wind-up gramaphone and a collection of records in Addis, and they all enjoyed the music as entertainment in the tent when they were not on duty. The person who was next on duty would be designated to wind up the machine, as he had to remain fully dressed, and the others could snuggle under their blankets during the cold evenings. Most of the records were in fact Italian and the only English one in the collection was 'Lady of Spain'!!

It was now the middle of November and the men could look down into the valley and see the South African planes dropping their bombs on Gondar at the bottom of the escarpment. The Italians were keeping the roads into the town under constant fire, so it was decided by the Commander, that the Brigades would make their way down to the plain by using the animal tracks. This meant that the trucks could not be used to transport the equipment, and mules were procured to carry the wireless sets and accumulators, which were strapped to their sides in such a way that the operators could continue to transmit as they travelled along.

The final battle took place on 27th November 1941 and the next day 28th November, General Nasi signed the surrender documents for his army of eleven thousand, five hundred Italians and twelve thousand native troops.

The Signals unit was able to retrieve their vehicles and continue down the winding roads onto the plain and into the town. They took over what had been the Italian wireless station and found their maps and charts still on the walls.

On December 1st, there was a victory parade, with representatives of each unit marching past Lieutenant General Sir Alan Cunningham. Each unit took part in the parade, the Free French, South African, Indian Signals and various native Regiments. This signalled the end of this part of the conflict.

The Signals unit stayed in Gondar for a few more days, so they had a chance to look round at the town and the countryside which was now peaceful. One building which caught Ron's eye, was an old castle which had been built by the Portugese in the sixteenth century. Gondar had been the capital of Abyssinia from 1632 until the mid nineteenth century when it had moved to Addis Ababa. Ron also had the opportunity to visit Lake Tana just outside Gondar, which is the source of the Blue Nile. The ancient fabled city was surrounded by mountains called 'The Mountains of the Moon' and the Queen of Sheba had lived there before leaving the area to visit King Solomon.

After the fall of the city, the unit was recalled to Addis so, once again they packed up their apparatus and moved out. The return journey was quite easy taking just three days to reach the outskirts of the town where they were to stay. They were shown into a large building standing alone, amidst acres of open flat country-side. The building contained many small rooms and a couple of very large ones and had probably been built about five years previously. It was later to become 'The Farmer's Club'.

In most of the small rooms there were three camp-beds placed for the soldiers, but in the one assigned to Ron, there were four, the other three occupants being from the South Wales area. Ron was intrigued to find that the daily topics of conversation were nearly always about Rugby football and the Welsh valleys. But Ron found them to be a grand set of lads and enjoyed being with them as they had much in common, all being of the same age, twenty three or four.

The dining room was in the main building, but the kitchens them-selves were in wooden huts a little way off. Each meal-time, the men had to take their dixie and mug to collect their food. Nearby a group of natives would congregate to attract the attention of the soldiers. Around their necks were hung small wooden boxes, each containing a number of eggs which the native youths encouraged the soldiers to buy. They would say 'Uncle La La' which Ron assumed to be what eggs were called in the local dialect of Amharic, the language spoken in Abyssinia. As there were no fresh eggs included in the army stores, the men would gladly buy the delicacies and the cook would fry them for breakfast. It was a treat to have an egg with their bacon occasionally.

Addis Ababa was situated about eight miles from the Farmer's Club. It was a dreary town with a European population five times that of Nairobi. It sprawled over an immense area but had no discernable town-centre, unless the crowded dirty triangle called The Piazza del Littorio could be classed as such. The roads wound past Blue Gum trees and the occasional residences, interspersed with squalid huts with rusting tin roofs. The shops held many articles of some value but, as their exteriors were ram-shackle and uninviting, they did not encourage customers to enter.

It was early December when the Signals Regiment arrived and the skies were grey, it was comparatively cold and there was rain daily to create an impression of gloom and depression. Along the main street, the excited tribal chiefs would rattle by in their little pony and traps or sitting astride mules, like medieval lords, which at least gave the town some local colour.

The unit remained in Addis for three months, until February 1942 with little to do in terms of wireless duties, and to relieve the boredom the soldiers would take weekly visits into the town. Even this would not have been possible during the holy month of Ramadan which was September. The Moslems fasted during daylight hours and the troops were not allowed into the town during the weekends until the period was over.

When they were allowed to go into the town, the soldiers would wait outside the Farmer's Club for a lorry which had been detailed to transport them. It could carry about twenty men and, after clambering into the back, they would discuss what they would do in Addis. When they jumped down from the truck, they made sure they knew what time it was going to return to pick them up. Ron missed the lift back only once but, in doing so, gave himself an eight mile hike back to base. The only consolation he had, was being able to observe the houses and buildings along the way in greater detail that he could from the truck.

The Piazza del Littorio was the place where the soldiers, Italian civilians and the Ethiopians gathered. There was a tall pole onto which was lashed a wireless speaker, from which music played and news flashes could be heard, in Italian, at regular intervals throughout the day. This spot was called 'Thieves corner' and goods could be bought and sold here. The first item which caught Ron's eye was a 35mm camera for which he bartered with an Italian. Later he bought an ornate ivory, ladies fan which when closed became a bird of paradise. He also acquired an Italian Berretta revolver and ammunition from an Italian civilian. His bartering got him the weapon for some of his cigarette supply and the rest in cash.

Ron would take a stroll around the streets with his Welsh buddies and they would usually end up at one of the many cafes. The one which they preferred was owned by a Greek man, not the usual Italian, so they always called it 'Joe the Greeks' (Joe being the owner's name.) Ron always had his coffee with milk and sugar, unlike the locals who preferred theirs strong and black in small cups or sometimes ice-cold in tiny glasses. Ron always liked to spend part of the time in town by himself, so that he could wander down the side streets to observe the houses and to see how the population lived. On one such occasion he found a small shop where he could have the film developed which he had taken with his newly acquired camera, and he could also have a new film put in to replace it.

The Catholic Cathedral was at the end of the main street, and one Saturday evening Ron found that a service was about to start as he was passing by. As he had time to spare before the lorry arrived, he decided to enter and participate in the ceremony and was pleased to note how easy it was for him to follow the procedings.

Christmas 1941 was fast approaching and word went round that the Officers and N.C.O.'s would be waiting on the men at the festive table. Some of the soldiers were a bit dubious, but sure enough when the day came, the cooks had put on a splendid meal followed by mincepies and beer and all served by the Officers. After a few beers, some of the ordinary ranks got a bit above themselves and began to act up, ordering the Officers to bring things to the table. Luckily the Officers took it in good part and there were no recriminations when the festivities were over.

Things returned to their hum-drum normality after Christmas until one day the Adjutant posted a notice with the daily orders, stating that the local Ethiopian Police had offered the soldiers the opportunity to ride their horses. Any interested soldiers were asked to give in their name. Having never ridden a horse, and glad of the chance to do something different, Ron added his name to the list.

They were allocated two hours early in the morning, which meant rising at six to get to the stables. They learnt the basics in the stable-yard, before taking the horses out for some exercise in the open spaces. Arriving back at camp, those who remained behind wanted to know how it had gone.

"Super!" said Ron, enthusiastically, "I'm really looking forward to next week".

Next morning he was not so sure, as he ached all over, and the inside of his thighs were red raw. He had forgotten the pain by the time he was due to go again, but remembered sufficiently to wear double under-pants under thick long army trousers for his second attempt. After this he decided that he would purchase a pair of riding breeches in Addis next time he went there.

The terrain over which they rode, was unlike any that Ron had seen in England. Once outside the town itself, the land opened out into rolling countryside, with no fences or hedges, just mile after mile of open space. Ron loved the freedom that these weekly rides gave him.

One event that was to disturb the peace of their early morning rides, occured just after another young soldier had decided to join the party and he was still very inexperienced. The group decided to have a good gallop out across the open plains and set off at a fair pace. The new comer was on a spritely Arab horse and as he galloped along, he lost one of his stirrups. The horse hit a pot-hole and unseated its rider. One foot was still stuck in his stirrup and he was left hanging from it, being dragged and bounced along the ground as the frightened horse raced away. Luckily, another of the party had served in the cavalry and was

Ron lying on his camp bed with a skin from a wild cat shot by him in Abbyssinia, 1941.

Ron and Frank with a family of Congo pygmies, 1943.

an excellent horse-man. He raced after the bolting animal and caught hold of the reins, bringing it to a halt. Another of the group shouted to Ron to take hold of his reins, while he jumped down to release the battered young rider. They slowly returned to the stables carrying their comrade carefully. He was taken to report to the Medical Officer, but fortunately he had escaped with quite minor scratches and bruising, to accompany his major fright. Ron was not surprised to find that he did not join the party the following week, as his pride, too, had taken a bit of a battering.

The men were continually trying to find ways of passing their time while they waited for new orders for their next assignment, and in January it was decided to hold a Sports Day on the open grass-lands opposite the Farmer's Club. All the events were to be fun races and games, three legged races, tug-of-war, sack-race and so on, and the day chosen dawned cool but dry. Teams were made up from the various European contingencies and the Africans at the camp. One race in particular caused great hilarity when the team that Ron was on, decided to play their game of 'musical chairs' on horse back. They had managed to borrow the same police horse that they used for their weekly riding sessions and six of the lads started out, circling the five chairs which had been placed in a line. When the music stopped they were required to dismount and, keeping hold of the reins, run to get a seat. The horses had other ideas, however, and as the riders pulled one way they pulled the other, and a game that was intended to last a few minutes took the best part of an hour to complete. It was great fun for all concerned, but when it was time for the African team to play this game they decided to do it on foot!

The weekends were still spent, whenever possible, investigating Addis Ababa, and Ron became more adventurous, venturing deeper and deeper into the heart of the town. He found the Emperor's Palace, where Emperor Haile Selassie lived and kept two lions, the presence of which gave rise to the leader's name 'Lion of Judah.' Ron was quite amazed when, at a later date, he finally saw the great Emperor. His reputation and the respect he commanded, gave the impression that he was a magnificent figure, whereas he was in fact a tiny insignificant little man to look at and not at all an awe-inspiring individual in appearance.

Ron penetrated into the heart of the native quarter and saw the conditions under which they lived. The roads were non-existant and the shops, ramshackle tin and mud huts. He used his camera to record the state of one butcher's shop, which had no shop window but two rusty corrugated sheets which were flung open to expose the produce hanging in the dust and grime, with flies buzzing all around it. He noticed too that the female vendor had beautiful nubian features and long, fuzzy hair which stood out from her head forming a dark halo.

On the road from the town returning to the camp, was a series of wooden buildings which were also places where trading was done and, when they were open for business, the front shutters would be removed to reveal the goods within. One shop which Ron remembered many years later, sold nothing but animal game skins, one of which he bought to hang on the wall above his bed. It was that of a spotted wild cat, and such things would be unavailable today because of the conservation laws, and even then, when the war was over he was prevented from bringing it back to England with him.

Despite the lack of a military assignment, the full ritual of the army still applied, and each morning, the soldiers had to make up their beds in strict prescribed fashion. After breakfast, the blankets had to be folded and placed at the foot of the bed with their haversack, and their pith helmet placed on top of them. Spare boots had to be stood at the bottom of the bed and the room made clean and tidy for the duty officer when he made his inspection. If the room did not come up to regulation standards, the men would be allocated punishment duties in the cook-house, 'spud-bashing' or cleaning the cook pots.

During this time, Ron was to recall a very tragic event, which was to affect the whole unit. One day while travelling in a fifteen hundred-weight army truck, along one of the narrow twisting mountain roads, two of their unit left the road and fell down into the deep gorge. When they were found they were both dead. As it was such a small unit, everyone knew everyone else intimately and they all felt the loss very deeply. It seemed such a senseless event. Their deaths had not been caused by any enemy action and yet two young lives had been lost. The young men left to grieve could make no sense of it. They paraded outside the Club on the day of the funeral, and marched solemnly to the cemetry which was situated on the higher ground above the town. Ron was one of the six chosen to be in the firing party, and they fired a volley of salute over the graves. These young men now lay buried in a foreign land, in a strange place where few people who knew them would ever visit. The young soldiers returned to the camp but none of them could satisfy the question on all their lips "Why should this thing have happened?"

By February 1942, they had been in East Africa for twelve months and no leave had been granted to anyone in the unit during that time. One day the daily orders contained the information that twenty of their number were to given some leave. The list of the lucky men was to be posted up the next day, following a draw which was to take place. To Ron's delight he saw his name up there, top of the list. He could not believe his good fortune.

The men were informed that the leave would be taken in Kenya, nearly two thousand miles away. The day arrived for them to leave, and they waited eagerly for their transport, with their bed-roll of blankets and ground-sheet and a few clothes. They were taken down to the main depot in Addis and there boarded an empty lorry with a canvas roof. This vehicle was returning to Nairobi, along with another ten or more which had been delivering supplies to the base. The first day the convoy covered a fair distance of a couple of hundred miles or more, on fairly decent tarmac roads, and at night they stopped to make camp off the road. They made a meal and a hot drink, before unrolling their blankets, laying down their ground sheet and settling down for the night, as near to the truck as they could get. They remained partially clothed as the nights were cold and they needed to wrap themselves up well in their blankets, out in the open air. The night closed in, the animal sounds were all around them and Ron found it impossible to get any sleep as he lay on the ground.

It was a moonlit night and Ron tucked the blankets under his chin as it got colder. He was just dozing off when he was suddenly aware of rustling sounds coming from the direction of their food tins and the remains of their supper. Ron did not move, but in the moonlight he could see, not ten yards from his head, a jackal attacking what was left of their evening meal. He dare not yell out, but slowly slid his hand under his pillow to feel for his Italian Berretta pistol which he always carried with him. He clutched the loaded weapon and it gave him a feeling of security as he waited for the animal to finish its foraging and, hopefully depart. It crept away as silently as it had come and Ron breathed a sigh of relief.

When they stirred next morning, the men had breakfast, threw their bed rolls into the back of the truck and hoisted themselves up after them. Ron found that many of the others had slept very little too, and they decided to unroll their blankets and lie down on the floor of the vehicle to catch up on their lost sleep instead of sitting on the rigid metal benches along the sides. So the second day passed and the convoy continued its passage through the area of Southern Abyssinia called The Great Lakes. On the fourth day they arrived at the walled fort of 'Fort Mega', which had been one of the first Italian forts to be captured. It had stately twin towers between which was a large entrance gate through which the convoy drove. Fort Mega was reminiscent of those held by the foreign legion in the romances of P. C. Wren.

The convoy stayed over-night in the shadow of the great walls of the fort, surrounded by the remains of a large selection of captured Italian artillery, most of which dated back to the First World War. The convoy re-assembled next morning for what they all hoped would be their last day on the road before reaching Nairobi. As they reached the border of Northern Kenya, they came to a precipitous escarpment which led down to the Chalbi Desert. This they crossed to reach Moyale, before encountering mile after mile of black lava, the remnants of an extinct volcano at Marsabit. The mouth of the volcano was about five miles in diameter and colonised by many different plant and animal species, but the lava-belt surrounding it had limited the movement of some of the animals over the years. The convoy itself made its way over this black desolate desert, arriving into more lush shrub and bush-land and encountering natives mounted on camels before passing small native villages. Now suddenly their eyes were drawn to the horizon ahead. There in the distance they could see Mount Kenya with its snow-topped peaks gleaming in the sun. As evening approached they arrived on the western slopes of the mountain and made camp in the car-park at Nanyuki.

They were now just one hundred miles from their final destination, and next morning set off to complete their journey. They crossed the equator sign at a small pub called 'The Silver Beck', where the actual line cuts through the middle of the building, so that one side is in the southern hemisphere and the other in the northern.

They passed through Nyeri, which is not far from the game-reserve of Tree-Tops where animals can be viewed from platforms built high up in the trees above the water-holes where the numerous wild species congregate each evening to drink. It was here that the young Princess Elizabeth was staying, ten years later, when her father died and she learned that she was now Queen.

The final part of the journey was much more comfortable, as there were good tarmac roads to take the place of the pitted dusty tracks over which they had been travelling for much of the time. They reached the outskirts of Nairobi and the convoy pulled into a base camp in the city, the men jumped down and their official leave began.

The young soldiers were shown into long wooden huts which were to be their quarters for the night, and they grinned, in delight, at the sight that met them. Real beds! And best of all, showers and facilities to have a good wash. After a good hot evening meal, that night they slept better than they had for many months and woke refreshed and ready for the fun they had planned for their leave. They were taken down to the station to catch the train which was to take them to their holiday destination of Soy, situated in Northern Kenya.

This was their holiday destination? As they jumped down from the train, all they could see were dozens of native children begging for money, scrawny hands outstretched and huge pleading eyes searching the travellers for some sign of giving. The soldiers had little to give, and passed on through the wooden station building to the yard beyond. They looked around for the transport they had been promised which was to take them the the hotel. Nothing, - unless a long flat open farm-cart drawn by six long-horned oxen counted as 'something'. They soon learned that this was in fact their transport, and scrambled on board to be taken on a half-hour journey to the single-storey building which was their home for the holiday. They were met by four native youths covered from head to toe in white gowns and just thin sandals on their feet.

The accommodation comprised a series of round thatched brick huts at the rear of the hotel. Each hut contained two single beds covered with mosquito nets, and an alcove contained a small wash-basin and mirror. They deposited their gear, freshened up and congregated in the hotel bar to decide how they would spend the next two weeks. Their options were pretty limited as the town of Eldoret was some way off and transport was hard to find, so, much of the time was spent in and around the village of Soy itself.

The first evening was spent relaxing in the bar after their meal which was served at seven, just as the sun was setting. It was always easy to guess the time for dinner, as here on the equator, the sun always set between seven and half-past.

When they did manage a trip into the town, they were accosted by the harsh sounds of Indian music emanating from the majority of shops and cinemas owned by the Kenyan Indians.

The time passed all to quickly, and soon they were retracing their steps back to camp. They got as far as Nairobi, only to find that there was no transport to take them back to Addis Ababa for at least a week. When the convoy was finally assembled, each truck was well stacked with boxes of supplies, and each man had to search the trucks for a space for himself and his kit-bag. The journey was even more uncom-fortable than the outgoing one and the small groups of men in each truck, peered out of the back of the vehicles as they passes through the bush, seeing the same animals again and the same pitted roads. Now they encountered rain storms which turned the tracks into muddy rivers, and at times they were forced to wait until the rain stopped and the water subsided before they could continue. Occasionally one of the trucks would get bogged down in the mud and another of the convoy, with better traction, was required to haul in out.

By the time the group of soldiers reached Addis Ababa, following their two weeks leave, they had actually been away from camp for a full six weeks. To their surprise they found that their unit was no longer at the camp in the Farmer's Club, but had moved to Harar, five hundred miles away. More trains, more trucks and more travelling finally reunited the soldiers with their unit. The Signals unit was now under canvas outside the ancient walled city of Harar, but Ron was delighted to be back in contact with all his old comrades.

Harar itself, reminded Ron of the stories of the Arabian Nights and noted one particular castellated palace, that he thought especially hideous, which was used by one of the sons of Haile Selassie. The five city gates were shut and locked at sunset each evening, but Ron found that within the city walls were many fine craftsmen, working silver into elaborate fine jewellery. The women had skin of warm, golden brown, their features were delicately carved and they wore colourful tight striped trousers. Outside the walls there were hundreds of camels waiting to be loaded up to transport goods to the south of the country.

Ron made a couple of forays into the city and on one occasion sat and watched one of the silver-craftsmen working a fine bracelet, which Ron bought after he had seen its completion. He was intrigued by the conditions under which the old Abyssinian worked. He sat in the doorway of his shop, with no artificial light, and a small tin with a hole in the lid, through which a wick protruded. The wick produced a tiny flame and the worker blew through a fine metal tube onto the flame, directing in onto the silver wire and rod, and the piece on which he was working. Using this make-shift 'blow-torch' he produced the intricate filigree patterns that were typical of the area.

Further along the cobbled streets Ron saw other craftsmen working on larger articles, one putting patterns, again in silver filigree, into plates, while a third was hammering patterns around the edges of plates, using sharp pointed implements and infinite patience. The pictures that this last man produced were typical native designs and Ron purchased two of them, one with designs of animals around the edge, the other more ornate, with perforated patterns around the outside. All these artisans sat cross-legged on the stone floor, often using their bare foot as a third hand to do their fine work.

Ron was now detailed to go, with two other operators, to relieve those working at Jijiga. This base was not too far away, and they departed from Harar early one morning, leaving the mountainous region behind to find the dusty plain below. Jijiga had a large gated entrance and they crossed the parade ground to be shown into the wireless station, within the Fort. They immediately relieved the operators who were working there and they in turn were able to use the same transport to return to base.

One man stayed at the radio while the other two took their kit-bags to the room assigned to them for sleeping. Ron saw that it was one of those previously used to house prisoners, and had one small window, high up in the wall, and a thick wooden door as the only means of exit. Mosquitoes flourished in this area, and they had to ensure that their mosquito nets were securely tucked under the mattress before dusk each night.

It had been some time since the men had worked the continual shift system required to keep the radio open round the clock, and they quickly established their rota. There was little to occupy their spare time and Ron, as usual, spent his time investigating his surroundings. Nearby there was a small airstrip, which was in the hands of the South African Air Force and the Royal Air Force. One small pre-war bi-plane sitting on the airstrip reminded Ron of the 1930's Bristol Bulldog in which he had once flown while on holiday with Reg, in Rhyl, and it had cost them two shillings and sixpence for a quick trip along the Welsh coast. This one had two cock-pits, the forward one where the pilot sat, the other equipped with a rear facing machine gun. Ron was smiling to himself at the happy memories, when one of the flying officers approached the plane.

"Ever been up in one of these?" he asked Ron.

Ron recounted his holiday jaunt.

"Want another go then ?" he was asked.

"Given half a chance," was Ron's quick reply.

Ron was never one to deny himself any new experience and did not question whether they should be doing this now. It was a beautiful day and the wind was blowing in their faces as Ron looked down on the town below and the plains surrounding Jijiga. It was an event that Ron would not have missed and he remembered it for the rest of his life.

Ron had been working the radio-set at Jijaga for about a week, when he was sitting at the equipment one evening. Around his head he could hear the persistent buzzing sound of a female mosquito, and occasionally would flap his hand to distract it. At times he could feel a sting, but got on with his job until the end of his shift, at midnight. Once in his

Ron showing his native servant Mwangi how to iron his uniform, Kenya, 1942.

A butchers shop in Addis Ababa, Abbyssinia, 1941.

bed, he could not settle, as he could feel and hear various 'creepy-crawlies' within the net with him. Unable to stand it any longer, he got up and shook out the bed and the net to release them. Maurice was grinning at him from his bed opposite, and the truth dawned on Ron.

"It was you!" he said.

Maurice admitted that he and John had got the idea after seeing a large insect, which had been attracted by the single bulb, flying round the light. They had caught it, and a couple more, and put them under Ron's net as a practical joke.

Ron was beginning to feel particularly unwell and crawled back into bed. He began to realise that he was coming down with a bout of the dreaded malaria, and hoped that if he stayed in bed he could sweat out the fever. Two days later he realised that this was impossible without some medication, and reported to the Medical Officer. Having taken Ron's temperature, and finding it to be dangerously high, the Doctor decided that he needed to be sent to hospital. The nearest field hospital was eighty miles away in Hargeisa, British Somaliland, run by Free Belgians from the Belgian Congo. The only available vehicle was a fifteen hundredweight, open topped lorry normally used for carrying mail between Harar and Hargeisa, and it was now commandeered to take Ron to hospital.

Ron felt too ill to care how he was transported, and was only just aware that he had arrived and was being put to bed. He knew no more for several days, when, upon opening his eyes he saw a number of hospital staff standing around his bed.

"You're a very lucky lad to be alive," the Doctor told him. Ron had survived a temperature .of over one hundred and five degrees, only because the staff had managed to find sufficient ice to pack around him to bring his temperature down.

Ron remained in the hospital to recuperate for almost a month, being fed on camel's milk and almost raw liver until his strength returned. Most of his red blood cells had been destroyed by the disease, and his blood count was monitored constantly. He was given iron tonic and injections into his back-side on a daily basis and even after a month of very careful nursing he was losing weight and making very little improvement. He was taken out into the grounds on a couple of occasions and once, saw the results of heavy rains high up in the hills. The normally dry river bed, at the bottom of the hospital grounds, was now full and flowing fast, carrying with it chunks of dead wood and even dead animals which had been brought down in the flood waters.

His condition was giving real cause for concern, and it was then discovered that Ron had contracted Black Water Fever. It was now necessary for him to be transferred to the main hospital in Nairobi.

Over two hundred million people a year suffer from Malaria. It is a desease caused by a minute parasite which is carried in the saliva of the female Anopheles mosquito and is transferred to humans when she punctures the skin and injects her saliva into the blood to dilute it, in order to suck some of it up. The blood is needed by the insect so that she can lay her eggs. As the saliva enters the human blood stream, the germ enters too, and travels in the blood stream to the liver where it multiplies rapidly. If an unaffected mosquito then bites the victim, it sucks up some of this germ and so the cycle continues.

There are four main types of Malaria, 'Falciparium' being the most dangerous, and the one which Ron had caught. The symptoms most commonly seen are; fever, rigors, episodes of uncontrollable shaking and chattering teeth, all associated with high temperature and lasting sweats, anaemia and jaundice. Left untreated, the first attacks are often fatal and even when treated, they are recurrent and may continue for up to thirty years after the first episode. Ron's were to last for twenty years, long after the war had finished.

The soldiers were exposed to many diseases during their time in Africa. Ron had succumbed to Dysentry, Malaria and now the more dangerous form, Black Water Fever, but others were affected by Yellow Fever and Bubonic Plague which they caught from fleas which lived on the rats in the more squalid parts of the towns.

The day arrived for him to be evacuated by plane from the hospital to Nairobi in Kenya, a distance of two thousand miles. The plane was a three-engined Fokker plane capable of carrying up to twenty passengers in small canvas bucket-type seats, at a speed of just over one hundred miles an hour. The height it could fly was limited as there was no oxygen supply and the cabin was not pressurised as in modern aircraft. Ron managed to sit upright with a number of military officers who were returning to their East African Headquarters in Nairobi. The plane had to make several stops in order to refuel during the flight. The first stop after about five hours flying, was at Lugh Ferrandi, in Italian Somaliland, the second at a small airstrip at Wajir. This was another of the Forts found in this part of the country, with its white walls enclosing mud coloured buildings around a central court-yard. It stands on an historic camel route across the Chalbi desert on Kenya's north frontier. The plane put down here for the night, as it had been in the air by then for most of the day. Ron was transferred to a long low wooden building where they all spent the night, before continuing their journey next morning. The second half of the trip was much more interesting as they could see the countryside clearly from their vantage point. The desert was left behind and the land became green and lush, animals could be seen, as could the native villages. The plane passed close to the slopes of Mount Kenya, its peaks rising high above them and the great forests looming dark around them. They flew over herds of zebra, giraffe, bison and antelope, the noise of their engines often startling the animals and causing them to stampede as the plane flew low above their heads. Passing so close to the mountain and in such a small plane caused distress to the occupants as it hit air pockets and plummeted down alarmingly several times. Ron, in his weakened state was particularly affected and although this only lasted for about thirty minutes, he suffered badly from air-sickness during this part of the journey. He was relieved therefore, when they finally arrived at Nairobi airport and he was met by medical personnel and transferred immediately to the hospital. Ron had been here before, but under happier circumstances, as the hospital was close to the base camp where he had stayed for one night, before starting his holiday in Soy.

Ron was taken to a bed on the top floor of the hospital, told to undress and get into bed, and a Doctor came to examine him. He was weighed, a blood sample was taken and he was given an iron injection. He was then brought his evening meal which was remarkable for its ordinariness; chicken, mashed potatoes, cabbage and gravy, followed by an egg custard which he hadn't tasted since leaving home. Ron was seldom home-sick, but here alone with none of his comrades around, having spent so long in hospital and seemingly making so little progress, he yearned for his family and the old familiar life.

After two months of this illness Ron had lost a considerable amount of weight, and the staff were trying to get him back to a more normal weight of ten stones, and gradually it did improve. He saw many other patients come and go as he lay there, including one young lad who was obviously suffering from Tuberculosis, and whose coughing was painful to hear.

When Ron began to show real signs of improvement, he was transfered, by train, to a nursing home near to Nakuru, so that he could regain his strength. This place appeared to be a large private house set in extensive grounds, overlooking Lake Nakuru, where thousands of flamingoes could be seen. The home was called Crumlin House, and a long low wooden hut at the rear of the main building housed the twenty military personnel who had all been sent there to recuperate. Most of the men, Ron discovered, were from the army, but there were also several naval ratings and one or two air force people too. They slept in the wooden hut, but ate their meals in the large dining room in the big house.

The owners still lived in the house but had decided that they would assist in the war effort by opening up their property in this way for injured or sick military personel to get well in pleasant surroundings.

On the first night, as Ron was preparing for bed, he was grabbed by two of the burly naval ratings, and dumped into a bath of cold water. "Not your usual hospital treatment!" he thought, as he dried himself off and got into bed. The next newcomer got the same treatment and Ron realised that this was their idea of an initiation ceremony.

Ron was to spend two months here while he regained his strength and vigour and found little with which to occupy himself, apart from walks in the grounds, down to the lake to watch the antics of the water-birds close-up. He was lucky therefore to get quite friendly with the owner, who offered to take him game shooting, up in the hills at the back of the house. Ron was given one of his guns to use, and at his first attempt did not manage to hit anything. On his second outing, however, he killed a small doe. It was retrieved by the master's dog and ceremoniously carried home by two native boys. The antelope was taken down to the native huts, skinned and divided up as tradition demanded, half for the 'Big House' and half for the natives. Next day the skin was stretched out on the ground, pegged carefully to preserve its shape, and the underside rubbed well with brine, then it was left in the sun to dry. It now became Ron's property, and he kept it as a reminder of the time he spent at Crumlin House. There were two types of antelope to be found in Kenya; Grant's and Thompson's Gazelle and it was the latter that Ron had shot .

His daily doses of iron tonic, the peace and tranquillity, and the good food were all having the desired effect, and Ron gradually regained his weight and restored his fitness. There were fruit trees in the orchard from which the men were allowed to eat freely and they enjoyed the oranges and bananas as they took their stroll in the gardens and down to the lake. It was difficult to realise, at times, that they were actually in Africa and that there was a war raging in other parts nearby.

During the time that Ron was at Crumlin House, a large python was shot near the swamp-pool. He had never seen one this size, and it took ten men to hold it out while someone took a photogaph. Full length, it measured over fifteen feet.

After eight weeks, Ron was considered fit enough to return to his unit. He was sent back to the hospital for a check-up and when this found him to be clear of the disease, he was discharged to resume duties. After saying his 'good-byes', he went first to the base camp, in Nairobi, to await transport to return to his unit. He was still waiting, when five days later he was stricken with a recurrent bout of malaria and had to return to the same hospital for treatment until it passed again. Luckily it was soon under control, but while he was there he discovered that his old unit had been reformed and sent to Burma to take part in that campaign.

Ron had been away from his unit for four months and much had been happening in his absence. When he had first fallen ill and been taken into hospital, he had travelled in the clothes he had on, and all his other garments and possessions had been left behind. While the unit remained at the camp, his mates ensured their safety as best they could, but when they were told they were on the move again, all Ron's belongings were packed into a trunk. No-one knew quite what to do with them. Ron was still in hospital and they were sent after him. By the time his possessions had arrived at the hospital at Hargeisa, Ron had long gone and the staff did not know his whereabouts. It was therefore decided that the only solution was to send them to his home for safe-keeping. Thus it was, that some time later, his Mother received the container of Ron's personal effects. She knew nothing of Ron's illness, as he had not wanted to worry her unnecessarily, but what she experienced now was every Mother's nightmare. No-one was permitted to divulge his exact whereabouts, so for some time she knew nothing of his actual condition. The contents of the box gave few clues and she wrote to her son and sent the letter through the usual War Office channels, in the hope of getting some early reply. She and the family had a worrying time as they waited for news.

Ron was back at base-camp, in Nairobi, and no-one knew quite what was to happen to him now, but he was not one to sit around idle for long, and he made himself useful in the main office of the depot. He designed a quantity of posters and signs to to put up around the camp. The Commanding Officer was quite impressed with this work and called Ron to him to tell him that the position of Draughtsman was coming vacant, and that if he was interested, he should apply. This sort of job did not come along very often, and Ron was delighted at his luck. He applied, was interviewed, assured the board that if he was given the position he would study hard and pass the exams and so impressed them with his enthusiasm that they gave him the job. The rank would only be granted when he had actually passed the necessary examinations.

Next day he was taken to his new place of work and living quarters at Killarney camp. His drawing office was small, and the lad who Ron was

Christmas Greetings from the Royal Signals, East Africa, 1944.

to replace stayed for a week to show him the ropes. Ron was told that the lad from Scotland was suffering from a nervous break-down and was being repatriated on medical grounds, but Ron learned from the boy himself, that he was actually making his condition seem worse than it was, so that he would be sent home. Either way, it had worked out well for Ron, as he would now be doing a job which he enjoyed, and using his innate artistic talents in the war effort.

Ron soon got the hang of the work and had sole access to his office as some of the work was top-secret, involving communications maps, referring to positions of various units, Brigades, and Divisional Head-quarters. It was now the middle of 1942 and Ron had access to some very intriguing information which he had to transfer to charts for use by the C.O.'s. He worked normal office hours, but was always on call in case he was needed at any time, and he did not have do any guard duties.

As it got dark at about seven, Ron would go back to his office each night after his meal to study for the examination, which he knew was not far away.

One day, one of the camp officers, for whom Ron had done some work in the first days before his official appointment, came to see him and told him that he would be the person setting Ron his test questions.

"I can't tell you the actual questions which I will be asking you on the day I choose to test you," he said "but I will give you an idea of the sort of things you need to know."

He then proceeded to outline the type of questions which would be asked. Basic maths, trigonometry and drawing were subjects with which Ron felt confident, and he knew, that these were topics on which he would be questioned, so it did not worry him unduly.

The day dawned for the testing and Ron answered all the questions to the best of his ability. He then went back to work and waited to hear the result. One week later, Ron was delivering some communications charts to the Adjutant's Office, when he looked up from his desk. "You passed your test, Baker. We have sent for confirmation of your new rank, and you will hear in due course." Ron was elated.

A month later this came through with army orders and was entered in Ron's army paybook. He was now 'B.3. Draughtsman Baker' and it meant that he could stay at the camp in a job he enjoyed for the foresee-able future.

Hut 26, in which Ron was billeted, contained a vast assortment of military personel who, before the war, had been employed in a wide variety of occupations. They now used their talents in the service of their country as wireless operators, electrical and mechanical technicians, over-head linesmen, carpenters, cooks as well as administrative staff, cyphers and decoders. Their characters too were just as varied, but one in particular was to be remembered by his comrades well after the war.

Jack was the cook and liked his drink but, because of a weak bladder, was continually having to relieve himself at all hours of the day and night. If he had partaken particularly heavily in an evening he would disturb the rest of the men in the hut when he went to the latrines during the night. One night however, he was so drunk that he could not even find the door of the hut, and they were all woken up by the yells of Corporal Taffy Jones who occupied the bed next to the door. He was shouting for someone to turn on the light as he thought that he was drowning. When the light came on, all eyes were turned in the direction of Taffy's bed and they were treated to the hilarious sight of him being showered with urine by Jack who in his drunken state had thought he had reached his intended destination and relieved himself all over Taffy's face. The poor Corporal soon used his influence to get Jack moved to a position where he could do no more harm.

The months passed by with Ron still doing his work at Killarney camp, and 1942 gave way to 1943. The men played sports or swam whenever they could, to keep fit, and they would vist the city of Narobi when time permitted. Ron noticed again the segregation on the buses they used to travel from the camp to the city and back, a partition separated the front half of the bus, where they sat, from the area at the back used by the native Kenyans. Apart from these occasional outings, life continued on each day in much the same way for Ron, except for a brief spell in the East African Command Headquarters situated in the 'Country Club'in Muthaiga. He was sent there for a period of two weeks to produce a series of posters and signs and he appreciated the change of scene and personnel. He was now mixing for a time with the 'Top Brass', and found them very easy to work for.

While Ron was in Nairobi he visited an Indian tailor's shop, with the intention of buying a khaki walking-out suit. He got into conversation with the owner and told him of his occupation before the war. The conversation continued while Ron was being measured for his suit, and Ron explained about his experience as a pattern cutter. The price for Ron's new clothes was negotiated at thirty shillings, which was three weeks wages and it was agreed that Ron could collect them the following week. On his return, Ron approached the owner who said to him that before he took his suit he wanted to ask Ron a favour.

He took him into the back work-room and put his hand on his shoulder, looking up at him earnestly.

"You did say that you could make a pattern for any garment," he said.

"Yes," replied Ron warily, wondering what was coming next.

"Well, I have an order for some riding breeches and I'm afraid that I haven't a pattern for this type of garment. Could you produce such a thing for me?"

This time Ron's reply was more assured and said "Yes", straight away, especially when he realised that he would be paid for, what for him, was a simple task.

The small work-room contained a couple of men, sitting sewing, cross-legged on the floor, and a young girl, working an ancient treadle-machine. Ron was shown to a long wooden table, given a couple of sheets of thick brown paper, a tape measure and graded tailor's square, and an hour later he presented the finished pattern to the owner.

"What do I owe you ?" he asked.

"Give me what you think it's worth" replied Ron, and both parties were happy when Ron walked out of the shop with his new suit now costing him only one pound, just the cost of the material.

Ron kept in touch with his new-found friend-in-the-trade, and would look in to see him whenever he visited the city. He was told that the client had been well pleased with his breeches and would be recommending the shop to all his friends.

Ron was now happy, and this year found him returned to good health, in a job he found useful and fulfilling and in pleasant company. He knew that the war continued, and he could not yet return to his home or his family, but his life was not too bad. It was at this time that, during one of his evening walks, he met up with a local Scottish family, (Mr and Mrs Tom Van Hegan and their daughter, Betty) who lived not far from the camp. They got to talking about life before the war and Ron explained what he had been doing. Betty, too was keen on dress design, so they were interested to hear about Ron's trade. They would part company, as the family reached their drive, and Ron would continue on back to camp. Another family called Maxwell also lived nearby and they too took an evening stroll at about the same time and would meet up with their neighbours and get into conversation, as they walked along. The Maxwell's daughter, Peggy, and Betty were at the same school and were great friends too. On one evening, as Ron was taking a stroll, he met up with both families together and was invited to dinner at the Van Hegan's. He thoroughly enjoyed his visit, and, as much of the conversation had revolved about his tailoring background, he had been able to help the daughter understand more about the business.

Tom Van-Hegan had left Scotland for Kenya in 1913, taking on the position of 'Saw Doctor' with a timber mill firm, before working his way up to becoming Managing Director of Equator Mills in Nairobi. He also had shares in a timber mill on the slopes of Mount Kenya near Nairobi and at one time had employed Jomo Kenyatta, who later went on to become an important figure in African politics. Ron was fascinated to hear about his life and grateful for their generous hospitality.

When Ron returned to camp, he designed a special card to thank them for his delightful evening. When he met them again out walking, they said how pleased they were to receive such an original message of thanks and Ron was asked to join them on other occasions. Through their introduction, he was also invited to the Maxwells home, and he joined both families, on Bank Holidays when they took a picnic up to the Reserves. His comrades back at the camp were surprised that the local white families had welcomed Ron into their homes, as it was not a very common occurrence, even for the officers.

During this time, Ron was granted a months leave, half of which was to be spent at a holiday village at Nyeri. Tom Van Hegan gave Ron an introduction to a friend of his, David Kerr, and told Ron to call on him while he was in the area. Ron was invited to the Kerr's home for a couple of days, and found it to be an unusual, but beautiful home with exquisite views out towards Mount Kenya. The house itself consisted of two round thatched huts connected by a long low room which was the living quarters. On the wall of this room was a glass display cabinet containing a magnificent specimen of a stuffed trout, and numerous water-colours of the surrounding scenes.

At dinner that night, Ron remarked on the beauty of their surroundings and said that he would like to paint the views. David said that many people felt the same and offered to show Ron his collection of paintings after dinner. The conversation then turned to the fish which was displayed on the wall, and his host said that he would take Ron fly-fishing next day so that he could experience the thrill of casting in the fast flowing river nearby. David had been a keen fisherman for most of his life, and was 'trout-warden' for that part of the river.

Next morning, the Kerrs took Ron to their favourite spot, close to The Outspan Hotel, where they parked their car. They walked down a steep path, through the hotel gardens, to the side of the fast flowing shallow river below. Mr and Mrs Kerr then took out their rods and began walking up stream occasionally stopping to cast a line into the water. They must have gone a couple of miles and had caught nothing. "It's no good today," David remarked "They're just not biting."

They all sat down on the rocks beside the river to rest a while, had a drink and a sandwich, before retracing their steps. Again they would flick a line into the water, more in hope than expectation, and all of a sudden, David called out "Hey! I've got a bite." Within seconds so had his wife, and very soon they were reeling in the fish with Ron unhooking and storing them safely in the bag. The smaller ones were returned to the water, but they had a catch of ten good-sized fish, averaging three to four pounds a piece, by the time they decided to call it a day and return home.

"These will do for tea," remarked Mrs Kerr, and to his surprise, when tea-time came, a whole trout was placed before him. Until that moment Ron had never experienced the taste of truly fresh fish, and he would remember that day for a long time.

The Kerrs had made Ron feel very welcome during his short stay with them and made him promise that if ever he was in Nyeri again he would give them a call.

Ron continued his holiday with the rest of the group, and now they moved up-country, by steam train, to Kampala, the capitol of Uganda. This was a round trip of a thousand miles, but the men were well compensated for the tiring journey, by the beautiful scenery they saw on the way.

The train passed through the rift valley, passing the Naivasha and Nakuru lakes. Then had to climb up out of the valley where a second engine was added to provide the power for this section of the journey, passing through Eldoret and the slopes of Mt Elgon. Which the panorama was an ever-changing scene of different wild game and the men gazed out in wonder at the views. They had left Nairobi early in the morning and they arrived at Kampala late that evening, to be met by a small bus which took them to their hotel.

Their accommodation was dull and uninspiring and after freshening up they had a meal before retiring to their rooms.

Kampala was a city built on seven hills, the tallest of which (Namirembe) held a religious building, which, Ron soon discovered, was a Church of England Cathedral. The shops in the main streets were, like those in Nairobi, owned bt Ugandan Indians, and were of a very similar type.

A Safari had been arranged for the soldiers, and a couple of days after their arrival, they packed up their things once more and climbed onto the small bus which had been provided for the trip. The luggage was stowed up on the roof and the men settled down to experience the wonders that lay ahead. The first stage took them along the side of Lake Victoria, and through Entebbe, where they stayed for one night on the outward journey. The lake looked inviting and at first they were tempted to take a dip, but they soon discovered that the water was covered in thousands of 'lake flies' and no way were the men going to venture in with those around, to say nothing of the hippos and crocodiles!

Continuing their journey they passed another lake which they were told held over twenty thousand hippopotamuses. These were difficult to see except for the snouts and ears poking up out of the water. At night, the huge animals would amble out of the lake to eat the lush, green vegetation which grew along the banks of the water.

They now entered 'The Queen Elizabeth Game Reserve', named after our present Queen's Mother, where there were some of the rarest animals in Africa and which was also one of the largest game areas in East Africa.

The bus stopped beside Lake Edward, where the road came to an abrupt end at the lake-side. The men watched as natives, who had been fishing on the lake came ashore and threw their catch up onto the bank. The women then took over and, producing long sharp knives, called 'pangas', proceeded to gut and clean the fish, throwing the entrails into the water. Flocks of birds appeared from nowhere to gobble up the tasty 'innards' out of the water, before disappearing as quickly as they had come.

The men were told that they were waiting to be ferried to the opposite side of the lake, but they were not prepared for the sight which met their eyes as a strange contraption approached them across the water. It consisted of two canoes lashed together, side by side, with wooden planks stretched across the centre. Four natives with paddles sat in each canoe to provide the propulsion. The men got back on the bus and the driver drove it up a ramp onto the 'ferry'. Ron tried hard to recall some of the prayers he had been taught as a child, and the other men seemed to be similarly employed! They were all relieved when they reached the opposite bank and the bus was again on dry land. The bus driver said that crossing the lake here saved them a journey of two hours, but the men felt that the two hours would have been well spent to save their jagged nerves.

They soon forgot their fears, however, as now, truly into game country, they saw what they had come to see. The bus drove slowly, but it had to stop completely many times to allow the herds of elephants, giraffe, zebra and antelope to pass by. Occasionally they were held up for longer periods as a group of baboons would be parked across the roadway and were not inclined to move off until they were ready. Continual hooting on the horn would eventually persuade them to decamp and move on. Ron saw wildebeest and lions, hyena and jackal, buffalo and warthogs, rhino and crocodile and occasionally maribou storks perched high in the tree-tops when a dead carcass lay beneath.

The tour next took the party past the Ruwenzori range, the third highest in Africa, at seventeen thousand feet, topped with more than twenty glaciers and known as 'The Mountains of the Moon'. Along their sides were deep impenetrable forests and the animals which they saw now were numerous and very varied. There was little civilised habitation in these parts and the only place that Ron saw any sign of buildings was at Fort Portal, which was the next place they stopped. A few Europeans lived in brick-built homes arranged around a central 'green'. A type of hotel also stood in the centre. It had a large main room, which served as dining room and bar, and the sleeping quarters consisted of small round thatched huts, called 'rondarels', each housing two people. There was a small wash/toilet area in the room, which held an enamel bowl and a large jug containing the water. The basic nature of the facilities did not faze the men as, after spending so much of the time sleeping under canvas, this was positively luxurious, and it became their domicile for the next few days.

After their tiring journey, the men rested for a day, but were then quite ready for what the driver suggested next. He offered to take them up the mountain-side so that they could get a good view across the top of the forest into the Belgian Congo. They climbed up high in the bus, so that they could see mile upon mile of Congo forest land, the vista broken only by the large river, Semliki which ran across it. It was a truly spectacular view and the men stood and gazed over the expanse of jungle which seemed to be never-ending. As they were returning, the driver took them to the edge of the dense forest, and there they got out and walked about half a mile into the trees. (This was Henry Morton Stanley's 'Impenetrable Forest'.) In a small clearing they met a family of Belgian Congo Pygmies; Mother, Father and two children. The father could not have been more than four feet tall, and all they wore was a tiny calico strip of cloth, front and back, hanging from a cord belt. Ron thought that this could never have been washed, as it matched the colour of their brown skin exactly. The natives allowed the soldiers to be photographed with them and the soldiers enjoyed their company for a while, before retracing their steps and returning to Fort Portal on the bus.

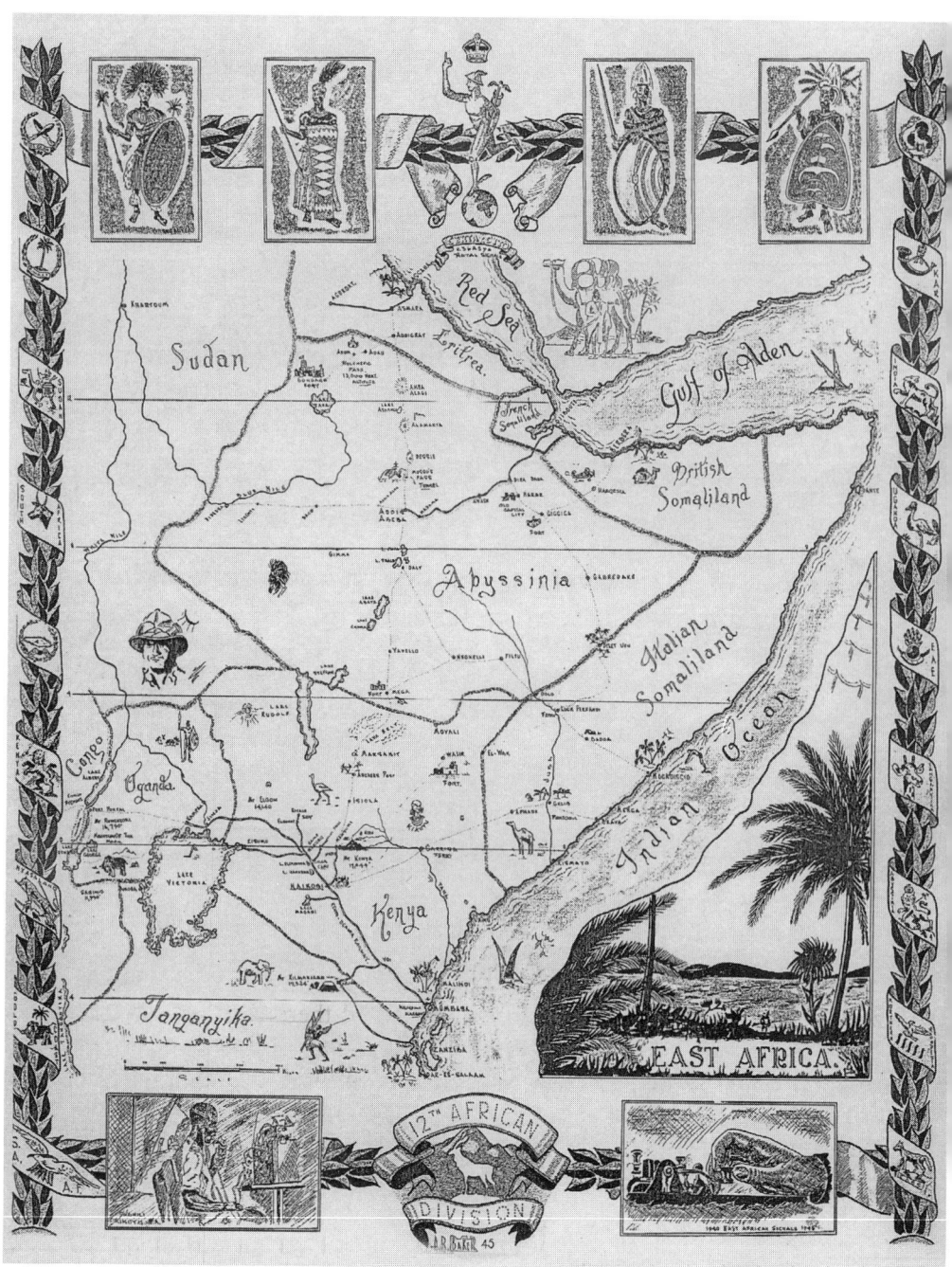

A map of East Africa drawn by Ron on linen.

Ron was well aware that this was 'mosquito country' and ensured that his net was securely tucked in under his mattress each night before he retired to bed. He did not want a recurrence of his previous experience, and he made sure that his colleagues were aware of the dangers too.

The group spent a few days in North West Uganda before returning to Kampala by a much more direct route. Another night was spent here before they again boarded the train for their return trip to Nairobi. Ron sat on the opposite side of the train to the one he had been on during the outward journey, so that he saw a different aspect this time. For most of the journey, the men sat without speaking, and just absorbed the sights of the animals roaming the territory, as they travelled back through Kenya and returned to Killarney camp.

Ron returned to Hut 26 after his holiday and was putting his clothes away, when he chanced to look up at the wall behind his locker and above his bed-head. There he saw the remains of a large black spider squashed across the wall. He was attempting to remove the mess, when Cyril came into the hut.

"Oh! I see you've found your intended assassin," he smirked and went on to explain, that while Ron had been away, one of the lads had seen the huge tarantula crawl from under Ron's bed-clothes and start to climb up the wall. Apparently the soldier had then reached for the nearest heavy object, which had happened to be Ron's own spare boots, and taken a mighty swipe at the venomous arachnid. The lads had decided to leave the evidence of his narrow escape for Ron to see. He was, once more, made aware of the perils that awaited them in the tropics.

Some of the pests which the men encountered were not so easy to see or to avoid as this large spider, but could cause considerable discomfort. One fly which was very prevalant in the area was the 'Jigger flea', which burrowed under the toe nails in order to lay its eggs in a sac. This sac had to be removed using a needle, and care had to be taken not to break it, to prevent the eggs from being released into the skin and causing infection. The natives were very prone to this infestation, as they walked about bare-footed, and they would show the soldiers how to get rid of the pests.

Another irritation to which Ron was particularly susceptible, was 'prickly-heat', which, in those temperatures was quite common. Ron was always very fair skinned, and had very light hair, but after a very short time in Africa, he became almost white-blond and stood out among the natives, much to their amusement.

The army employed the local inhabitants to take care of the day -to-day chores for the men, such as cleaning and washing, and each soldier had one native specifically assigned to him. The native boy assigned to Ron in Nairobi was called Mwangi, and belonged to the Kikuyu tribe. He would always call Ron 'Bwana Baker' to his face, but Ron was very aware that the boys had nick-names for each of the soldiers, and knew that his referred to his pale colouring. Even Mrs Van Hegan always called him 'Blondie' and this name stuck to the day she died, back in Scotland.

In general, the natives were quite trustworthy, but occasionally, an event would show how careful the soldiers had to be. Early one morning, Jack, the cook, rose as usual to begin the preparations for breakfast. He leaned towards the box where he had left his jacket and shorts and realised that they were no longer there. Thinking that some of the men were playing games, he let out a yell to waken the rest of the hut. "Where've you hidden my uniform?" he bellowed.

"Shut up, Jack" was the reply from most of the beds, but as he persisted, one by one the men stirred and realised that their clothes too were missing. Jack, being the most wide-awake found himself something to put on and went out of the door towards the wash-hut. On stepping out-side, he almost fell over a pile of army garments piled on the ground. They all then realised that, during the night, someone had crept in, collected up armfuls of clothes and taken then outside so that the thief could go through the pockets for anything of value, undisturbed. The men had known that the perimeters of the camp were well guarded, and had not thought it necessary to lock the door of the hut, until this episode, but from then on they certainly did.

Another cunning attempted robbery took place while Ron was at Nanyuki camp. The men had learned not to leave money in their clothes and slept with what little money they had, tucked under their pillow. The native boys must have heard about this habit and on one occasion had devised a method of getting at the 'loot' without waking the soldiers. The intruder would creep in barefoot with a long feather in his hands, carefully search under the part of the pillow which the sleeping man was not covering, then gently tickle the ear of the man so that he stirred just enough to shift position. The intruder could then search the other part and usually find what he had come for. The more honest of the natives warned the men of this practice and they again ensured that the huts were well protected at night. Ron was staying in Nairobi, at 'The Norfolk Hotel,' when this method of theft was used on him, and on waking in the morning, discovered that his wallet had been taken from under his pillow. Petty theft was to be found in all places, and it was very difficult to protect themselves completely.

1943 was drawing to a close as Ron settled back into the routine of his work, after his holiday, and caught up with that which had accumulated in his absence. His artistic talents were, by now, well recognised, and he was called upon to prepare menu-cards for the Christmas tables, both for the Officers and the other ranks. He was in the habit of painting pictures of scantily clad young women which adorned the walls of the 'mess' and his colleagues had noticed, too, the cards which he drew to send home to his family and friends. Christmas cards were unobtainable here, and Ron was asked by several of the men to draw a card for them to send home for the festive season. He was usually paid in kind, with chocolate from their meagre rations or with a small item of equipment for his drawing or painting.

Christmas dawned and the men enjoyed the festivities and the special meal which was prepared for them. After the meal, they all donned funny headgear, to accompany their best khaki uniform to attempt to get into the spirit of the occasion. Some wore Bush hats, others peaked caps and the rest, special-issue small side hats.

Transport was arranged for the men to go into the city and once there, Ron and a friend, Cyril Trewitt, a lad from North Shields, would take off together to taste the delights of the city. They had to ensure that they caught the last bus back along the Ngong road to prevent themselves having to return to camp on foot.

The new year dawned and Ron found that he had less and less work to do. The wireless operators would be taken to the Kenton wireless station about eleven miles away, and decoders and maintenance personel still had tasks to perform, but Ron's work was now nearly finished. The population of the camp gradually diminished and the lads were posted to other parts of Africa. Some were sent to Rhodesia, others to Tanganyika and others to Uganda, but for the time being, Ron remained here at Killarney camp.

It was in January of 1944 that Ron had a very disturbing letter from home telling him that his tin trunk had arrived home and asking for news of his condition. He had kept his severe illness a secret from his family, in the hope of sparing them worry, but events had conspired to cause them even more heartache when his belongings had turned up in Sedgley, with little or no explanation. Ron now wrote home giving full details of his illness and ensured them of his complete recovery. So many families had received their loved one's personal effects after the death or capture of the soldier, that this must have been a great shock to

Ron's parents, and he realised, now, that he had been mistaken in the decision he had taken not to tell them the full story from the start.

Now that the time required for working was very short, the C.O.'s. asked for suggestions for events or activities to occupy the spare time. Ron suggested establishing an Arts Club in Nairobi, to encompass drawing, sculpture, various musical instruments and theatre production. This was one of the ideas which was taken up and a society was formed which was called 'The Nairobi Five Arts Club'. It met once a week at The Norfolk Hotel in the city and continued until Ron left at the end of the year. Sgt Segal took a life class for the group as he had had formal training at Art school, and the group did splendid views of the scenery, as well as the studies of local people and buildings. In time, the group was able to put on a creditable art exhibition, with each of them entering a number of their pieces which were offered for sale to the civilian and military personnel who came to view. They each put a price on their work, and as Ron did not want to lose his pictures, he marked them at a figure which he hoped would discourage buyers. Fifty shillings a painting was a full five weeks wages and he knew that army pay would not stretch to this amount, and the locals certainly did not have that sort of money. He was pleased, therefore when the exhibition was over to take his pictures down and keep them for his family to see when he returned to England. He had done black and white pen drawings of native people, one of a young Toto, another a young Bibi of the Kikuyu tribe with shaved head and elongated earlobes distinctive of her kind. The lobes had large holes through which hung cords containing beads, coins and jewellery items. Two more of Ron's contribution were stippled water-colour landscapes of the area around Fort Wajir. All of these Ron still has in his personal collection.

Another event which came out of the Art's Club, was a show called "Klowning Kudos". Ron was responsible for all the set-design and for the wardrobe. One item on the programme, which would not have been allowed today, was a Black and White Minstrel Show. All the camp took part in this, including the Major, and Ron designed tall banded hats and the men sang well-known songs of the time such as 'Night and Day'. They were accompanied by a makeshift orchestra comprising; piano, drums, saxophone, violin and trumpet, being the only instruments that any of the soldiers could play.

To advertise the event, Ron designed two large posters, on which he had drawn a large man carrying a bill-board containing the name, times and dates of the show. It ran for a full week and many of the civilians came to see it and were well entertained as Ron learned when he visited the Van Hegans. They, and the Maxwells, had been to the show and were very impressed by it. The write-up in the East African Standard was very complimentary and all the people Ron met for several weeks afterwards were full of praise for their efforts.

The camp also managed to put on a few dances during this quiet period, and Ron was allowed to take Betty Van Hegan to these and on one occasion to a dance at the Kudu Club in the city. He enjoyed her young genteel quality and was careful to live up to the trust her parents had placed in him, in allowing him to escort their precious only daughter.

October 1944 saw the end of Ron's time in Nairobi, as he was, at last, transferred to another camp. This time his destination was Nanyuki, near to Mount Kenya, where the R.A.F. had left a large camp empty. It was decided that it would make a good training camp for the Africans to learn signalling techniques and it was to be renamed 'The H.Q. of the STC and D East African Command.' (The Signals Training Centre and Depot).

Ron had been delegated to help in setting up the school, ready for its first recruits, and it was with a heavy heart that he said goodbye to his civilian friends and thanked them for their hospitality over the two-and-a-half year period that he had been at Killarney camp.

Just before he left the camp, one of his friends, Vic Korris (son of Harry Korriss, who took part in 'Happidrome', a radio show at that time,) got married to one of the A.T.S. girls. His father was often heard on the radio back in England. Vic had been granted permission to marry and take a week's leave in Mombassa, on the Indian Ocean coast. The couple were married in Nairobi Cathedral and the reception was held at the 'Fair's Residence' on the Ngong Road.

Ron had prepared a banner to tie to their carriage as they left for their honeymoon. On it he had printed; 'Best wishes to Vic and Maud on their marriage--going away for their son and heir- not sun and air'

Ron was now leaving behind one of his best army friends, Cyril Trewitt. Each week they had enjoyed a game of tennis on a court a hundred yards from the camp. It was owned by one of the local civilians (a Doctor) with whom Ron had become friendly, and who had offered him the use of the facilities when they were not occupied. They would play a few games on the court after four o'clock in the afternoon when the sun had lost some of its 'bite,' and they were not obliged to wear their pith helmets. Ron knew that Cyril was one person he was really going to miss and hoped that when the war was over, they would meet up again.

Ron boarded a lorry for the journey to his new destination, a distance of a hundred miles or so. It was the end of the rainy season, and they could travel on the better dry sandy road instead of the hard bumpy road which they had to use during the wet weather. It was a quicker route, but left a trail of thick dust behind the lorry as they drove along.

On arrival, Ron was shown the hut which was his sleeping quarters, and he quickly deposited his few possessions and checked out his surroundings. Next morning, he was taken to meet his C.O., Colonel Tanner, and his new office where he would be working. It was larger than his previous drawing-office and better equipped, having two drawing boards and sets of drawers for his work. His first task was to produce sets of charts to show war establishment H.Q.'s, indicating times and places for the new recruits to use in learning about signalling procedures.

He was allocated a native 'Dobie Boy', a native Kikuyu from one of the local tribes. He would bring Ron a drink first thing in a morning, and like the lad Ron had left behind in Killarney camp, his job was to look after his clothes. He never needed to be told which clothes to wash, he would pick them off the bed, wash them, dry them in the sun and have them ironed before lunch-time. The irons were hollow and contained red-hot charcoal. The boys had to take care that the embers did not fall out as they worked and burn holes in the garments they were ironing. The army employed these boys, but the soldiers to whom they were assigned, would often give them little gifts to ensure their loyalty.

Each soldier was given a regular ration of cigarettes (one hundred each week) and could buy half a bottle of spirits quite cheaply each week too. As Ron neither smoked nor drank, he usually gave his cigarettes to the natives to share between them. His comrades soon learned that he did not drink and would be only to happy to buy his ration back off him. The officers would go into his office, on the day the spirits were to be distributed, and ask if he had already promised it to anyone if not they would obligingly take it off his hands!

Although Ron did not enjoy these army treats, he received regular parcels of 'goodies' from an old friend from back-home. Father Esau from the parish church in Coseley had been married to a woman from South Africa, and when he died, she returned to her native country. She learned of Ron's whereabouts and sent him parcels about twice a year, when she sent one to her brother who was serving in North Africa.

Ron was soon settled into his new life, and began to make friends among the personnel at the camp. He joined in with the sports and enjoyed playing in the hockey team, which would travel to other units to play matches at regular intervals. Once or twice they travelled as far as Nyeri, and Ron took the opportunity to look up David Kerr whom he had met previously while on holiday there.

Ron had more time now to indulge his passion for art, and designed a Christmas card for a few of the officers which he printed by hand. It depicted a scene which included part of the camp site with a few of the native Askaries marching to their lessons, set against a back-ground of Mount Kenya covered in ice and snow. It was very well received and the officers were pleased to have such a personal souvenir of their time spent in East Africa.

Earlier in the year, a monthly army magazine was produced called 'Jambo.' It was made available to all East African troops serving in Kenya, and was printed by 'The East African Standard'. The stories, photographs, drawings and cartoons were all submitted by military personnel serving in Kenya. Sgt. Spinks who was made editor, had been at the same camp as Ron, knew of his talents and got in touch with him, asking him to submit some drawings, cartoons and stories for the paper. This he did, writing a couple of short pieces about his time in Abyssinia and illustrating them. He would have liked to submit cartoons too, but, although he could draw the cartoons well enough, he could never think of a witty caption to accompany them. A fellow in the camp who could not draw but could come up with a witty remark at the drop of a hat, added the necessary captions to some of Ron's sketches and they too found their way into the army journal.

Christmas 1944 arrived and Ron was granted a week's leave which he took back in Nairobi. While speaking to Colonel Tanner about his plans, the officer said that he would be travelling there too and offered him a lift in his staff car. This was quite an honour as well as a much more pleasant mode of transport than Ron had envisaged for his trip. They agreed arrangements for the times of departure and they set off for Nairobi. Ron was deposited at the door of the Norfolk Hotel and he was to be picked up there at the same time one week later.

The cost for the week was just five shillings, and this included breakfast. Ron used his holiday to renew old friendships and establish some new ones. He looked up the Van Hegans, who were delighted to see him again, and he visited the Kudu Club where he met an East African girl called Lulu. She invited him to her home for a meal to meet her family and he was pleased to accept this invitation. He had to take a taxi to her home, which was on the other side of the city, but on arrival, was shown to the long low wooden bungalow where she lived.

A watercolour drawing from Nanyuki Camp of Mount Kenya, early morning 1945.

INGIA KUJIFUNZA · STC · ENTER TO LEARN
NENDA KUFAA · GO TO SERVE

A drawing taken from Ron's office window of the signal training centre at Nanyuki Camp, 1945

132

He was introduced to her father, who was an Indian Doctor, and to her mother who was French. Her brother was present at the meal too, and he was about twenty. They all sat round the table as the food was carried in by native servants. It was indeed a memorable meal for Ron as it consisted of rice and meat cooked in a Madras curry. After a few mouthfuls he felt as if his throat was on fire, his eyes were watering and the perspiration was glistening on his forehead. Luckily there was a large jug of iced water in the centre of the table and Ron poured himself a large glassful and swallowed it down. Not wanting to seem ungracious, he continued to eat the food, but ate slowly and made sure that the cooling water was never out of his reach.

The Doctor drove Ron back to his hotel, after a very pleasant afternoon and evening spent with the family, he thanked them for the meal and their hospitality, and Ron continued his holiday. He saw as many of his old friends as he could in the short time he had at his disposal, and soon it was time to return to camp.

Colonel Tanner picked him up at the time they had agreed and on the journey back, discussed ideas that he had for building a radio set. The signals staff were to build the set and he wanted Ron to design the dial, which was to show the positions and names of all the local stations. He wanted this as a reminder of the time he had spent in Nanyuki. It was completed to his specification in due time and transported to his home in Nairobi.

There followed an exceptionally dry spell and by the end of January the camp was completely out of some basic foodstuff, including potatoes. The catering officer sent Sgt. Rice out into the surrounding villages to try to buy some replacement supplies. He travelled within a forty mile radius of the camp, but could not persuade any of the tribal chiefs to part with any of their stocks. They too were running low and naturally, did not want to leave their own people hungry. When the catering officer received this news, he immediately cut rations back to a minimum to conserve what stock they had. This did not affect the native diets, as they ate rice and not potatoes with their main meals anyway. One of the natives, returning from a more distant village over the other side of Mt Kenya, brought news that there were plenty to be had in that direction where the rains had still fallen normally.

Sgt Rice was detailed again to go and obtain supplies, and, as the distance was over one hundred miles, he asked if he could take Ron with him for company. This was agreed, and they set off in a small truck, to bring back whatever they could find. They were given directions to the villages to the east of the mountain and off they went, driving first over decent roads for fifty miles, but then getting into thick bush territory for many miles seeing nothing of human life, until the land changed to an area of well cultivated terrain on the outskirts of Meru. Here a different type of native lived, but they could still converse with them in the universal language of East Africa which was Swahili. Eventually, the Sergeant and Ron were able to track down one tribal chief who had sufficeint stock to be prepared to sell some to the army. Ron had seen in England how potatoes were stored in small hillocks under a mound of earth, but here they were taken to a place outside the village. There was a small round wooden building standing on stilts, about three feet off the ground. When it was opened up, the hut revealed a healthy supply of sweet potatoes, not the white European ones which they were hoping for. Never-the-less the Sergeant and Ron bartered manfully for some of the precious commodity and managed to acquire three sackfuls from the chief, for a reasonable price. By this time it was too late for them to attempt the return journey, and they found a small, cheap hotel to stay for the night.

Next morning, they were able to appreciate the pleasant surroundings, and notice how green and fertile this area was in comparison to where they were camped on the other side of the mountain. They drove back with their load and, now that their mission was accomplished, were able to take in the views of the bush, the luxuriant forest and the mountain beyond. Ron tried hard to commit these views to memory so that he could paint them on his return. Sgt Rice asked Ron if he would like to drive for the last fifty miles and of course, he agreed, although he had been enjoying just taking in the splendid scenery and making mental notes for future use.

The two men were greeted by a delighted group of soldiers as they entered the camp, despite the load being the native variety of potato and not what they had hoped for.

The weeks were passing and sport took up most of the soldiers leisure time. Occasionally, Colonel Tanner would make the journey into Nairobi for a weekend, and would offer to take Ron in for the company on the way. Ron looked forward to these trips and again was able to meet up with those poeple who had been a part of his life for so long. He always looked up the Van Hegans and would take Betty to the local dance in the Kudu club. On one occasion Tom allowed him to use his 'Austin' to take his daughter to the dance, which Ron felt very honoured to do. Betty was still only seventeen years old and he always had to be sure that he brought her home at a reasonable time.

On one of these weekend visits to the city, Ron had a pair of shoes made in the native quarter. He was measured for them in the morning, chose the leather and the design and was able to collect them by mid-afternoon. He also bought his Mother a crocodile handbag which cost him four weeks wages, but which he looked forward to presenting her with on his return home.

During the time they were in Kenya, the soldiers were allowed to send a package of local treats home every four months. Ron, being a non-smoker, would send his father a box of fifty cigars and to his mother - sugar, tea, tinned pork sausage, glazed fruits and lengths of local fabric for dresses.

Easter was fast approaching, and the soldiers could look forward to a few days off. They discussed together what they could do during this break, and someone came up with the idea of an expedition up Mt Kenya to the edge of the glaciers. The plan was put to the C.O. who gave his permission with the proviso that an officer accompanied them. On asking around, the men found one young lieutenant, who had only been abroad for eighteen months, who was willing to go with them. They were allowed to use an army truck and they set off at day-break, a total of five men, in British battle dress and carrying their great-coats to protect them later from the cold they knew they would encounter as they climbed up high.

They left Nanyuki behind and climbed steadily up the mountain road, passing a small church and a collection of native huts, before the road began to deteriorate and the going got rough. They crossed the Nanyuki river and Tom Van Hegan's 'Equator Timber Mills, so called because the equator passed through the middle of it. They drove on, managing to negotiate the tropical forest before reaching the bamboo forest beyond. At ten thousand feet all this changed and they encountered a completely different zone of flora. A long wild type of grass was interspersed with large species of groundsel, and amazing coloured 'everlasting flowers' were seen nestling amongst the rocks. Finally, when they could take the truck no higher, the men climbed out, donned their coats and thick gloves and prepared to continue on foot. They climbed up towards the main twin peaks of the mountain, called Batain and Nelion, passing a large lake in the valley below and aiming for the base of the Lewis glacier which was still some fifteen miles away. Reaching the edge of the snow line, they came across a locked hut, which they assumed to be owned by the local farming community and probably used as a base for skiing or mountain-climbing. They had now covered well over twelve miles on foot and had still not reached the glacier and knew that they had to turn back and return to their vehicle.

The views as they returned were breath-taking. They could now look back over the Nanyuki Plain and could see in the distance, the Aberdare Range that parted Nanyuki itself from Nakuru and the Thompson Falls. The men gasped now, not with the exertion of the climb but with the wonder of the scenes, as they made their descent.

The return journey was uneventful and they arrived back at the camp in time for a late evening meal, a warm shower, and a change from heavy winter clothing back into tropical wear after their tiring but exhilarating experience. They all slept well after their exertions and next morning Ron arose, dressed and went to the door of his hut. He looked up to Mount Kenya, in all its glory, rising now out of the morning mist, fresh snow glistening on its peaks, and glaciers sparkling in the early sunlight. He shivered with the thrill of the memory. "To think, I stood up there yesterday," he thought.

This was the view that Ron had always hoped to see, but many days the summit was clouded in mist and its outline was indistinguishable. Now, on this special day, Mount Kenya stood clear and proud. Ron took out his pad and started to draw. The foreground showed the medical huts and the entrance gate with its flag flying, beyond lay the tropical forests and grasslands drawing the eye to the majestic mountain peaks above. He was oblivious to the rest of the men passing by, going to eat and they did not disturb his work, appreciating his need to capture the scene and record the moment.

Easter passed and they resumed their normal day to day activities, until on 8th May 1945, they were sent news that the war in Europe was over. Ron had by this time been away from home for five years and he, along with many of the other young soldiers were inclined to think of East Africa as 'home'.

In Narobi there were victory parades to celebrate V.E. Day. All the services took part, with bands playing, people shouting and singing and everyone making merry. But in Nanyuki the day continued as normal with only twenty or so whites there who all continued working as usual. Ron still had plenty of spare time and filled it with his drawing and painting, sitting at his drawing board in his office. He felt sure that before the end of the year, the army would see fit to send them all home to England, and at last he dared allow himself to think of that as a real possibility.

He now decided to produce a detailed map of East Africa which had been his home for the past five years. It had to be special. He decided it would be drawn on linen, and he found a suitable piece of cloth and coated it with a white solution, so that the black ink would adhere to it without running, and it would show up well.

The map covered most of the North Eastern tip of Africa. Kenya, Uganda, British and Italian Somaliland, Abyssinia, The Belgian Congo and Tanganyika were all included. The map was bordered by the badges of every unit that had taken part in the East Africa Campaign. Various South African Units were depicted as were representatives from West Africa - The Gold Coast and Nigerian regiments from East Africa. The King's African Rifles, Ugandan and Rhodesian forces, as well as The Royal Corps of Signals and The Royal Tank regiment from England, and The Highland Light Infantry, and the Cameron Highlanders from Scotland. He illustrated the map with sketches at various strategic points to show events that occured during the campaign and used red ink to indicate where the major battles and unit camps stood. It became an historic diary of that part of the war and Ron hoped that in time the original work could be placed in the war museum as a lasting reminder of the events that occured in Africa during that period. He made a couple of dozen copies from the map and presented them to the officers and other ranks who had shared the experiences with him and always hoped that looking at it would bring back memories of some of the happier times they had spent together.

One morning, Ron noticed that all eyes were turning upwards towards a black mass in the sky, slowly approaching Nanyuki. He watched too, as the thick cloud got nearer. The soldiers assessed that it covered an area of twenty miles long by ten miles wide and it took six or seven hours to reach them. It was a swarm of locusts, the first that Ron had seen during his time in Africa. He learned that locusts do not fly too well, but rely on the prevailing winds to carry them along. As it grows dark the insects drop to the ground and feed on whatever they land during the hours of darkness. This time the swarm landed on the camp and the surrounding fields. As the men walked out of the huts in the evening, they could hear the crunch of the locusts as they trod on them, lying thickly on the ground. Hundreds of birds were flying overhead to pick off the last few remaining insects still flying about, and they circled around swooping in to catch them in their beaks, and when none remained in the air, the birds dived in to snatch them as they fed off the ground.

Next morning Ron went out to see the result of the invasion, and was amazed to see that the swarm had vanished, leaving just one or two stragglers lying scattered about in between the huts. Ron walked down to their little patch of garden which they had carefully tended, in order to give them some fresh salad and the occasional tomato. The little green plot was now a red plot. Every leaf had disappeared leaving only the red tomatoes among the debris. Not one salad leaf remained. Ron and his comrades stared in horror at the devastation, they could not believe that this could have happened in such a short time. But this loss was nothing compared to that experienced by hundreds of farmers every year in Africa.

The Kenyan government monitors the movement of these large swarms which breed in the sands of Persia, (now Iran), and when mature, cross the Red Sea, making their way south along the rift valley, sometimes travelling as far as South Africa.

Information about their whereabouts is transmitted to the farmers to warn them of their approach, not that there is a great deal that can be done to protect their crops from the swarm if they are unfortunately in the line of their flight.

Ron had been in Africa for five years and this was the only time he was to see the effects of these creatures.

Now that the war was over, the men had little to do and Ron again had time to make the acquaintance of the neighbouring white settlers. He particularly enjoyed the company of one farmer who could keep him enthralled with stories of the early days, when the British people had first gone to Kenya and began farming. Most of the homes were constructed of wood, and were situated at some distance apart. This farmer had arrived in Kenya in 1913 and knew Ron's friend Tom Van Hegan who had emigrated at the same time.

He told the story of one Scottish lad who lived alone some distance from the man's own farm. The lad had a small wooden house and, as the nights were cold, kept a fire burning, and had an oil lamp glowing dimly to conserve his fuel. The door was shut but not bolted when suddenly it burst open and a huge snarling leopard bounded into the room and went for the lad, sitting close to the fire. He grabbed for the first thing that came to hand, which was a chunk of half-burnt log from the grate, and tried to defend himself. The animal dealt a blow to his head, but then, frightened off by the burning branch which the lad was vainly waving about, departed through the open door as suddenly as it had come. The lad was in a bad way and there was blood pouring from a gaping hole in the side of his head where the animal's claws had landed. Self preservation took hold of his actions now, and he wrapped his head in a sheet, got into his truck and drove to the nearest neighbours' farmhouse before collapsing in a heap on their floor. They bundled him into their vehicle and drove him the twenty miles to the nearest doctor.

"Did he survive?" asked the incredulous listener.

"Yes, he's still alive today, and living near Thompson Falls" was the reply, "but bald as a coot and the hole made by the leopard visible for all to see, so big you could almost put your hand in it."

After a few more stories of the early days, the man offered to run Ron home. They went outside and Ron saw to his delight an old 1920 Model 'T' Ford which the farmer used to transport him back to camp. He learned that the car had been owned originally by the man who had been attacked by the leopard and was now only used around the farmland.

David Kerr, who lived at Nyeri had many similar tales to tell of their hairy predicaments in the early days in Africa, before they got used to the different way of life and the dangers which lurked in the forests and bush-lands. He, himself had lost a leg in the First World War, but it did not hamper him or prevent him keeping up with anyone. He was a match for even the youngest around, especially when swimming, out game shooting or climbing ladders when he built his house.

The dangers of the country were to be brought home to Ron again a little while later, when a small group from his camp decided to go out on a game-shoot. They went towards the out-skirts of the Mount Kenya Forest, when the Sergeant in charge of the party moved on ahead to have a look for a suitable area to hunt. He was about a hundred and fifty yards ahead of the main group when a massive bull-rhino took his scent and charged him. By the time the men had got to his aid he had been savagely gored. The stunned soldiers could do nothing but carry his battered body back to the lorry and silently return to camp. He had been killed outright and he was buried with full military honours in Nanyuki.

Ron had not been on this expedition, for which he was very grateful, but in such a small camp, he had known the man well.

He looked back, and realised that he had experienced the death of three soldiers during his time in Africa, and not one of them had been the result of enemy action. He had joined the army and entered the war, knowing what was involved, but he had not appreciated that the dangers would have come from such unexpected sources. He sat and reminisced on the times he himself had been exposed to the natural savagery of this continent. He had survived one of the worst diseases which the area produced, he had come face to face with the deadly Black Mamba, whose bite could kill in seconds, and he had slept in the forests containing these very animals which had now killed his sergeant. The war may be over but the dangers still existed and Ron

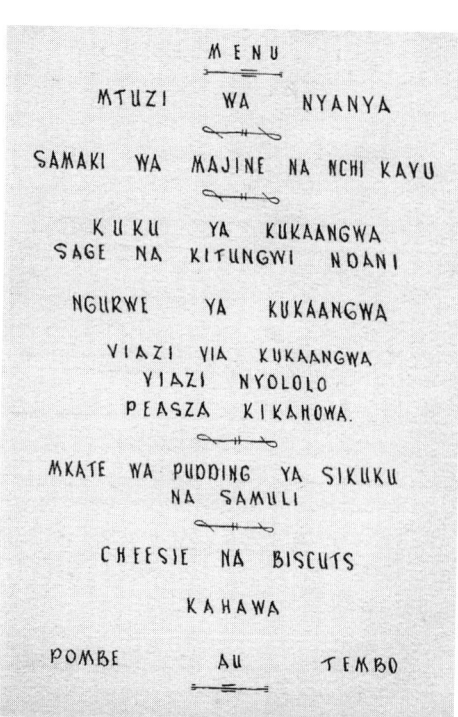

NANYUKI

STC&DS

MENU

BOR's DINNER

SATURDAY

12TH MAY 45

RON BAKER 45

MENU

MTUZI WA NYANYA

SAMAKI WA MAJINE NA NCHI KAVU

KUKU YA KUKAANGWA
SAGE NA KITUNGWI NDANI

NGURWE YA KUKAANGWA

VIAZI VIA KUKAANGWA
YIAZI NYOLOLO
PEASZA KIKAHOWA.

MKATE WA PUDDING YA SIKUKU
NA SAMULI

CHEESIE NA BISCUTS

KAHAWA

POMBE AU TEMBO

Menu Card for the Other Ranks Celebration Dinner, May 12th, 1945.

A Christmas Card for the Royal Signals, Salisbury, Christmas 1945.

looked forward, with ever increasing fervour, to being safely back in Sedgley.

On the eighth of June 1945 that day seemed to be coming increasingly near, as an important message was posted with daily orders. It stated that continual overseas service had been reduced to a maximum of four years. As Ron, and many of the others still at the camp had left England in that same convoy in October 1940, they had already surpassed that limit and were due to return home. There were many happy faces around the camp that day, especially those of the few married ones. They continued to wait for the information of their repatriation, and at the end of July it was announced that a draw would take place to decide which half of the group of thirty still in the camp would return in the first batch.

The soldiers stood around the C.O. as the draw was made.

First out of the bag was Sgt. Vicar, next was Second Signalman A. Carter, (a friend of Ron's from Willenhall) then Lance Corporal A. R. Baker No. 2362396. Ron was in such a daze he heard no more names. He was going home!

When the draw was complete, a couple of the married men clambered round the ones whose names had been drawn, begging to exchange their repatriation dates so that they could get back to their families. Ron was sympathetic to their pleas, but reluctantly had to refuse them. It would be another five months delay before the next group would leave and he knew that much could happen in that length of time. He was definitely going home.

Before he left the camp, Ron was presented with a book on Arts and Crafts by Vernon Blake, and written inside the cover was the message; 'With compliments of Officers Signal Training Centre & Depot, East African Signals, signed Major Lindque P.M.C. August 3rd 1945.' Ron was really delighted to receive such a personal gift and felt that it was a really nice thought.

The group was sent back to Nairobi at the end of July and stayed there for two weeks while plans were finalised for their journey back to England. Ron used the opportunity to look up his friends. He saw Betty Van Hegan and her parents and other white families who he knew, living along the Ngong road. The Van Hegans and the Maxwells were pleased to see him safe and well, and to hear that he was now on his way home. They invited him and a couple of his Scottish comrades to go with them on a picnic up into the Ngong Hills. The lads came from Largs, which was where Mrs Van Hegan's parents lived, so that they had much to talk about and messages were sent with the soldiers to her parents. The hosts matched the carefree mood of the soldiers and Mr Maxwell excelled himself, entertaining them all with his funny antics. They took lots of photographs to remind them of the happier days they had spent in East Africa.

The day was clear and bright, and from their view-point, high up in the hills, they could look south over the plains and see Mount Kilimanjaro with its snow topped crest, over one hundred miles away. Turning round, they could see Mount Kenya, almost the same distance away to the north. It was very rare to find the right conditions to see both mountains at the same time in this way. Ron had seen Ruwenzori and Mount Kenya too, but now he was seeing Kilimanjaro, the highest mountain in Africa, and thought himself very fortunate to see it before he finally left the African continent.

The men had left the base camp in Nairobi and moved to Lagata camp on the Athi Plains, when the ceremonies took place to celebrate V.J. Day on 15th August 1945.

Lagata camp was used by all personnel waiting to return to England. It was surrounded by barren land, full of a variety of wild animals. Ron saw a pride of lions just off the dirt road as they approached the camp on their arrival. The men did not stray far from base, and luckily they did not have to wait there long. On 17th August they were on the move again going to Mombasa by train to board the S.S. Franconia for the next part of the journey home. When Ron first saw the ship in the dock, he thought that it looked more like a luxury cruise ship than a troop carrier and, when they boarded her, they were not disappointed. The soldiers were shown to their sleeping quarters and then went to look around the ship before it sailed. They were surprised to find a fair number of young ladies also returning home. Ron got into conversation with one young girl who must have been in her late teens. She was a Jewess and had been sent from her home to Mauritius to escape the war in the Middle East, and was now returning to Israel and her family. The army had taken up the extra berths on the ship to take some of the soldiers part of the way home to England. Compared to the transport on the way out this seemed like heaven; good food, fresh water for washing and shaving and a comfortable cabin to sleep in. The mood was different too, of course, as now the men were on their way home, and everything seemed better and brighter and their spirits were high.

The weather was fine, the sea was smooth and the ship left port following the coast-line past Mogadishu, turning into the Red Sea, passing Berbera and Aden and eventually entering the Suez Canal. The ship negotiated the canal under a full moon and the men stood on deck to watch the manoevre. Many nights it was too hot to sleep below, and they slept on deck, feeling the warm breezes on their bodies. During the day they were free to do as they pleased, and they struck up conversations with the Israeli girls who enjoyed the company of the young men.

Seven days after setting sail, they passed Port Suez, and the following day, on the 25th August, they put into Port Said, where the men grabbed their kit-bags, said their 'good-byes' and disembarked. This ship continued on its way to Haifa in Israel and the men walked along the docks to find their next means of transport, which turned out to be a troop ship which ran between India and England. The soldiers had to walk about a quarter of a mile along the docks to reach the ship and they were laden down with all the items they had accumulated during their time in Africa. Kit, presents and souvenirs all contributed to the hefty load they carried. A few Egyptian boys stood around the docks and some offered their help in carrying the bags. Ron, by this time, had become very wary of these individuals and was not inclined to release his precious load, but one of the lads who was particularly heavily laden did. He gave one of his bags to a young lad to carry, and the boy walked ahead of them for a while. Suddenly the boy was off, darting down a side-alley and out of sight before the soldiers could stop him. There was no point in even attempting to follow. The men had too much to carry to try to run after the thief and they knew that he would be well hidden in the maze of alleys that bordered the docks. Ron clutched his bags even tighter, relieved that his presents, African drawings and accumulated memorabilia were safe, at least for the time being.

The men found the ship which was to take them back to England and boarded it with a sigh of relief. It already contained a large number of soldiers on their way home from India, and as the last group settled into their quarters, 'The Orantes' set sail.

On 27th August they passed Malta, on the 28th, Bizerte, on 29th, Algiers, and on the 30th, Gibralter. Ron plotted the journey in his head and felt himself drawing ever closer to his family. They sailed safely through the Bay of Biscay and into the English Channel and back onto home territory after all that time away. The soldiers hung over the rails of the ship as they sailed close to the Isle of Wight and they could see how green and lush it looked compared with the countryside they had got used to in Africa. On 2nd September the ship docked in Southampton and the soldiers disembarked to be taken to the railway station to board a train to carry them to the army camp in Ripon. The camp was situated on the race course grounds, but Ron was not destined to stay there long, as two days later he was off again. This time the destination really was HOME! A whole month of leave before having to return to the camp for his next official posting.

Ron had sent a telegram the day before he left the camp;

"EXPECT A STRANGER HOME TOMORROW."

He arrived at the station and slowly carried his packages towards the home he had thought about so often, and the family who he had not seen for nearly six years. 'Stranger?'- perhaps he was not so far off the mark after all. He had left home no more than a lad and was returning a mature man having seen parts of the world his parents had only read about.

His parents were waiting for him, and, although neither of them was given to shows of emotion, they both clasped their son, before taking some of his load and leading him into the house. Ken was in India and Gordon had taken to sleeping round at 'Aunt' Hilda's for company since her parents had died. Ron had the big double feather bed to himself that night and revelled in the warmth and comfort as he snuggled between the clean sheets.

Next morning he opened up the tin trunk which had been sent back home while he had been ill in hospital. He had almost forgotten about the existence of some of the items. Most of the contents were his army clothes and tropical pith helmet which had been replaced when he had started his new job at Killarney camp, but he was pleased to see that his drawings and books were all present and correct.

Ken had got married while he had been away and Ron lost no time in visiting his new sister-in-law next day. Elsie lived in an end-of-terrace house at the top of Jew's Lane in Upper Gornal and when Ron entered the house and began to introduce himself to her, was surprised to find that she already knew him. Elsie told him that she, too, had worked at Town Mills, his old clothing firm, and she remembered him from before the war. Ron was rather embarrassed that he could not place her at all. She told him that her parents kept 'The Pear Tree' public house in Lower Gornal. Ron offered to take her out one evening as soon as he was settled and they parted company so that he could continue looking up family and friends.

The next person that Ron met up with was his old buddy Doug Holmes, who he had worked with at the Mill and who, now, had moved to Clifford Williams and Son's at Handsworth. He was delighted to meet up with Ron again, and offered him the use of his car while he was on leave as he had used up all his petrol coupons. Ron was allowed a supply of coupons and was happy to take his friend up on his offer.

Ron's next port of call was to another pre-war friend; Mabel Roberts, who, with her brothers, kept horses in the field next to their home at Mons Hill, Woodsetton. He told her that he had been horse-riding while he had been in Abyssinia and asked if it was possible for him to take one of their horses out occasionally. She said that he could exercise one of her brother's horses and he immediately went home to change into the riding breeches he had had made in Africa. He took the horse out and enjoyed again the feel of the wind in his face as he rode along. Mabel and he arranged another ride for the following day and this time they rode together all along the verge of the Birmingham New Road, and his companion marvelled in the changes she saw in the young man beside her.

Now that Ron had transport, he went for drives out into the country, to Bridgnorth or Bewdley to sit by the river and to enjoy the feeling of freedom as well as to spend time with the friends that he would take along for company. During his second week of leave, he went to visit Reg Reynolds' mother at the Summer House pub, and she mentioned that a friend of hers Adi Bradley, who also kept a pub, had suggested that Ron went to make the reaquaintance of her younger sister, Vi. Ron had known Vi Raybould before the war and, finding that she wasn't married, decided that he would look her up.

Ron called to see Vi and he arranged to take her to the Clifton Cinema in Sedgley that evening. On returning her to her home he asked her to a dance the following week at the Civic Hall in Wolverhampton. Very soon, Ron began to realise that his feelings for her were rather special, and although he spent time with other friends and family during his leave, he also saw rather a lot of Vi.

The time came for him to return to Ripon and he made arrangements once again for his departure. He returned the car to Doug, giving him the rest of his petrol coupons to use himself. He said his good-byes once again and made his way back to the station to return to camp, on the 4th October, to be given his next posting.

An interview was arranged for Ron the following day with the Posting Officer. The officer had all Ron's details and service records in front of him as he entered the room, but asked him about his previous positions. He listened carefully to the description of his experience and then looked at Ron and asked him, "Where do you actually live, in civvy street?"

Ron told him, "A few miles from Wolverhampton, in the West Midlands."

Ron in dress uniform, 1940.

Ron in Nairobi, East Africa, 1944.

"Well, as you have spent so much time away from England, we shall be looking for a posting near to your home. You'll hear something over the next few days."

Ron was moved out of the camp to accommodation near the town centre, which suited him very well. He had nothing to do but explore the lovely Yorkshire town with its cobbled square and interesting northern-style buildings, and visit its cinemas and dance halls. The days expanded into weeks and still he continued to wait to see where he would be sent.

On the 12th November the information reached him. Ron was being sent to Southern Command Signals H.Q. Harnham, Salisbury. He was somewhat dazed as, once again he packed up, made his way to the station to take him first to Waterloo in London to transfer to a train for Salisbury. He reported to his new Commanding Officer, who told him that he would be working directly under his command as H.Q. Draughtsman.

"Any questions?" he was asked.

"I am rather puzzled," replied Ron, "Why have I been tranferred down South, when I was promised a posting in the West Midlands?"

"I think that it was considered, after working so long in Command H.Q.'s, that it would be degrading for you to finish your service in some small brigade office." he explained. He continued reassuringly, "Don't worry, now that the war is over, I doubt that you will be here for very long, and if you want a week-end rail-pass, just let me know and I will make sure that you get one."

Ron settled in to his new office and found that there was very little to do by way of official army work, and resorted to his art to fill the time. He designed a couple of Christmas cards. One showed Harnham gateway, the other depicted a 'Signals' motor cyclist pulling a sledge full of presents. When they were finished, he showed them to the C.O. who thought it a splendid idea to sell them to the personnel at the camp for Christmas, and told him to take them into the town to get them printed. This he duly did, and while he was there asked if he could have them trimmed with blue and white ribbon. He was told the cost.

Ever the shrewd person where money was concerned he replied, "Don't bother. I'll do it myself."

Ron very soon made friends with some of the other men at the camp, and they would visit the city centre at the weekends and go to the local cinema, the dance hall or indulge in sports. Occasionally they would walk into the city along the river bank, past the water-mill and the weir, arriving near to the Cathedral, with its tall spire and elegant facade.

One of the Nissan huts at the camp had been designated as a recreational area, and was set aside for reading and relaxation. It was seldom used and, knowing that Ron had the ear of the C.O., one of the other men, who had previously played in a band, put it to him that he should ask for permission to turn the hut into a dance hall in time for Christmas celebrations. This Ron did, with a favourable response. They were to put the idea to the officer in charge of leisure and, if he agreed, they could go ahead. This officer, too, thought it be a good way of keeping the men amused at weekends, and together they formulated a plan to change the hut into a dance hall. He was able to allocate a small amount of money from camp funds, and with these they bought paint and materials to brighten the place up and to build a stage for the band. Ron designed the decor, and turned the ceiling into a beautiful night sky with stars of different sizes stencilled onto the deep blue background. A small working party completed the work and were quite proud when it was finished and they could stand back and view their handiwork.

The band comprised four musicians and, when they had practiced, sounded good. They were ready for their first event, and Ron made posters to advertise the dance in the camp and in the surrounding area. They were all delighted when quite a few girls from the district turned up, and their first effort was a complete success. They immediately arranged a second dance for the following weekend and although Ron again made the posters and helped with the preparations, this was one that he would miss.

Ron was granted his first pass for the weekend of 23rd November to attend the wedding of his best friend Reg Reynolds, back in Sedgley. He intended to make the most of his time off, and left on Friday afternoon to arrive late in the evening. The wedding took place in the local chapel and Ron got dressed in his best battle-dress for the ceremony. After the speeches to Reg and Freda, Ron was impatient to be off, and wishing his friends well, he departed early to take Vi to a show in the evening. Ron had to be back at camp by Sunday evening, but this time he had a pretty lady to accompany him to the station and wave him off.

Many young men, returning from the war had taken no time in renewing old friendships and tying the knot with their girlfriends from before the war, and Ron found himself attending another wedding the following weekend too. This time it was one of his soldier comrades who was getting married. Cyril Trewitt was marrying Cath, whom Ron had heard so much about in the long lonely hours in Africa. Again Ron was granted leave to attend, and again left camp on Friday to travel all the way up to Bakewell for the ceremony. He found the address where he was to stay and next morning made his way to the church to witness another of his friends getting married. They had a wonderful reception in a room in the Town Hall building. The meal was accompanied by wine and they drank champagne to toast the happy couple. When the guests were able to mingle later, Ron made his way to his friend and his new bride.

He hugged Cath, "I feel I know you already," he said, "Out in Nairobi, Cyril talked a lot about you. I've seen your photo so often and heard the things you said in your letters, that I think I would have known you anywhere." Ron was really happy for his friend and left the party, after promising to keep in touch and bidding Cath's parents 'goodbye'.

He intended to stop overnight at home once more and had a special lady of his own in mind as he made his way south on the train. He saw Vi for just a short time on the Sunday afternoon, and again she went to the station to see him off. When he arrived back at camp, he was delighted to find that he had been granted ten days leave and knew that he intended to use the time to get to know Vi better.

His parents saw little of him during his leave, but they were pleased to see how happy he was looking and to know that he was seeing 'a nice young lady' on a regular basis.

He returned to camp after his leave and was able to pick up the Christmas cards and prepare them for distribution. He bought the blue and white ribbon and the cards were made available to the soldiers to commemorate their stationing at Salisbury. The cards were soon sold out and although they made a small profit, Ron was disappointed that he had not had more printed as there were insufficient to satisfy all those who asked for them, but he gave the profits back to the C.O. so that it could be used for further projects.

The men were now granted seven days Christmas leave, and once again Ron spent much of his with Vi, before retuning to camp on 27th December to await his 'demob' date. They each had a 'group number' based on their age service and the date they had joined the army. Ron's number was 26, and meant that he would be demobbed sometime in January 1946.

On 2nd January he was presented with his C.V. and his reference which could be used when he applied for a job in civvy street. It read;

"An excellent and skilled draughtsman. His work has been charac- terised by originality and care. He has taken immense trouble over every task he has performed. He has undertaken commercial poster work for this unit, all his work showing most excellent taste.

He has a most pleasing personality, is thoroughly trustworthy and loyal.

I have no hesitation in recommending him to any employer.

Captain J. Yardley Headquarters Southern Command 2nd Jan 1946."

On 21st January, Ron left Salisbury to go to the demob station in Hereford. He slept his last night as a service-man at the camp before rising and eating his last army breakfast. He walked slowly towards the Quarter Master's store, opened the door, and looked inside. He gasped in amazement, thinking that he had somehow been transported back seven years in time to Dudley before the war. What he saw was row upon row of gent's suits hanging on rails, just as he had left them in the warehouse at Town Mills. He laughed out loud and got some very strange looks from those already in there. He didn't attempt to explain. They wouldn't understand. He moved on in and was duly issued with a three piece suit in a choice of blue chalk stripe or brown. Ron chose the blue. White shirt, tie and hat and a selection of underwear lay in piles ready for handing out. When the collection was complete, each man was sent to the corner of the hut to change into the new civilian clothing before handing back the army uniforms for the last time. Ron stood for a moment, free now to come or go as he pleased. It felt strange. For six and a half years he had been subject to the instructions of army officers and that was now over. His last task was to pick up his free rail ticket to take him home. He walked quickly now to the station, boarded the train to Birmingham, changed to a local Wolverhampton train that stopped at Tipton, and made the short journey on foot to 17 Sedgley Road, Woodsetton and home.

Ron had four months paid 'demob leave,'a total of £119-2/6d pay for the time he had served abroad and when he had arrived back from Africa he had £206-2/10d in his bank account. He soon made a hole in his savings as his first purchase was an Austin Seven Ruby 1936 motor car, which cost him £180, which he bought from an old friend of his, Les Nicholls from Clifton Street. This car was to serve him well over the next two years, both for business and pleasure.

Ron thought hard during his leave, trying to formulate his ideas for the future, and after three months his mind was made up. He was going to set up his own tailoring business. He applied for an allocation of clothing coupons and, when they arrived, started to look around for suitable premises from which to work. One place,particularly, took his eye. It was now empty, but was in the Sedgley Bullring area and had been a greengrocers before the war, and run by a family by the name of Barnett. Ron visited the landlord, Mr Arthur Collins, who kept a tobaccanist shop a few doors away, and a rent of ten shillings a week, plus expenses, was agreed upon.

Ron now went back to his old firm and saw his previous boss. He told him what he was planning and said that he would not be returning to Town Mills.

"I'm really sorry about that," Sydney Fryer said, "We had hoped to see you back in your old office, but if it doesn't work out there will always be a place for you here, you know." Even the information that they would give him five pounds a week, which was way above the going rate, could not tempt Ron to change his mind. Syd warned Ron of the difficulties that there were now that the war was over and money was still scarce in most homes.

Ron knew that he was not in for an easy life. Supplies would be difficult to come by, hours would be long and he had a lot to learn in the business world . But he knew that this was what he wanted to do.

He wanted to be his own boss, answerable to no-one.

With Syd's warnings still ringing in his ears, he made his way down the stairs, out of the gate, climbed into his little car and drove home to start his new life.

BUSINESS AND FAMILY LIFE
(1946 - 1977)

O N 20th April 1946 Ron collected the keys to 14, High Street, Sedgley, and began the task of turning it into a tailoring business. The premises had been built as a house, but as far back as 1910, it had been used for retail purpose, with the front down-stairs room converted into a shop. This room measured just twelve feet square and still contained the original fire-place. Ron stood in this bleak room and took stock of what he would need to start his business. He knew that he would need a cutting table, a changing room and most importantly, some novel way to attract customers to enter the shop. He came upon an old shop sign behind the Clifton Cinema, just across the road from his new premises. It measured fifteen feet by three and was solid mahogany. "Sproson Vinrace - General Grocers" was still visible on the sign, which had lain there for ten years since the grocers had moved to the opposite side of the street. Ron cut the sign into a long table top, ten feet in length and as he constructed the basic piece of furniture, hoped that it would soon be put to good use.

"Now what?" he pondered. A long mirror was his next acquisition. This he bought from Arthur Croyden, who, besides being the local hair-dresser and chiropodist, also dealt in second-hand furniture, from his shop next to "The Red Lion Inn."

The mirror was placed in the corner of the room and Ron then set about constructing a small changing room. He had acquired a quantity of black-out material, left over from the war-time, and with this he made some curtains which he hung from rails in one corner to make a cubicle. The curtains could be drawn back when not needed so that he had more space to work.

He now began work on the window area. It had been used previously to display a selection of fruit and vegetables and the racks had to be removed before Ron could put his own individual stamp on the premises. He used the shelving which he had removed, the black-out material and some of the wood left over from his cutting-out table, to construct a narrow, flat shelf. He then found a piece of stout cardboard on which he drew the figure of a tailor, sitting cross-legged, sewing a coat. The right arm was hinged at the shoulder so that it could be moved backwards and forwards to give the impression that the figure was actually sewing. Ron was pleased with the final effect, but then wanted to find a way of really making the arm move. He went to discuss the problem with Roger Fellows, who ran an electrical shop, round the corner, in Bilston Street. They put their heads together and Roger came up with the idea of using a windscreen-wiper motor, which could be attached to the arm in such a way as to make it move to and fro. It turned out to be a marvellous idea and, soon, Ron had the figure fully working and sitting in his shop window to attract the attention of passers by. He carefully wrote on the window what services he could offer, and arranged the small quantity of material he had been able to acquire around the window display. He offered, as a bespoke tailor, to make, alter or convert any item of clothing which the returning service-men could no longer fit into. Finally Ron had to buy a second-hand sewing machine and he placed a small advertisement in the 'Express and Star' announcing that his business would be open for trading on the last Saturday in April 1946.

He needed to register a name for his business and he thought of two possiblities:- 'County Clothes' or 'Quality Clothes'. When he applied for registration, he was told that the first name was already in use in the area, so 'Quality Clothes' it became.

Opening day dawned and Ron arrived early to ensure that his shop looked attractive and welcoming. The Sedgley folk had been watching the preparations as they went about their business in the days before trading began, and were keen to see what Ron could offer. Many young men had, like Ron, recently returned from the war, only to find that what few civilian clothes they possessed, did not fit them, and they were pleased to find someone near home who could solve their problem. They seemed happy, too, to support a new Sedgley trader in his attempts to get his life back on track after the horrors and hard-ships of the previous five or six years. In the first months of trading, Ron was inundated with garments for alteration and found himself working flat-out to meet the strict dead-lines which he had set himself for providing this service. As luck would have it, Ron was speaking to a young man who had come to live, with his young bride, in rooms behind the gas showroom near to his shop. During the course of the conversation, the man happened to mention that his wife had worked in the tailoring business and was looking for work. By the end of the week Ron had appointed his first employee and could delegate some of the work to her and devote more time to other ideas which he had.

The business was soon prospering as a result of word-of-mouth rec-ommendations and the advertisements he had placed in the paper, and within six months he was considering opening a second shop. He learned that some premises had become vacant in the High Street in Brierley Hill, which he knew to be a very busy shopping area. Ron realised the potential of such a prominent position. Business in the district was booming, with Round Oak Steel Works and Marsh and Baxters factories nearby, together employing thousands of people. He couldn't see at first how he could manage both shops, but, during the negotiations for the new premises, he met up with Doug Holmes, an old friend. Doug said he would like to work for his friend - an offer which was the answer to Ron's prayers. Doug had been in a 'reserved occupation' during the war, as a designer and pattern-maker with Clifford Williams & Sons. Ron knew and trusted Doug and was pleased to give him the job as manager of the Sedgley shop while he himself set up the new business. Typically, Ron was disappointed that, because Doug had not himself seen active service, he did not have a supply of clothing coupons to bring with him into the business! He did, however know Doug's skills and was pleased to be able to welcome such a trustworthy friend into his business.

Clothing coupons were as important a commodity in the tailoring business as any item in the shops, as without them, Ron could not obtain the material to make the garments. He was allocated a specific number for each business and as he made a suit, skirt or coat for a customer, they had to bring the corresponding number of coupons into the shop when they came to fetch and pay for their clothes. The tailor then had to retain these coupons and bank them in envelopes with the relevant details of all his transactions. Anyone found to be mis-using these coupons or not accounting for them correctly would be prosecuted and could be fined heavily or imprisoned.

The use of clothing coupons continued until the middle fifties and on one occasion, when Ron had not been his usual meticulous self, a spot-check was made on his coupons and a discrepancy was found. He was still experiencing some sleepless nights the following week, when it was announced that rationing was to cease and the coupons would no longer be required. The investigation into the short-fall in his collection was stopped and the supply of cloth became de-regulated over-night.

The rent for 152, High Street, Brierley Hill, was £2 per week, at the end of 1946, and this only allowed Ron the use of the shop itself; no extra store rooms or upstairs facilities were included, and he had to pay the rates as well. The living accommodation upstairs was, in fact, rented out separately. Still, he was satisfied with the deal, and once more set about establishing this second business while Doug continued to look after the Sedgley shop.

Ron fancied himself as a fairly good judge of charactor, but was well aware that some of his customers would try to put one over on him if they got half a chance. One day he had just finished measuring a local man for a new suit, in the Brierley Hill shop, and had just seen him off the premises, when the window cleaner finishing off the front door, remarked, "You don't want to trust him, he's known round here as a bad payer."

Ron thought he ought to give him the benefit of the doubt and made up the suit and the man came back when it was ready, and paid in full immediately. Ron was pleased and when he returned three months later, with his son, to have suits for both of them made in readiness for the son's wedding, he had no qualms in giving them his best efforts. The father offered to pay for both the suits when they were ready, and did so with a personal cheque. Unfortunately the cheque wasn't honoured and it took Ron nearly twelve months to get any of the money back for the two suits. This incident made him very careful in dealing with customers he did not know.

The next few months passed by very quickly and people in the trade soon became aware of Ron's success. The owner of the rented Brierley Hill shop premises, a fellow by the name of Horace Naylor, was himself the manager of a tailoring shop - 'Fred Terry's'. He approached Ron one day and indicated that he would like to join him in his business ventures. Ron was never one to miss out on a good opportunity and told him that this might be possible in the future, if Horace were to sell him the premises which he was then renting off him in the High Street. This was agreed and 'Quality Clothes' became the proud legal owner of 152, High Street for the princely sum of £1400. The tenants who had been renting the rooms above the shop, moved out very soon after the transaction was complete and Ron had his own workshops up and running within a week of their departure.

Doug and Ron continued to work hard and by the end of 1946 had acquired another shop to rent in Summer Lane, Lower Gornal, and a young lad called Sam Smith, who lived within a few hundred yards of the new premises, was taken on to manage it.

So, the new year dawned with Ron running three premises and all this had been achieved in a matter of months. The workshop above the shop in Brierley Hill employed a number of young women, and Ron made good use of his little Austin motor car to travel between the three establishments. It was just as well that he had this means of transport as the late winter from February to April of 1947 proved to be one of the worst on record, and Ron found himself having to negotiate huge snowdrifts as he made his way between them. Public transport was at a standstill and several roads were completely cut off for days on end. The road from Swan Village up to Sedgley was impassable and Ron had to detour along the New Road as far as the Guest hospital and then back through Dudley and Upper Gornal, past thirty foot snowdrifts at Jockey Fields before reaching his shop at High Street, Sedgley.

While Ron was working at his Brierley Hill shop, he would leave his little motor car on a small piece of land to the rear of the shop. During the 'Big Freeze' of 1947, he had to protect the radiator from the chill winds by covering it when he left it. He always had his old ex-army great-coat (which he had had dyed dark blue) in the car, and he would carefully cover the bonnet and front of the radiator with it. One evening, on returning to his car in the bitter winds, he noticed that the coat was not in place. Ron looked around on the ground, imagining that it had been blown off. He scoured the vicinity in vain and returned to the car to see a piece of paper stuck behind the windscreen wiper. He could not see what it said, so took it to the corner of the street so that he could use the street-light to read it better.

"Dear Benefactor," it said, "It was kind of you to place your great-coat over the bonnet of your car. On passing along Level Street, I felt the cold east wind on my body. I looked at your small car, saying to myself "I need the warmth of that coat more than the car does." So I decided to try it on. It covered my very cold body and so I thank you for your kindness in leaving your coat for me." The note was signed "An unemployed ex-soldier, and finished with "Thank-you once again."

Ron could not begrudge the man his coat, and luckily his little car's engine had not suffered in the freezing weather.

Ex-servicemen were having a hard time in getting back into employment in some cases and one chap, a neighbouring tradesman in the High Street, Brierley Hill, helped them out when he could. He had a butcher's shop opposite Ron's tailoring business and in the early days was known to bring in a young soldier who had fallen on bad times and ask Ron to make him a suit and he would pay for it himself. His name was Mr Freddie Nott and he must have paid for half-a-dozen suits for these unfortunate young men and Ron admired his generosity.

The early days after the war were difficult for everyone. Food and materials were still scarce, and, if available, had to be exchanged for coupons as well as hard cash. One day, a gentleman came into the shop and ordered a suit. In due time it was ready and he came to collect it. It was then that he informed Ron that he did not have sufficient clothing coupons to cover it. However, he came up with a novel way to pay the difference. He said he would give Ron a hundred-weight sack of sugar in lieu of the coupons. This was a bit of a problem for the tailor. He did not want a made-to-measure suit left on his hands, but on the other hand, he was not sure that he knew what he could do to get rid of that quantity of sugar either. In the end he agreed to the arrangement and the man brought the huge sack of sugar and plonked it in the middle of the fitting room floor, paid for his suit and left, well satisfied.

By coincidence, that afternoon, Ron was fitting another customer in the back room, when he saw the sack. He looked puzzled, and Ron related the story. "Goodness knows what I'm going to do with that," he said.

"I'll tell you what," was the reply, "I'll buy it off you. I run an ice-cream business and I can never get enough sugar."

Ron was delighted. "You bring me some clothing coupons and it's a deal," he said.

He was back in the shop within the hour with the coupons and Ron was glad to see the back of the sack. Everyone was happy and each had what they most needed.

It was during this bleak cold winter that Vi's Mother was taken ill and, after a short time, died. Vi and her brother, Bill, went to live with their sister Adi after the funeral. Adi kept 'The British Queen' Pub in Parkes' Hall and Vi did not like the place at all, so after a matter of a few weeks, moved out and went to stay with her older sister a short distance down the road. Ann and her husband Frank Addis, and their son Robert, made her very welcome, but Vi felt, as the year unfolded, that she was prevailing on their hospitality, and this feeling prompted her to set a date for their marriage. Ron and Vi's relationship had been developing well and, by the autumn of 1947, they both knew that they were ready to commit themselves to marriage. Ron set about in his usual methodical way to provide a home for himself and his future bride.

Ron and Vi Raybould's friendship had developed from the time he left the army and they had become engaged soon after he was demobbed. Vi had lived with her widowed mother in Kent Street, Upper Gornal, together with her brother, Bill, until her mother's death in March. The snow still lay thickly and the roads remained difficult to manoevre as Ron tried hard to join Vi as she sat at her mother's sick-bed, each evening after work. When her mother finally died, Vi and Bill moved in with their sister and the contents of the family home were dispersed between all the children.

Vi was the youngest of a large family. Her mother had given birth to ten children, but two of the brothers had died before the last was even

Sedgley No. 10 High Street showing Ron's 1936 Flying Nine Standard car.

No. 152 High Street, Brierley Hill, 1949.

born so Vi had known five sisters and just two of her brothers. John, the eldest was eighteen years older than she was and Bill seven years her senior, and although he was thirty five when his mother died, he was still unmarried and did not marry until some time later. He was happy to make his home with Adi at the pub when Vi moved into their other sister's house.

Vi had had other boyfriends before Ron but showed no great enthusiasm for what most girls saw as their inevitable destiny. She saw marriage now as a solution to her domestic problems and looked forward to the ceremony as the beginning of a new life. Ron was left to sort out the practical details of their marriage and to find them a home to live in.

While he was having his hair cut in Arthur Croyden's barber's shop, he overheard some news which he felt might be useful. Number 52, High Street, Sedgley was being vacated and the barber thought that the present owner would be willing to sell it. Ron wasted no time in visiting the man who lived in Hill House, Hill Street, Upper Gornal. The owner was a Mr Fellows, a batchelor and an habitual snuff-taker. It fascinated Ron who noticed that the fine powder was always sprinkled down the front of his waistcoat which covered his well formed pot-belly! At first he seemed reluctant to commit himself to a sale, but when Ron promised that he was prepared to offer him a price above the market value, he relented and finally a figure of seven hundred and fifty pounds was agreed upon.

Ron had a good commercial reason for his interest in this property. He was only renting his premises at 14, High Street, and knew that his landlord had sons of his own for whom he would have to find homes as they grew older. Ron felt that by having a property of his own in the neighbourhood, he had 'back-up' plans if ever Mr Collins failed to renew his tenancy. So, number 52 High Street became his new home and could be used as his business premises should the need arise.

The wedding was planned for Friday, 26th December, Boxing Day 1947. Vi decided to get married in a tailored suit rather than a wedding dress, and Ron made his bride's navy-blue outfit and she bought a small matching hat and carried a bouquet of tiny blooms and trailing fern. The venue was Ron's family church; St Chad's in Coseley, as Vi did not like the Vicar of her own church. The reception was booked at the rooms behind Upper Gornal Co-op store. The cake was made by a lady from Brierley Hill who worked for Wimbush Confectioners in Birmingham, and Ron managed to collect together enough ration coupons to provide food for the wedding guests. Wine and beer was brought from the family pub - The British Queen, and Ron's younger brother, Gordon took the photographs. Unfortunately, a box camera was the extent of his photographic equipment, and he had no flash light. By the time the wedding finished, it was almost four o'clock, on a dark winter's afternoon. Although Gordon did his best, when the films were developed a week later, there was only one picture recognisable. There was no pictorial record of the day except a picture of the wedding cake taken in the reception room, earlier in the day!

John, Vi's oldest brother gave her away and Ken stood as Ron's best man. Vi had no brides-maids and the service was simple, watched on that cold winter's afternoon by a small collection of family and friends.

Despite her lack of enthusiasm for the whole idea of marriage, Vi was to say after her golden wedding had come and gone, that she could not have hoped for a kinder or more considerate husband than Ron.

This might not have been so apparent on the day following their wedding, however. It had become the habit at that time, for Ron and Vi's brother-in-law, Frank to go to the football match, and, right on cue, Frank arrived at Vi and Ron's new home. (It had already been decided that paying for their home was far more important than having a honeymoon, so they had gone straight there after the reception.) So it was that twenty-four hours after their wedding, Ron was watching Wolverhampton Wanderers win at home 2-1 and Vi was walking to spend the afternoon with her sister 'Nan.'

"This is a fine thing," Vi thought philosophically as she trudged along the road alone, but she was not the kind to complain to her husband.

It was not until a few days later, when Ron was mulling over the events of the previous week, that it suddenly occured to him that it might have been better if he had stayed at home with his new wife!

The newlyweds' new home was the middle house of a terrace of three and had been built in 1910. It consisted of a front room, large back living room, which led into a scullery and veranda which itself led into a wash-house. The outside toilet adjoined the scullery and was reached by walking down the bricked path which extended from the back-door to the small gate at the rear of the house. The gate opened onto another similar pathway which also allowed access to the other two homes in the block and met up with the side road - Brick Street.

Brick Street was a short, narrow road, along which were a few small houses, a number of 'Nail Shops' and a small safe-works owned and run at that time by a Mr Lee and his son. A small cottage lay at the bottom of Ron and Vi's land. Here Mr Garland lived. He was a cobbler and used one of the old, small nail shops for his business. His son followed his father into the business, but in 1947, he was employed by

Wolverhampton Wanderer's Football Club to maintain the players' football boots. Another of the cottages was owned by Mr Nicholls who was a saddler and leather-goods manufacturer, and the end house next to Brick Street itself was owned by a builder - Mr Hunt. He and his son worked together and stored all their equipment in a 'lock-up' across the road from their home. Few houses had garages of their own at that time, but Ron was lucky to find a small one nearby where he could store his precious motor when it was not in use.

The house fronted onto the High Street and the front door opened onto the pavement. The road was therefore very close to the actual house and trolley-buses passed very regularly, and would keep them awake some nights as they trundled by. Occasionally the electric pole would come off its wire, resulting in a hail of sparks and flashes which could easily be seen through their bedroom window, which faced the main road.

The hardworking traders of Sedgley lived in harmony with one another in their little enclave, and Ron and Vi settled down to married life in their midst. Ron held the view that it was a husband's duty to provide for his wife and he did not expect Vi to go out to work. He had seen the way his own parents had conducted their lives and believed that it was a satisfactory arrangement, with the wife and mother at home to look after her husband and family and the father bringing in the money to keep them warm and fed. Before her marriage, Vi had done several jobs, but just before she married, had been employed alongside her sister, Irene, as a receptionist to a private Doctor's Surgery in Waterloo Road in Wolverhampton. Now Vi stayed happily at home, keeping house and preparing meals for 'the breadwinner' - Ron.

He provided well for his wife and, later, when she had passed her driving test, he bought her a new Morris Minor for her own use.

Rationing was still in full swing, and there was some strange bartering went on with some valuable essentials. On one occasion, a traveller came in to the Sedgley shop, and as it was the height of summer, Ron was surprised to see that the usually immaculate man had on a raincoat, fully buttoned up. Ron looked puzzled and the young man soon explained his predicament. The zip on his trousers had broken and the fly was wide open. He had spent the sweltering day visiting clients in his coat. Ron put him in the fitting room and replaced the zip for him making him respectable once more, and the man left to go to his van outside. He returned a moment later with twelve, quarter-pound packets of tea which he gave to Ron as a 'thank-you' for saving his dignity.

By March of 1948, Vi and Ron discovered that their union was to be blessed with their first child, and before the year was out their son was born. Ron prepared for its arrival as he did with everything. He decorated the house in what spare time he had, and enjoyed tending the garden - grassing over the small vegetable plot, so that their child would have somewhere safe to play.

The baby was due in November but, by September, Vi's condition was beginning to give cause for concern. Her legs had swollen up alarmingly and she was admitted to 'The Women's Hospital' at West Park, Wolverhampton in an attempt to alleviate the situation. Ron, and their own Doctor, Dr Summerville visited her regularly and it was a very worrying time as there was a very real risk that Vi would lose the baby that she was carrying due to the toxaemia. After three weeks, it was decided that, although it was early, it was necessary to start the labour and bring the baby prematurely. Vi was taken to the delivery room late on the evening of 5th October and, after a long labour, gave birth to a healthy boy next day. Although early, the baby weighed in at six-and-a-half pounds, to the great joy and relief of his delighted parents.

Vi remained in hospital for a further week to regain her strength, and Ron was thrilled when he finally got the 'phone call that he had been waiting for, to tell him that his wife and son could be collected to go home. When he arrived to fetch them he found that another mother and baby from Upper Gornal were also being released and he had been volunteered by the ward sister to drive them home too. Ron, two new mothers with their infants packed themselves into his tiny motorcar and he set off gingerly to transport the precious load to their respective homes.

The young family had a few sleepless nights to contend with for a time, but soon settled into a happy and contented ritual. Ron registered his son as 'Anthony Ronald Baker of 52, High Street, Sedgley', and later the child was christened at St. Chad's Church, West Coseley by the Rev Bourne, where Ron and Vi had been married the previous year.

Their home did not possess a bathroom, and while Ron and Vi made do with a tin bath in front of the fire on bath-night, little Tony had his own enamel bowl which was placed on the kitchen table for his nightly bath. The young parents watched in wonder as their son grew and developed as time passed. When they felt confident enough to leave him for a short time, they would ask Doug and Mary Beck who lived next door with Mary's parents to babysit for them. They seldom went farther that the Clifton cinema, which was a short walk away from their home and they knew that they could be reached quickly should the need arise. In truth these outings were very rare, as Ron often worked well into the evening, transporting work between his various shops and from his 'outworkers' who completed tasks in their own homes.

Not long after Tony was born, television came onto the market and Ron decided to invest in one. He dropped into Tom Hartland's electrical and wireless shop, a few doors along from his own shop on the High Street, to enquire about purchasing one. He was informed that, as television had only just come into the area, he would have to wait for a few weeks until it could be installed. He was impatient and when a fellow walked into his shop to order a suit and Ron realised that he was a Director of an electrical wholesalers, he complained about the delay.

"Leave it with me," the man said, and when he came back for his first fitting, he brought with him a telivision set. It was one of the first sets in Sedgley; a nine-inch Bush model costing just forty nine pounds. It was black and white of course, and Ron soon had it rigged-up in his dining-room. The neighbours were intrigued by this new form of entertainment, and were often dropping round at odd hours to watch it. None of them was such an avid viewer as young Tony though, as he could be placed in his high-chair in front of it, and he would sit mesmorised for hours, watching the small flickering screen. The Bakers were never short of baby-sitters once they had aquired this new 'toy'.

Tony was soon up on his feet and walking around, and like all young children, very inquisitive. Ron and Vi were very aware of his safety and the coal fire was protected by a stout fire-guard. One evening, after supper, the parents were discussing the day's business while the child was playing on the carpet nearby. They were so engrossed in their discussion that for a moment they took their eyes off their son, and he reached up to the overhanging table-cloth in order to pull himself up. Unfortunately, the tea-pot was on the edge of the table and down it went, spilling its scalding contents down the lad's right arm. The pair were demented as the child screamed in pain and fear. They wrapped him in a towel and Ron raced around to the nearest Doctor that they knew, who was Dr Chand living in The Manor House, opposite his shop. He sent them straight to the casualty department at The Royal Hospital in Wolverhampton. There he was treated and luckily there were no permanent scars as a result of this episode. Tony was to put his parents through several more scary moments as he was growing up.

Ron was beginning to feel that he would like some diversion from the responsibilities of work and family and discussed with his wife if he could be able to spend some time at college, studying more formally, the subject so close to his heart. Vi was happy to agree to this, and Ron made arrangements for someone to keep her company while he attended Dudley Art College one evening a week. This was the only formal art training Ron had had since his one hour classes at secondary school, and he relished the opportunity. He had been drawing local buildings in his spare time ever since being 'demobbed,' but felt he still had much to learn. His first evening was a life class, and when he entered the studio, he was met with the sight of a series of wooden 'donkeys' facing a central pedestal. At the front end of the donkey was a large easel with a container along the bottom to hold all the drawing implements and a sheet of paper covering the face of the easel itself. The students entered the room and took up their positions astride the donkeys facing the pedestal and, when they were all assembled, a female nude model entered the room and took up her pose on the pedestal. Each student had a slightly different view and they could draw any aspect of the model they wanted to. Ivor Shaw, the lecturer walked behind the students as they worked, giving advice and instruction.

Ron met one young man that first night at the college who was to remain his firm friend for the rest of his life. Basil Grainger had known Vi since birth as they had lived opposite each other as children and after church on Sundays, their families would join together round the piano for a sing-song. Basil always referred to Vi's mother as 'Nana Raybould' so closely were the two families linked. Now Ron and Basil were to estalish a friendship which continued until Basil died in 1999.

Ron really got bitten by the 'Art Bug' and wanted to experiment in different media. The next to take his fancy was clay and he soon learned how to work the malleable material to expel the air-bubbles and then deftly throw it onto the wheel. When he had produced a reasonable specimen this way, he found that he had much more control over his work by using long thin pieces of twisted clay and shaping them to create different objects. This gave him much more flexibility and he produced some interesting work using this technique. One of his pieces - a modern type of bird form, was accepted to be exhibited at Dudley Museum and Art Gallery.

After the first year, when Ron felt that he had mastered the techniques of drawing and pottery, he went on to enlist in classes for sculpture and wood-carving. He loved the feel of the various materials between his hands, and eagerly worked to produce new and exciting shapes. His teacher now was Mr Bridgewater from Edgbaston, and under his tuition, Ron produced some interesting stone figures, one of which, again, was accepted to be shown at the annual art exhibition.

Mr Bridgewater, while working at the college was commissioned to produce sculptures for both the police station and the college in the Broadway. That at the latter was a large eagle which was initially made out of clay, then a cast made and a model produced in bronze. This has stood for many years over one of the entrance doors to the college. The artist's work, depicting the form of two early policemen, still stands at the entrance to the police station in Tower Street, Dudley.

Ron's enthusiasm for the Arts did not wane, and he continued for a third year, studying lettering on slate and marble, and also woodcarving. When he had proved himself proficient in all these skills he told his wife that he was quite satisfied to stay at home on the evenings when he used to go to college and, from then on, only went out sketching with the class if they went on field excursions. He would often be asked to participate on these occasions as he was one of the few people who actually owned his own transport, and he would be able to carry several other members of the class out into the countryside to paint and draw. Petrol was still strictly rationed, but, as he had three shops, Ron had a reasonable allowance for business purposes.

It was now 1951, little Tony was nearly three years old and Ron felt that it was time to buy a more modern home for his family. Very few houses came on the market, materials were hard to come by and special licences were required in order to build new property. Ron applied for, and was granted, a permit to build his own home and he then had to find land and a builder to actually construct it. While he was in the midst of all these plans, a young couple who lived above one of the local shops in Sedgley heard that he had been granted a permit and were furious as they themselves had recently been refused one. They complained to the council that, as Ron already had a home, he should not have been granted the permit. Councillor Mrs Williams came to visit Ron and informed him that his permit had been revoked. Naturally, he was annoyed as well as disappointed, but decided that he would have to revert to the original idea of buying a second hand house.

One of his customers gave him some good advice on the subject of buying property, and Ron resolved to try to heed his word.

"When looking for a house, always buy the best you can afford, but don't buy a good house in a bad area. You would do better to pay the same money for the best you can in a good area, and then when you want to sell again you will always find someone willing to buy."

Ron kept this wise advice in mind as he hunted for a suitable property, and in October he found just what he wanted. No. 7 Richmond Road, Sedgley, had been built in 1938, just before the war

Castle Street, Dudley showing Ron's car outside the shop on Sunday afternoon.

No's. 8 and 10 High Street, Sedgley showing Ron's Vauxhall 1031 UK.

started. It was in a quiet cul-de-sac, within a short distance of shops, school and bus routes and perfectly situated for all the family's needs. It cost them £2200, and had three bedrooms, a bathroom and toilet upstairs, and a lounge, dining room and kitchen downstairs. The kitchen had a fireplace and outside was a coal-house which stored the fuel to keep the fire burning. The house also had its own garage and was named 'Padua.'

52 High Street had been sold for £1200, and the extra thousand pounds bought the Bakers the home of their dreams where they were to remain for seventeen years.

The family moved into their new home in November, which meant that the child now had a safe back-garden in which to play and was soon provided with a swing for his amusement. Ron also bought a load of sea-sand and made his son a sand-pit at the bottom of the garden in front of the shed, where Vi could watch him playing from the kitchen window. Tony had a collection of model army vehicles; tanks, ambulances, guns and soldiers which he treated with meticulous care, cleaning and packing them away in their boxes after each use.

The following year Vi became pregnant again and Ron was determined that she would not experience the same trouble that she had at the end of her first pregnancy. In February 1954, Vi went into a private nursing home in Riley Crescent, Penn Wolverhampton, and to everybody's great relief and joy, Diane Elizabeth Baker was born on 26th February, weighing 7lbs 8ozs after a very easy birth. Vi was soon home to her husband and son with the new baby. This child was provided with a luxury 'Windridge' baby carriage and Vi proudly pushed the new offspring around the village with little Tony holding onto the handle. When Diane was six months old, Tony was of age to start school. Vi would walk round to Queen Victoria Infant School, in Bilston Street to deliver him first thing in the morning, fetch him home for lunch, return him there in the afternoon and then fetch him again when school was over for the day as many mothers did then and still do today.

If the weather was fine, Vi would leave the pram outside the High Street shop when Ron was working there, and he would keep an eye on the baby while Vi did her shopping in the village unhindered. There was no fear for the safety of the child in those days and could be left to sleep in her pram in the street while her parents went about their different activities nearby.

As Tony got a little older, he would finish school and run along the pavement and around the corner into High Street to his Dad's shop and wait with him until he closed up and then return home with him in the car. Vi's life took on a full and happy pattern, looking after her children and her husband, who was making a good living at his trade.

When Tony reached the age of eight, Ron and Vi felt that he was quite old enough to walk to and from school on his own, and the only time he was supposed to drop into his father's shop for a lift home, was when it was raining. He tended to stretch the definition of 'rain' somewhat, and on occasion Ron would be surprised by the appearance of his young son.

"What are you doing here?" Ron would demand, and on going to the shop-door would see the tiniest spots of moisture in the air. "You're old enough to get home under your own steam," the busy man would direct, and pack him off home.

Business was booming, and in 1955, "Quality Clothes" acquired another shop, this time in Dudley itself - 149, Castle Street. These premises were in a very good position, next to Bellfields' Restaurant, a pork sandwich shop and just a few yards from the open market. This shop was rented for three pounds ten shillings a week plus rates, but as well as the ground floor rooms there were two further storeys above which were very useful. Another tailor, Mr Cobden, worked nearby and produced clothes for the London market. Ron had been cutting some of the garments for him prior to his move into the Dudley shop and knew that it did not threaten his own trade as all the work went down South. Now that there was extra space available, Ron was able to rent some of it to Mr Cobden who built up his business and was able to employ more local people in his workrooms above the shop. Each weekend, Mr Cobden would hire a taxi, pack it with all the clothes that had been produced during the week and take them down to 'Burberry's' in London.

Ron found a manager for his new shop. He was an excellent find and soon the shop was showing a good return. The Brierley Hill premises were bursting at the seams with all the sewing girls who worked there for him, and it was decided to expand the business by building a large workshop in the garden at the rear of the shop. Ken, Ron's brother, was asked to build it, and he and his work-mates came each weekend to do the construction. Within three months it was completed, the sewing machines were installed, a foreman was found to oversee the workshop and they were up and running.

Materials were still in short supply and the intention had been to mass produce men's trousers in the new premises. The four shops produced enough orders to keep the workers in the workrooms above the

Brierley Hill shop busily occupied but Ron wanted to produce garments which could be sold to the ready-to-wear men's outfitters.

All the orders for made-to-measure suits were produced by skilled, trained personel who had been gathered together over a time by Ron. He managed to find a very good tailor by the name of Mr Williams from Chapel Ash in Wolverhampton, who began his professional life, working in the old-fashioned way, sitting cross-legged on top of his table sewing by hand. Now he expertly supervised the cutters and machinists from early morning, arriving promptly at eight o'clock no matter what the weather. He remained a faithful employee until he retired at sixty-five.

Ron now remembered his promise to Mr Horace Naylor, who had sold him the Brierley Hill shop. He was taken into the business to manage another acquisition that Ron had made. He bought a ladies' outfitters in High Street, Sedgley near to his first shop, and Mr Naylor was employed to look after both No. 10 and the new premises at No. 14, with a Mrs Simner being taken on to manage the ladies' outfitters. This arrangement left Ron free again to travel between his various outlets and to his 'outworkers', collecting garments and transporting them to the relevant shop for fittings or sale when complete.

Ron found that certain jobs were more economically done by women in their own homes. Young mothers, who had babies at home to look after, needed extra cash and were happy for the opportunity to work at home. Ron would deliver pieces of cloth cut out for a pair of trousers, together with the relevant pieces of lining material, rolled into a bundle ready for the worker to sew up. He would later collect the garment and return it to the workshop to be finished off, pressed and hung up ready to be paired up with its jacket to make a suit. The jacket would at first only be tacked together, ready for its first 'skeleton fitting'. After this fitting, any alterations needed could be made easily without any machining having to be unpicked. When the fitting was corrected, the garment was then sent to a coat-machinist to be sewn up.

Two of the outworkers who Ron regularly employed were especially reliable and he gave them work whenever he could because of their circumstances. One young woman lived in Ruiton Street, Lower Gornal and, as she had a little baby was unable to go out to work, and she would sew trousers for him. One of the coat machinists he relied on, lived in Holly Hall and looked after her handicapped brother at home. As the lad needed constant care she, too, was unable to go out to work and Ron took the work to her home. Both of the houses were on the way from Brierley Hill to Sedgley and Ron could arrange his journey to transport work for the women at suitable times during the day.

If a second fitting for the suit was required, this was undertaken, adustments made and the garment finished off before it was taken to have its hand-made button-holes sewn. For many years this last task was done by Rose Jackson from Burton Road, Upper Gornal, who was an excellent 'button-hole-hand'. As the work-load got too much for her to cope with, her sister Olive would help her out. She, too made a good job of this intricate task. Ron would collect the garments again, returning them to Brierley Hill workshop to have the buttons attached with special waxed thread. One more trip took the suits to another Mr Baker, living in Laurel Road, Priory Road, Dudley, who would steam press the clothes with infinite care before hanging the jacket, trousers and waist-coat carefully together. Ron would them send a card to the customer to tell them their suit was ready to be collected. The whole process took up to three weeks from the first measurements until the customer picked up his completed suit, and many skilled people were employed in its production.

Ron knew the sort of impression that he wanted to project in all his shops, and was very careful to employ people who maintained that image. He had advertised in 'The Express and Star' for sales-assistants, when he first opened the ladies-wear shop in Sedgley. One of the first ladies he interviewed in response to the advertisement was a young lady by the name of Margaret Poole. She arrived promptly, smartly dressed and carrying a slim, rolled up umbrella, all of which Ron took note of, as she entered the shop and asked to speak to the boss. He asked her several relevant questions about her experience and her responses were precise and confident. He liked the way she presented herself and her self-assured manner, and did not take long in deciding to offer her the vacant position. She lived up well to his expectations and became proficient in displaying the garments in the window to best effect, and in dealing with customers. While working for Ron she married a local man by the name of John Cooper and they lived, first in Kingswinford and then later in Sedgley. When Margaret left, she was replaced by another lady of the same name, this time Margaret Willis who was married to an Eric Willis, who was, at that time doing his two years national service in Germany.

At about this time, Ron began to acquire seven-yard-lengths of fine quality worsted suiting from a firm called Henry Mellor of Huddersfield. This quantity was significant as it took three-and-a-half yards to make an average suit. If an unusually large man came into the shop requesting a suit, Ron would have to keep his eyes open for a small customer so that he could compensate for the amount used by the other client.

One Saturday morning a sturdy lad, by the name of Bill Toogood, entered the shop and chose a blue striped worsted cloth for a suit. Ron took his measurements and realised that he would be using much more than half a length of the precious material. He told Bill that he could return on the following Saturday for a fitting. As luck would have it, within a couple of hours, another man came into the shop looking for a new suit.

"I don't want grey or brown," said the short, stocky Mr Phipps.

"Well let's see what we have here," said Ron, his mind quickly seeing the opportunity to use up the small quantity of blue worsted. "I think this would suit you very well," he said draping it over the man's shoulder.

Measurements were taken and again a fitting was promised for the following week-end. All went well and in due course both suits were ready for collection. The suits were hung on the racks and first Mr Phipps came in to collect his suit one Saturday afternoon. He tried on the jacket and stood in front of the mirror obviously pleased with what he saw. The suit was carefully folded and wrapped up, paid for and off went the satisfied customer. A little while later Mr Toogood came in to fetch his suit and the process was repeated.

On Monday morning, Mr Toogood was back, this time, looking far from pleased. "The jacket and waistcoat are a perfect fit," he said, "but the trousers are about four inches too short."

Ron was most apologetic but soon realised what had happened, and promised that he would retrieve the correct ones before the day was out. Ron was looking for Mr Phipps' details in order to contact him, when the phone rang and who should it be but Mr Phipps.

"I just thought I'd let you know that the jacket and waistcoat are a perfect fit, but the trousers are about four inches too long," he informed the harrassed tailor, but continued in carefree tone, "but not to worry, the wife is a dress-maker and she can shorten them for me."

Ron was frantic "No, No! Don't do anything with them. I'll come and fetch them back and bring you your own trousers."

"But they fit around the waist O.K. They must be mine." He insisted.

Ron had to convince him not to let his wife take a pair of scissors to the trousers. He then dashed off to retrieve them and managed to accomplish the exchange before any damage was done. It was sheer coincidence that the waist and hip measurements for both men were the same, and the mix-up had been made at the final stages of production.

Some of Ron's early art work.

A stone carving by Ron.

Ron put this down to experience and resolved never to let it happen again.

A number of local Sedgley charactors crossed Ron's path during his early years in business in the 1950's. Walter Parker was a batchelor who farmed High Arcal Farm and was passing the shop when Vi was visiting her husband there with Diane in the high pram. Talk was of the following day's treat which was to be pancakes, as it was Shrove Tuesday. "Oh, it's ages since I had them," said Walter. "I haven't had any since me Mam died."

Vi promised that she would make extra so that he could have some and it was agreed that he could pick them up at the shop the following afternoon.

Sure enough, Vi did as she had promised and made an extra half-dozen, tea-plate-sized pancakes for him to collect, and he arrived eager to pick them up next day.

He took one look at them and retorted scornfully, "Them bay be 'ponkerks'. Me Mam's were twice that size!"

It was the last time Vi put herself out for him.

That evening, over tea Vi and Ron laughed over the irrascible old farmer and Vi related an event which she remembered from her youth. Her childhood home had backed onto Walter's land and the youngters had dared to trespass over the fence one day, into his corn-field. He had seen them, and come after them, brandishing a pitch-fork, threatening to put two holes through them if they ventured on his land again. Seeing the look on his face and hearing the tone of his voice, the children believed he meant every word of his threat and kept well away from him from then on.

'Big Ben' was another chap who Ron remembered from those early days of trading in Scdglcy. Ben was a batchelor like Walter, and was a simple fellow, doing odd-jobs to earn a few coppers in the village. He was noted for his huge feet, at least a size eighteen, that seemed to spread all over the pavement as he delivered groceries and bread for Arther Jeavons. If Ron should happen to be standing in his shop door-way when he was passing Ben would approach him and say "I bet you can't show me a silver thruppenny- piece."

Ron would keep his face straight as he searched in his pocket for the tiny coin, then place it on the palm of his hand and hold it out to show him. Whereupon the chap would snatch it up in the blink of an eye and scuttle off giggling to himself. Ron let him get away with his trick several times as he felt sorry for him.

Tom Haywood was another man who helped out around the village during this period. He had a club-foot, but this did not prevent him from shinning up ladders all day long to clean windows, which was what he did unless the weather prevented him from doing so. When there was heavy snow, he made himself useful clearing pathways in front of the shops to allow people to get about more easily.

The people of Sedgley were a hard working lot and one woman who made a name for herself on that score was Lucy Edwards. She had a young daughter to keep and found that the only way she could do this was by getting a job as a 'char-lady.' She spent her time scrubbing the floors in many of the shops in the village, including Ron's. She would get down on her hands and knees with her bucket and scrubbing brush and do a really good job. When Ron suggested one time that it would be easier if she used a pail and mop, she replied that it might be easier but it wouldn't do such a good job! She was always cheerful and did not mind that she was a char-lady, she was happy in the knowledge that she did her job well, and she was sorely missed by many of the shopkeepers when she died.

Mr Jones, an old fellow who lived above Barclay's Bank in the Bull ring, was someone who Ron would always stop and have a natter to if he could spare the time. He had worked for the local Doctor at the turn of the century, as his coachman and later as his chauffeur. He had driven one of the first cars to arrive in Sedgley. He was full of stories about Victorian times, recalling the days of horse-drawn trams, the first electric trams and the trolley buses. It all added to Ron's desire to capture what was left of Sedgley's history with his drawings.

1956 was a busy year in the Baker household. Ron and Vi had decided that they needed more space for their growing family. They planned to extend the back of the house to enlarge both the kitchen and the living room and at the same time to install central heating. One of his customers was an engineer working in that field and ran the system from a boiler at the back of the fire in the kitchen. Ron began to realise that his hard work should be bringing his family a few more creature comforts and, while on holiday in Aberdovey, in 1958, found a way by which this could be accomplished.

The family were out walking along the hillside overlooking the sea when they saw some new building in progress. There was a marvellous view from the development and Ron soon learned that the brick bungalows were being sold for £2,950 each. They looked around the site and chose a position at the top of a very steep hill which gave the most splendid aspect over the Dovey estuary on one side and Borth on the other. Ron paid a deposit and by the main August school break the following year, their new holiday-home was ready for occupation. Ron went to Montgomery's Wholesalers in Birmingham to order beds, blankets, dining furniture and kitchen equipment to be delivered to Aberdovey, in time for their arrival.

Ron now had another way to take his mind off work for a while, give the growing family a regular change from Sedgley, and, although only a two hour journey from home, being on the west coast, was considerably warmer than home.

Ron still enjoyed gardening when he could spare the time, but one incident during this period could have had dire consequences. He cut the forefinger of his right hand while he was digging and, although he washed it and covered it up, he spent a week of increasing discomfort and sleepless nights before seeking medical help. When he could stand the pain no longer, he visited the family doctor; Dr Donaldson, who took one look and sent him straight to the Dudley Guest Hospital. There he was immediately operated on to release the poison, which, by that time, had travelled up his arm into the glands in his arm-pit.

"You've only just caught this in time," he was told, "Another day or two and you'd have been a 'gonner.'"

It took another two weeks before Ron could hold a pair of cutting shears again, but eventually he made a full recovery and resolved to take more care of himself, as much for his family's sake as for his own comfort.

He had never had good teeth and had lost some during the early days of his war service. Now he began to experience trouble again and when a local dentist came to him for a suit took the opportunity to ask his advice.

"Pop down to my surgery after you finish here this evening, and I'll have a look," said Mr Ken Waterhouse.

The tremulous tailor made his way down to Five-Ways Tipton. The inspection revealed that the 'good' teeth to which the partial denture was attached were in a bad state and needed to come out.

"I'll have to think about it," said Ron and made his way home to Vi to tell her. After some discussion it was decided that he would have the work done and before he had time to change his mind, he rang Ken to make an appointment

The day fixed for the work was a Monday, and he would require gas because of his fear. The mask was applied and Ron drifted into oblivion. When he came round, he looked up into the dentist's face. "I did'nt feel a thing," he mumbled. "How many did you take out?"

"All of them," was the reply!

"Come back on Friday and I'll take an impression for your dentures."

Ron kept out of people's way during the week and returned for his appointment as arranged. Ken brought Mr Baker, the dental mechanic into the room and introduced the two men.

"This is Mr Ron Baker, my tailor, and I want you to make him a nice set of teeth with the materials left over from that last private patient."

Ron was a bit worried as he believed that he was having the work done on the National Health and knew how expensive private treatment could be.

"Don't worry," said the dentist, "my main concern is to get you a set of well-fitting teeth that will last you a life-time."

The following day he had to attend Sedgley Rover's football club annual dinner at the Red Lion public house in Sedgley as he was their vice-president. He kept his head down and his mouth shut as much as possible until it came time to eat. He took up his position at the top table and the first course was brought in. Soup; he could manage that and did so, sipping slowly and discreetly. Then the main course appeared; cold roast beef, pickled cabbage, pickled onions and salad. Ron took one look at the plate in front of him, decided it was quite beyond him and went home hungry!

The following week Ron went to collect his new dentures and after they were fitted in place he was told not to remove them for a couple of weeks to let them settle properly. He then waited to hear the cost of all this treatment and was pleasantly surprised when told that he had to pay only three pounds nineteen shillings and sixpence, knowing that private false teeth cost over thirty pounds.

Ron returned to work in his shop, trying to get used to the feeling of a mouth full of such strange structures. Speaking, too, was difficult and he hissed and spluttered as he spoke, much to the amusement of customers and family alike. He gradually aclimatised to the new experience and after two weeks he did as he had been told, and removed the dentures. The lower set were released with relative ease, but the top ones were another story. He tugged and pulled and was getting very hot and bothered as they would not budge. Eventually he released them and found that, not only had they taken on the shape of the gums, they were fitted with a small suction pad which held them in place. He wore these same teeth for over forty years and never had any discomfort from them.

1959 was an exciting year for the family. Diane became old enough to start school and Tony was of age to sit his '11 +' examination. Mr Bill Slater, his Headmaster told Ron that his son would have no difficulty in passing the tests which would gain him entry into the Grammar school. Ron remembered back to his own school days and the opportunities which had been denied him, so it was with a great deal of heart-ache that Ron and Vi received the information that their son had failed the exam. They were both determined that he would have the best that they could afford and decided to enter him for the entrance examinations for a place at the fee-paying Tettenhall College. This he passed and the delighted parents took their son to start his new school, fully togged out in his smart uniform when the school-year started. The suppliers of the school clothes was Alfred Hall and Co. in Wolverhampton. Here he had been kitted out with blazer, shorts, shirts, tie, cap and sports gear together with two badges, one for his cap and the other for his blazer pocket. The journey from home was thought to be too long for the lad to undertake alone, so Ron would take him by car each morning and Vi would pick Diane up from infant school each afternoon and then continue on to pick up her son.

Two years later Tony was entered for a scholarship examination which he passed with flying colours and allowed him to continue his education at Tettenhall at no cost to his parents.

During the summer of 1963, Ron was visiting a neighbour of theirs; Dr O'Neill, and during the course of the conversation, the doctor happened to remark that he did not think that Vi was looking very well.

"I don't think it would do any harm for her to see her own doctor and have a check up," he said.

Ron, naturally, was concerned and rang Dr Donaldson, asking him if he would call in and see his wife. It was a Saturday morning, June 15th 1963, when the Doctor visited Vi at home to examine her, before going to the shop where Ron was working.

Ron was rather disturbed when he saw the doctor and noticed the serious expression on his face. The doctor's words struck like a mallet.

"I have some bad news for you, I'm afraid. I'm sure that your wife has breast cancer. I haven't told her, I thought it better to see you first."

Ron stood rooted to the spot as the doctor continued gently. "Would you be prepared to pay for private treatment?" was his next question, as the stunned man tried to assimilate the dreadful news.

Money didn't come in to it. Ron's only concern was the health of his beloved Vi.

Doctor Donaldson said that he would contact a cancer specialist, Mr Hershman, immediately, and arrange for him to visit them at their home and examine Vi himself.

"Whatever you suggest," Ron replied. "You're our Doctor, I trust your judgement."

Ron left the shop and returned home, still in a daze. He could not tell his wife what had been said, but only that their doctor had suggested that a second opinion was called for.

The following day, a Sunday, Dr Donaldson rang to say that the specialist would visit them at eleven o'clock. Ron told Vi.

The Doctors arrived on the doorstep promptly and Mr Hershman took Vi upstairs so that he could examine her. They were soon back and Vi went to sit beside her husband on the sofa. He took her hand in his and they looked into the man's eyes.

"I have some sad news for you," he said, with no unnecessary preamble, "I'm afraid that you have cancer in your left breast, and, by the look of it, you have had it for some time. I suggest that you come along to the Corbett Hospital on Tuesday and I will operate on you there."

When the children, who by now were fourteen and nine, had left for school, Ron took his wife to the hospital as instructed. He waited with her in the private room, as long as he could, but eventually had to return home to be there when the children returned from school.

In a matter of days, Ron's tidy, organised and successful life seemed to have collapsed around his ears. He not only had his many businesses to be concerned with, but his wife in hospital in a potentially life-threatening condition and his two children to look after. He looked to Vi's sisters for help, and they rallied round him, feeling the anxiety as keenly as he. He visited them at Parkes' Hall after leaving his wife, and Ann responded promptly to solve the most urgent concern which was the care of the children. She offered to come to the house early each morning and remain there until he finished work each evening. Ron was grateful for her suggestion and returned home after arranging to fetch her early the following morning.

He knew that they would be operating on his wife that evening and he fed the children as best he could, while he waited for the time when he could ring the hospital to get news of her condition. He was told that the operation would take place later that evening and that he could ring next morning to be told more information. Ron tossed and turned all night and by six o'clock decided that there must be information available and dialled the number with trembling hands.

He was told that she had come through the operation and was resting in her room and that he could visit her at any time during the day. Ron got the children off to school and then drove over to the hospital. She was recovering from the effects of the anaesthetic and her first concern was for the welfare of Tony and Diane. Ron was able to reassure her on that score, telling her how her sister, Ann, would be helping out each day until Vi was back on her feet. She wanted to see the children as soon as possible and Ron brought them in to visit her that evening after school and most evenings as she recuperated.

Vi made good progress and within seven days she was discharged to return home to her grateful and relieved family. The private room was costing a great deal of money, Vi had her sister to care for her at home, and as another patient was waiting for the bed it was decided that Vi could be discharged early and continue to be cared for at home.

When Ron took Vi back to see Mr Hershman to have her stitches removed, he remarked on the beautiful, tailored suit which she was wearing. Vi told him that Ron had made it and he laughingly remarked, "Oh, you're the expert with the stitches then. What do you think about the quality of mine then?"

Ron was then presented with the bills for the private treatment which his wife had received. The surgeon's account alone, amounted to a thousand pounds, the room and hospital facilities were separate, as were the anaesthetist's fees. He paid them gladly and regarded it as a small price to pay for the life of his wife.

Further physiotherapy was needed, both in the hospital and at home to help Vi regain the use of the left arm which had been affected by the radical surgery. Ron, ingeniously rigged up a pulley contraption in the garage for her to use to exercise her arm, and she continued to use it until she could lift her arm without discomfort.

Vi continued to vist the hospital for over twenty years before the Doctor discharged her as being finally clear of the disease.

For the rest of the summer of 1963, Vi's illness hung, like a black cloud, over the family, but Vi and Ron tried desparately not to let it affect their children's lives and activities. Both children were musically gifted though, for the life of him, Ron could never work out where they got it from.

A month after Vi's discharge from hospital, Diane sat her grade one piano test and a few days later Tony passed his grade three test on the

High Street, Sedgley, 1946.

High Street, Sedgley, showing Brick Street, 1947.

clarinet, which he studied privately under Mr Skoon at Tettenhall College. At last the family felt that there was something to celebrate and life began to get back to normal.

In March of the following year, Tony undertook the first of several exchange visits to France. He stayed with a lad called Xavier Nivea, his parents and Grandmother in Orleans for a four-week period, in an attempt to improve the standard of his French. The visit worked well, and from being one of the bottom of the class in the language, he became one of the high-fliers. A return visit was made by Xavier in July, and he stayed with the Bakers for a corresponding length of time. He proved to be great company for all the family and his presence cheered Vi up no end and they were all sorry to see him depart.

The new year came in and Ron decided to buy Vi a new car. The year was 1965, and the model which Ron had chosen was one of the first of its kind to be produced. It was a Super De Luxe Mini, registration number DDA 137C and cost him just under £500. This car proved to be quite a favourite of both Vi and Tony, who was approaching the age of seventeen. Ron would drive over to Milford Common and there let his son take the wheel, as he was still too young to get his license to drive on the public roads.

Exchange visits between Tony and Xavier were again arranged for this year and the French lad attended school with Tony for the last few days of the summer term before they broke up for the holiday. This time Ron managed to obtain a bicycle for Xavier to use and a group of teenagers would cycle off across the fields, enjoying their freedom and each other's company.

Ron was not enjoying himself during this summer, however, and it was he now who had occasion to visit Mr Hershman at Burton Road Hospital as a result of chronic renal pain. It was discovered that he had developed kidney stones as a bi-product of the malarial fevers which he had suffered in Africa. He was prescribed medication to try to break down the stones and luckily surgery was not needed.

In November he became a member of the Masons that met at the Birmingham Masonic Lodge of St Francis - No. 4899 Province of Warwickshire, and Ron added another activity to his already full life.

At that time there was a great deal of mystery surrounding the Masonic institution, and its members were sworn to keep their membership and its activities a closely guarded secret, but Freemasonary can be dated back to 1646 in England and Royalty, Presidents and even Robbie Burns can be found among its membership at some time or another.

The following year was particularly eventful for all the family with Diane's confirmation in May, a visit to Poland by Tony later in the year, and a move by Ron's aged parents into a small flat. They had lived in the house in Sedgley Road since their marriage and, now that it was to be demolished, they were finally able to make use of more modern kitchen and bathroom facilities. Joseph and Lilian were now in their early seventies and, although it was something of an upheaval for them, the move to Regent Street, Woodsetton, gave them a much more comfortable existance.

Ron always encouraged the interests of his children and when Diane was twelve he bought her an accordion and arranged for her to take lessons with Mr Arther Jones so that she could learn to play it. Diane was small and of slight build so that the instument dwarfed her when she began to play. The family would enjoy listening to the melodies which she produced on it, and it was very soon that she became as proficient on this as she was on the piano. Before very long, Mr Jones came to Ron to tell him that there was nothing more that he could teach Diane, as she was now as good as he was. Her piano teacher died at this time and Ron had to find his daughter a new Music teacher. The new teacher was Mr Jeavons who lived on The Broadway in Dudley, and was the organist at St Chad's Church Coseley.

Ron and Vi were very proud of their children's accomplishments and made sure that they always knew it. They watched Diane as she entered a public speaking contest at school and glowed as she was named as the winner and went up to collect her prize of five shillings. They attended events where she entertained at musical evenings at the old people's club and Ron remembered how he had ached for some recognition or sign of approval from his own parents as he was growing up.

Ron's businesses were doing well and 1968 saw some more changes to the family's lifestyle. Firstly he decided it was time for him and Vi to have new cars. He had a Morris 18. A good-sized family saloon and he exchanged Vi's Mini for a blue Singer Chamois Coupe. He also decided that a change of home was called for and in the Autumn they moved into 'Rivoli' a four bedroomed detached house in Cotwall End. Vi was sorry to leave Richmond Road, but Tony and Diane were delighted to have the extra space; larger rooms, bigger gardens and room for three cars in the garages!

Tony had, by now, passed his driving test and was the proud owner of a Morris Minor split-windscreen motor car, which he had bought off Mr Greenway (who lived nearby in Richmond Road) for the princely sum of £10.

By the time the family had moved into their new home, Tony was one year into a seven year course at Leicester University studying Architecture.

Health worries reared their ugly head again the following year, when Ron's father Joseph was diagnosed as having throat cancer and had to attend The Royal Hospital in Wolverhapton for a series of twenty-five treatments of Cobalt.

The family continued to enjoy their holiday home in Wales, and it was here that Ron experienced the next of his health scares. One weekend after a good meal, he suffered excruciating chest pains. Naturally, Vi was extremely concerned, and called in the local Doctor, a man by the name of Tom Davies. He arrived quickly and examined Ron. His investigation showed no heart trouble, but told Ron that he probably had a peptic ulcer. He was instructed to see his own Doctor on his return to Sedgley. This of course he did, and Dr Donaldson told him to keep off fried foods and stick to a light diet and there was a good chance that the ulcer would heal itself. For three weeks Ron stuck to the rules that had been set, but during a trip to Birmingham to buy some new crockery, he decided to pop into a nearby pub for his lunch. He thoroughly enjoyed his meal of curry and rice; food that was definitely denied him on his new regime of careful eating. But he was soon to pay for his folly. He awoke at three o'clock in the morning, writhing in agony and Dr Donaldson (who lived a few doors away from the Bakers now) was called out to see him. The doctor immediately called for an ambulance and Ron was transported to Wordsley Hospital. Once there, a drip was attached and a tube put down into his stomach to drain the contents. He was then given a 'Barium Meal' and X-rays taken to discover the extent of the damage. These did indeed show a peptic ulcer, but Doctors were hopeful that it would mend without the necessity for an operation as he neither drank nor smoked. He remained in the hospital for six days, and upon his discharge, the importance of sticking to a very careful diet was once more stressed. This time he understood the warnings, and the diet regime, together with the medication which was prescribed, soon returned him to his old self.

1969 was proving to be a very eventful year, as Ron now learned that his two shops in the High Street were part of a demolition programme. Ron was fortunate that a shop nearby, not affected by the demolition, was up for sale, and he gratefully snapped it up for £10,000. He cleared out the contents of the old grocers' shop and had his own belongings installed with scarcely a hiccup in his business dealings. His Dudley shop was also demolished as a result of on-going modernisation, but Ron decided not to find premises to replace these. He had had a few health scares himself and he still felt 'raw' from Vi's illness, and although still in his early fifties decided that it was time to ease off a little and devote more time to his wife and children.

The following year became another memorable one for Ron. He was approached by a Sedgley librarian, Tom Sankey, who asked him to think seriously about producing a book of his drawings of the buildings in the Sedgley Manor. Ron had been compiling a portfolio of drawings of local old buildings, ever since he left the army in 1946, and now, that collection had become quite extensive. Some of the buildings which he had captured on paper were no longer standing, and his work was a valuable historical record to locals and those from farther afield.

Ron knew a young man by the name of Peter Garland who worked for Kenrick and Jefferson, a firm of printers in West Bromwich and Ron approached them to see if they would print a small number of books for him. Ron was very conservative in his estimation of the interest that there might be in such a book, and asked only for two hundred to be produced. The firm replied that this was far too small an order for them to be bothered with, but allowed the lad to use the presses after working hours so that he and Ron could do it themselves. And this is just what they did.

Peter made lithograph plates from Ron's black pen and ink drawings. They bought the paper, and the prints were reproduced on the machines when the presses had finished each day. Then, over one weekend, the pair of them sat and painstakingly collated the pictures into the order required for the book. They were then taken over to Birmingham to be bound with hard covers. This work took a few weeks, after which time the two hundred volumes were returned to Ron. He had arranged for the local paper to write about the project. He provided Dudley and Wolverhampton libraries with twelve copies each and all local schools were also given one. All the rest were signed and numbered and put on sale in his Sedgley shop for fifty shillings. The book was entitled: "Sedgley. A Pictorial History by Ron Baker". All copies were sold in a very short time.

The following year saw Diane well estalished at Dudley Technical college studying for her 'A levels', having completed her secondary education at Dormston School in Sedgley. She was now old enough to take driving lessons. Tony was taking a year out from University working for Warwickshire County Council, and he moved in to a flat above the stables of a large house on the Kenilworth Road for the duration of his contract. Xavier had got married this year too, and spent part of his honeymoon with Nicole (his bride) with the Bakers in Sedgley, and the rest of it at their bungalow in Aberdovey.

Ron's father died in Wolverhampton Royal Hospital on 2nd May 1971 in his 82nd year. He had paid into two life policies all his married life; one for tuppence a week and the other threepence. His widow picked up the grand total of eighty pounds from these, plus a 'Death Grant' of fifteen pounds, and she had her husband cremated at Lower Gornal Crematorium.

In February, Ron took his wife on what was to be the first of many trips abroad. Foreign travel was in its infancy and they flew to Palma Nova, in Majorca, to stay at 'The Hotel Tabago' for five nights full board for twenty five pounds each. Later in the year, all the family went by car, to visit Xavier's family in Orleans, stopping on the way for a six-night stay in Paris. Here, the total bill for four of them for the six nights bed and breakfast, was only thirty nine pounds.

The new year started happily with Ron's nephew, Philip (Ken's son) marrying Maria at St. Mary's and St John Catholic Church at Snow Hill Wolverhampton. Maria was the daughter of Polish parents who had come to live in England after the Second World War.

Ron was being true to his resolve to spend more time and money on his wife and family, and now, he and Vi took off, this time on their own, to the Algarve.

Diane passed her examinations and her parents took her down to Wall Hall Teacher Training College near Watford for an interview. She was accepted for a place in that college and began her studies there in the October.

The year ended on a sad note, when Vi's brother, John, who had had a series of heart-attacks the previous year, suffered yet another one, which finally killed him.

1973 saw the final year of Tony's course and he attained his qualification - R.I.B.A. (Royal Institute of British Architects). He took up a position in Leicester at a handsome salary of £2200. Ron was delighted to see how well both his children were doing and relished the thought that his hard work as much as theirs was responsible for their success. He had missed out on the chance of higher education, but he had made sure that they had not.

Ron and Vi again took a holiday abroad, this time to Switzerland, staying in a hotel by the side of Lake Lucern. They travelled by train, and Ron began to notice how prices were beginning to escalate. He had always been very aware of the cost of living and kept a careful eye open

Ron, Worshipful Master of his Masonic Lodge, 1977.

for a bargain. He knew how hard it was to make money and never was one to waste it. Now he began to see signs of more spending money around after the long years of austerity after the war.

Ron sold the bungalow in Aberdovey for £7000, and the Brierley Hill shop for £10,000. Decimalisation was in full swing, and petrol now cost 55p a gallon. Tony bought himself an end-terrace house in Leicester for £5,500 during this period and settled there with his new bride Carys.

Ron and Vi were seriously looking at the possibility of him selling the businesses and retiring from work completely. Although there had been no recurrence of Vi's illness, it had shaken them both and they devoted more and more time to themselves as each year passed, although Ron was still working hard at his tailoring trade and his businesses were flourishing.

They first took a short trip to Jersey, this year, before deciding to be much more adventurous and took a two-week cruise on 'The Blenheim' on the Fred Olsen Line to the Canary Isles. They were accompanied by their friends, Hugh and Mary Murray, and the foursome enjoyed it so much that on their return, booked for another one the following February. Unfortunately, before the time for their departure, Hugh had died. Ron had invited a few more of their friends to join the party the second time and they hired a minibus to take them down to the ship in the London Dock. They boarded the ship and settled themselves into their cabins, fully expecting the same sort of pleasurable experience as the first time. It was not to be.

The ship steamed out into the Channel on the Thursday evening and it soon became apparent that a storm was brewing. For the next two days, passengers were advised to stay in their cabins as there was a force twelve gale blowing. The storm had struck so quickly that the crew had not had time to make all the necessary adjustments. Water poured into some of the forward cabins, making them completely uninhabitable and the occupants had to be moved elsewhere. Signals were received for the ship to go to the assistance of another vessel which was in trouble but, because they themselves had lost power in one of their engines, they were unable to respond. Most items in the lounge and dining areas had been fastened down and ropes were strung along lengths of the corridors for the passengers to cling onto as they moved about the ship. Ron was heaving himself along to try to reach the forward lounge, when a huge wave struck the side of the ship, causing it to lurch alarmingly. He saw the grand piano which had been bolted to the floor, breaking free of its mooring and being flung across the floor smashing against the opposite wall. Ron made his way precariously to the Pursar's office to report the incident. The crew was incredulous, having never experienced weather condition like it before. It was lucky that no-one was seriously injured as furniture was flung about in the public rooms. One of the old ladies in Ron's party was particularly distressed and grabbed his arms, imploring him to take her home.

"Take me home. I want to go home now, please," she begged him, and could not understand why he wasn't able to do so.

She shared a cabin with a friend who was designated the top bunk for sleeping. This lady made it perfectly clear that she had no intention of climbing up there while the ship was rolling around in this manner, and Ron had to fetch her mattress down and prepare a bed for her on the floor of the cabin.

The storm subsided to force ten, which allowed the ship to make a little progress. The Captain informed them that he was taking them into the Bay of Biscay to avoid the worst of the storm and two days late, they put into dock at Madeira. A young Portugese couple on board the ship, made the acquaintance of Ron and Vi. The young couple kept a restaurant in Windsor and were returning to their family home in Madeira for a holiday. Ron and Vi were invited ashore to meet their families. They were relieved to set foot on steady ground once more after the buffeting they had experienced, and followed the pair to their home. It turned out to be a flat above a cafe and upon reaching it, they found a welcoming meal and drinks laid out to greet them. They were made to feel like part of the family and when they had eaten their fill, the lad took them down to his local bar. They did not drink any of the alcoholic beverages on offer but instead asked for coffee and were amused to see that it took some searching to find suitable cups to serve it in.

They were then taken on a tour of the little fishing village in which they lived and Ron was happy to study the ancient architecture and picturesque views. He was intrigued to learn that it was a place that Winston Churchill came to paint, and he could understand the attraction for him.

The ship continued its voyage, stopping off in Lanzerote and Tenerife. Here Ron became quite ill with sickness and severe colic. The ship's doctor kept visiting him in his cabin, supplying him with medication to relieve the worst of the symtoms and watching for signs of dehydration. The second week of the cruise Ron was confined to his cabin and by the time they docked at Madeira again on the return journey, the young Portugese couple came back on board and visited him in his cabin, as he was still in his sick-bed. Ron had more than one reason to remember this particular holiday.

Before they reached home, the Captain gave everyone a copy of the ship's log for the first two days of their cruise as a momento, telling them all that in twenty years of sailing, it was the worst storm he had ever experienced!!! He also told them that they had been delivering a hold-full of cars and the storm had been responsible for damaging more than half of them before they reached their destination.

Upon returning to Sedgley Ron visited his Doctor and it took another four or five weeks before he was back to normal again, and rid of the 'bug' that had affected him.

The following year was a happy one for the family, seeing the wedding of Diane to Andrew Carr, at All Saints Parish Church in Sedgley. The marriage took place on August 6th 1975 and the day was fine and warm. A friend of Ron's, offered the use of his own Rolls Royce to take Diane to church, where a total of eighty guests saw the couple take their vows. They held the reception at 'The Littleton Arms' in Hagley and afterwards many of the guests returned to Ron and Vi's home where they sat in the garden in the warm evening.

Diane and her husband made their home in Edlesdborough, a small village near Dunstable in Bedfordshire. She was twenty-one years old by now and a fully qualified teacher.

The following year was the fiftieth anniversary of the Masonic Lodge to which Ron belonged, and he was afforded the great honour of being installed as Worshipful Master for this celebration year. On November 5th, Ladies' Evening was held at The Botanical Gardens in Birmingham. This was always an especially grand event, with the women wearing long evening dresses, long gloves and fur stoles, and the men decked out in dress suits. Upon their arrival, each couple was introduced formally to Ron and Vi, in their official capacity as hosts for the evening, and a photograph was taken of each greeting, in front of the Lodge Banner. Each couple was given a copy of their own and the presiding Master was given an album containing a copy of all the photographs, as a momento of his year in office.

During this period, the miners had been on strike and there could be electricity cuts at any time as a result of their action. Candles were to hand in case of this happening during the evening, and right on cue, the lights went out just as people were taking their places at table. The candles were lit and the gas lights, which still existed in the dance hall adjacent, were turned on to give sufficient glow for people to find their seats.

It had been Ron's job for many years to use his skills to produce the table plan for these events and he had done so this year too. He always found a different way to decorate the top of the plan in a way specifically related to the current Worshipful Master. He found it particularly difficult to find something to represent himself, but came up with a view of Sedgley Bull-ring and church, in the style of a watercolour by David Cox; an English artist whom he particularly admired and collected.

As the first course was being served, the lights came back on, and a great cheer went up. They could now see those sitting around them, conversation became a lot easier, and the meal continued pleasantly. It was the tradition that the Grand Master would present each lady present with a gift on these occasions so Ron had to produce one-hundred-and-twenty-two small suitable items for them this evening. He had asked his friend Ray Hindmarsh, who was a rep. for Brierley Glass, to provide him with one-hundred-and-twenty-two, four-inch cut-glass specimen vases, each boxed and a card inside from Ron and Vi. Ron decided that as this was a special anniversary for the Lodge, the gift that night should be something that the couple could keep as a lasting memory of the evening. It was Vi's task at the end of the meal, to stand up and thank Ron on behalf of all the ladies for the gift. She was very apprehensive about this but she coped well in the event. Another of her duties was to declare the name of the charities who would benifit from the collection which was made during the evening. The amount that was collected was three hundred pounds and together with Ron, she decided that half would go to Cancer Research and half to the Masonic Schools. Everyone declared the evening a complete success and all went home replete and with many happy memories.

By now, Ron had disposed of all his business interests except the Sedgley shop and he fully intended to sell that in the near future. His customers soon heard about his intentions and some of them were quite concerned. None more so than a gentleman by the name of Leslie Pugh who was six feet four inches tall, weighed twenty-seven stone and had a waist measurement of sixty-seven inches. He always had great trouble in finding clothes to fit him and came to Ron regularly to have suits made. Ron kept his details on file and over the years had produced a pattern to his configuration. Mr Pugh now came to the shop and ordered three suits to be made for him in case he could not find another tailor to make them for him after Ron had finished.

Ron started on this mammoth task and one day was hanging up one of the pairs of trousers, when his assistant, Jean Webb, saw them.

"Good heavens!" she said, "We could both get into those."

After a bit of banter they decided to give it a go, with Ron down one leg and Jean down the other. They were standing in this ridiculous pose looking at themselves in the mirror and giggling at their reflection, when who should walk into the shop but Leslie. Ron was rather shame-faced but his immediate response to the look on the customers face was "Just trying them on for size, Les."

Mr Pugh was rather taken aback, but realised the humour in the situation and soon joined in with the laughter.

Ron by now had become a bit of a joker and on another occasion, a young lady came into the shop, asking if he could shorten a pair of slacks for her. Ron sent her upstairs to the fitting room and asked Jean to go up to pin them up. After a while Jean returned to say that she had done it, but asked him to check to make sure that she had done it correctly. Up they both went to find the lady standing there waiting. Ron thought that she looked the sort who might have a sense of humour and taking his tape measure from round his neck, proceeded very seriously to take measurements of her bust, waist and hips, with Jean looking on.

"Excuse me, but I just wanted my trousers shortened," she said.

"If you go to the Doctor, and he says take your clothes off so that he can examine you you do it don't you? Well, I'm a tailor and if I think I need to measure you, I didn't think you would object."

She saw the funny side of it too and Ron checked the trouser length properly and she left the shop, chuckling at his cheek.

He would have been lucky to get away with such antics today.

Nothing more was said about the incident by Jean, but the following day a friend of hers came into the shop and asked Ron to take up a pair of trousers for her. "And I want the full service too," she said with a twinkle in her eye.

Ron looked at Jean who he suspected of having told her friend about the previous incident, but she kept her face perfectly straight and denied any knowledge of it.

1977 became a very important year for Ron as he finally decided to dispose of his last business interest; the ladies and gents outfitters in Sedgley. He knew that he would have great difficulty in selling it as a going concern, as the bespoke tailoring trade was in serious decline and ready-to-wear businesses were growing in popularity. All the girls who had been trained by Ron in the tailoring trade had found work in other areas and the factories, once producing made-to-measure suits, now mass produced clothes for the large department stores. Ron had made a good living from the tailoring trade, but now it was time to move on.

He was fully aware that his shop was in a good position in the High Street, and suitable as premises for any kind of business enterprise. A close friend of his, by the name of Eric Phipps, worked for The West Bromwich Building Society, looking after all their properties in the area. One day, when he was fitting Eric for a suit, Ron told his friend that he was selling the premises in order to take early retirement. Eric pricked up his ears and told Ron that if the building was for sale without the business, he felt sure that the building society would be interested in opening a branch in Sedgley. Ron told him the price that he was expecting for the shop, and within a week, the Board had met and agreed to the asking price of £16,000. They also agreed to Ron remaining in the shop until he had concluded all his business.

Over the next three months Ron wound up his business, held a closing-down sale and disposed of the contents of the shop bit by bit. He took all the clothes that fitted himself or Vi, so that for many years they seldom had to buy anything new to wear. Suits, blazer, underwear, overcoat, even socks and hankies were stored away for himself, but Vi was reluctant to fill up her wardrobes with the clothes and chose just a few jumpers, petticoats and stockings from the stock. Neither of them required gloves, as they had been kept supplied with the latest styles by the traveller who brought them samples each Christmas, from Millingtons their suppliers. This traveller had been a good friend to Ron while he had been in business and often referred him to his old army friends, who came to the tailor for their hand-made suits. One Army Major referred in this way became a firm friend of Ron, who would visit him in London whenever he was down that way.

Ron decided that if he watched his weight and was careful with his wardrobe, what he now had would last him for his life-time.

He had spent his life working hard for his living and now that his working life was over, he was not going to waste anything.

On June 11th 1977, Ron shut the door for the last time having sold or given away all its contents. He didn't look back, he knew that he had plenty to look forward to and he intended to make the most of it.

Retirement
(1977 onwards)

RON'S retirement did not have a very auspicious start. One evening, in August, as they were returning home from a dance at eleven o'clock, Ron and Vi were forced to stop their car to allow an ambulance out of School Street. They thought no more about the incident until the following day, when they were informed that Gordon, Ron's brother, had died during the night. It was he who had been in that ambulance and had died a few hours later, alone in hospital. Gordon was divorced and had lived by himself. Their Mother, who was by then eighty two years old, lived in a one bedroomed flat and had always been very close to Gordon and would have taken him in to live with her if she had had the space, but it was not to be. Now at just fifty-three, he was dead and the duty fell to Ron to make all the funeral arrangements and dispose of his possessions.

Now it was September and Ron could lie in bed in the mornings without having to worry about opening the shop on time or wondering if the staff would turn up for work. He did not have to concern himself with latest styles, price of material or even whether his customers would settle their accounts on time. He was carefree and for the first time in his life he could devote his attention to doing all the things he had been promising himself he would do over the years. He began in earnest to add to his collection of his own paintings and drawings, to augment his collection of antiques and oil paintings and document as much as he could of the local history.

The next couple of years saw the demise of some of Ron and Vi's closest family and friends. Ann, Vi's older sister died in 1978 at Burton Road Hospital and just two months later, Mrs Van Hegan (whom Ron had become aquainted with in Africa during the war) died in Largs in Scotland where she had returned to live with her husband and daughter, Betty. The following year, Tony Grace, another friend of theirs, died of a heart attack at the young age of forty-seven. Ron was glad that he had decided to retire when he had, before the age of sixty, while he still had his health and time to enjoy himself.

Ron spent time with friends who shared his interest in art and local history. Eric Phipps, a fellow art collector also retired about this time from the West Bromwich Building Society, which gave them both the opportunity to indulge their hobby as they travelled around the country together, visiting art exhibitions and galleries. Eric decided to raise some cash to finance his retirement by selling half of his collection of pictures. The pictures were sold at Christie's Sale Rooms in London at the beginning of 1978 and made a figure of £65,000.

Ron had in his possession a beautiful Victorian cameo dress-button, which had been owned by his Mother's grandmother, and he now asked a friend, Ray Hindmarsh to set it into a gold frame so that it could be hung on a chain. Ron was thrilled with the result and thought that it looked magnificent when he gave it to Vi and she wore it as a necklace. Many people admired it and found it difficult to believe that it could actually have been a button. One had to look very closely to see the two tiny holes in the centre which still showed its original use.

In June 1979, Ron and Vi became grandparents for the first time when Diane gave birth to Daniel. They had enjoyed their trips down south to visit their daughter in the past, but now had the added incentive of visiting their grandson and baby-sitting while his parents went out occasionally.

Tragedy struck some more close friends in1980, when firstly, Ken Bullock died of a heart attack. (Ken had worked with Ron in the tailoring trade in the early years), Ken's wife Mary died of cancer in the same year and then her brother Bob Allen died of a heart attack shortly afterwards, on the evening before he was due to attend a Masonic Ladies Evening with Ron and Vi. They were all roughly the same age as Ron and he felt their loss very greatly.

In 1981, Ron left, along with Howard Nicholson, Harold Sylvester and Bill Parnham for their first trip to the sites of the First World War battlefields and graveyards. They drove down to Dover, crossed the Channel, continued to Dunkirk and on to Ypres in Belgium, where they made their base. They stayed in the hotel opposite the Cathedral for three or four days while they looked around. They continued their journey down into France where they visited all the battlefields and grave yards in the Mons Valley. Some of the British graves could only be reached by trudging over ploughed fields, which at the time of their visit were thick mud. They could see, as they passed that, after the Spring ploughing, unspent, and possibly live shells were still being brought to the surface. Each year after the ploughing was complete, the Army personel would come along and collect up the shells and explode them safely elsewhere. Ron and his friends were careful not to touch the shells, but photographed them where they lay in the mud.

Three years later Ron and his mates made a second similar visit, this time to the Second World War battlefields and found it a very different experience, seeing the Normandy countryside where men they had actually known had fought and died.

The family were again to experience tragedy in 1983, this time with the untimely death of Ron's sister-in-law, Elsie, Ken's wife. She was walking home after finishing work at the Doctors's surgery and had collected fish and chips for the family's supper when she collapsed and died on the pavement, having suffered a heart attack. She was only a few hundred yards from home and her sudden and unexpected death was a great shock to all the family. She was only fifty-nine years old.

Ron and Vi had treated each other to new cars that year. Ron had a Ford Cortina (Reg. No. ROA 419Y) which cost £5000 and Vi a Ford Fiesta which cost £3185 (Reg. No. TOL 166Y) and later they decided to take their daughter, son-in-law and grandson on a cruise.

On 23rd September they set off together for a fortnight's cruise on the Sea Princess around the Eastern Mediterranean. They flew out to Greece where they boarded the ship. They visited Egypt, South Turkey, North Turkey, the beautiful volcanic island of Santorini then returned to Greece before continuing up to Dubrovnic and finally up the Adriatic to Venice. They stayed in that beautiful and historic city for two days before flying home again.

In November Ron finally reached sixty-five years old, which meant that both he and Vi could start collecting their pensions. They were happy to have a regular weekly amount coming in to the house and no longer needed to rely on savings for their every-day expenses.

The following January, their little grandson, Daniel, started at the school his mother Diane taught in Edensborough. Ron and Vi had begun to realise that all was not well with their daughter's marriage and the following year, she approached them to ask for their help. Ron visited his solicitor, Mike Timmins on February 18th 1985 to ask him to act for Diane in her divorce from Andy. Diane and Daniel had to vacate their home for it to be sold and the proceeds used to pay off the debts which Andy's kitchen business had accumulated.

The mother and child were now homeless and a close friend of Diane's, Sue Loch, offered them the use of a cottage until they could find somewhere more permanent to live. Diane continued to teach at the local school during all this upheaval. Ron and Vi looked around the area for somewhere suitable for their daughter and grandson to live, and came upon a small development of three cottages being converted at the edge of the village. They looked perfect and after Diane had seen them, negotiations began with the builder. Ron agreed to buy the end cottage for a price of £41,000, and in a few short weeks, the cottage was ready for occupation and Ron and Vi saw Diane and Daniel happily installed in their new home.

There was one small glimmer of joy during this unhappy period when Ron bought a raffle-ticket from a friend. The raffle was organised by the Lion's Club, the president of which was Alan Brookes. The first prize was a three minute 'trolley-dash' around Marks and Spencer's food hall. Ron had forgotten all about the ticket, when Alan's son David knocked on his door one evening to tell him that he had won.

There were quite strict rules as to what could be chosen from the shelves. There could be no wines or spirits (which, considering Ron did not drink, was no hardship) and only one packet or tin of each type of food. Despite this, Ron managed to fill three trolleys in the three minutes, and when they were added up at the end, he had managed to collect £216 worth of food. He realised when he got it all home, that all the frozen foods which he had picked up would not fit into his freezer and he had to ask his butcher if he would store some of it for him in his large shop freezer. The fresh cream-cakes he shared with his friends and the rest kept Ron and Vi happily fed for some time. The incident provided a bit of light relief from the sad business of their daughter's divorce.

The following year saw the initiation of a local historical society. The study and recording of Sedgley's past had always been one of Ron's great interests and now he met up with two other like-minded fellows and their discussion led to the formation of the group. Andrew Barnett, a local historian and Headmaster of Redhall School in Lower Gornal, and Trevor Genge, Headmaster of Lanesfield School and Ron, called a meeting of any other interested locals and it was proposed to form 'The Sedgley Historical Society.' Twenty-six members joined at first, with Andrew elected as President, Trevor as Chairman and Ron as Vice-President and Treasurer. The annual fee was set at one pound and during the first year of it's existance, members gave talks on aspects of local history. They met once a month during the winter and spring months and gradually the membership grew to fifty people. The old Nail Works in Brick Street was being restored and Andrew negotiated for a room to be available for their meetings, rent-free. It was gradually turned into a museum showing trades and professions from Sedgley's past.

A lease was drawn up for the property and three trustees required to officiate. Ron, Andrew and Trevor duly signed and took responsibility on behalf of the Society. The official opening ceremony was performed by Lord Harmer Nicholls. This gentleman was a local land-owner and the father of the actress Sue Nicholls who is famous for her roles in the original 'Crossroads' and later in 'Coronation Street'.

Brian Hollis was chosen to be the museum's curator and Margery Ellis, his assistant. The Society grew and the museum was soon bulging at the seams with all the exhibits that the members collected. Antiques, tools and documents were either given to the museum or loaned to members and the society applied to the council for a grant in order to improve the room.

This was awarded and William Burgess, a local Artist and Potter, was commissioned to produce a tiled mural to adorn the wall above the entrance to the museum.

The museum is still open to the public on Tuesday and Thursday afternoons, and Brian continues to hold the position of curator.

Many of the contents of the museum were objects which had lain around in old factories in the area or items from people's homes, but occasionally discoveries were made of items which had lain hidden for many decades and came to light quite by accident. One such find was unearthed by Frank Huband who was clearing out his attic above his shop in the High Street, prior to his retirement. He discovered a large collection of early nineteenth century documents. Amongst them were letters dating from 1810 to 1817, addressed to 'ELWELL NAIL FACTOR, SEDGLEY, BEWDLEY.'

Postage stamps did not exist in those days, and the letters were folded, sealed with red sealing wax and marked in pencil with the cost of the carriage, which was between five and eight pence. The reason for this strange address was that, as there was no station in Sedgley, items had to be sent through the nearest River Port which was Bewdley. Small ships would carry the orders for nails and chains from all over the country to Bewdley and then they would continue by horse and cart over bumpy unmade roads to Sedgley. The completed orders would return to customers in the same way.

The death of the owner of Hill House, in Hill Street, Upper Gornal also gave rise to an interesting find for the museum. The gardener had been instructed to clear out some of the out-buildings and Ron got to hear that many of the contents were being burned indiscriminately. He had had dealings with the previous owner of Hill House when he had bought his first house in Sedgley and believed that he could have items of interest to the Society. He hurried along to Hill Street and found the gardener shovelling papers onto the fire.

Ron asked him if there were any more documents left unscathed and was shown up to a loft above the garages. One box remained and Ron asked if he could have it for the Society. This was agreed and he took the grubby box back home to inspect its contents carefully. He found that the contents consisted of numerous rent books belonging to a previous owner of the house - a Mr Hall who had been a solicitor. He must have owned several properties which he rented out, as the books covered 'The Malt House' and a 'Candle Factory' in Upper Gornal, and a number of small back-to-back terraced houses in Lower Gornal. The rent books covered the years from 1830 to 1890 and Ron noted that the rent for a tiny house in Dibdale Lane, had been one shilling and ninepence during this period. He kept a selection of the documents for the Sedgley Society and passed the remainder to the newly formed Black Country Society for their Archives in Dudley.

Andrew Barnett, the President of the society died on November 9th, 1989, aged eighty, and for ten years thereafter his contribution was recognised by calling the September meeting "The Andrew Barnett Lecture", when someone who knew him, would give a talk in recognition of the part he played in the society's formation. Ron gave one of the first of these talks and a total of eighty people came to honour Andrew as Ron described what it was like growing up in Woodsetton in the 1920's.

At the end of June 1986, Ron and Vi went down to Edelsborough in Buckinghamshire so that they could 'baby-sit' their grandson, Daniel, who was now seven, while his mother, Diane went out for the evening. Since her divorce two years previously, Diane had tried hard to get her life back on track and her parents were pleased to play their part in allowing this to happen. When they arrived home on the Sunday evening, however, they were greeted with the sad news that, in their absence, Ron's mother had died. Ken, his elder brother came round to their home to deliver the news and to give him the details of her demise.

Ken had gone to her flat on Saturday morning, to visit his mother, Lilian, and, on finding her front door unlocked, had assumed that she was visiting her friend, Mrs Wainwright, who lived upstairs. Up he went to look for her, and not finding her there had returned to her flat to take a look around. He discovered her under her bed which was an old, high brass bed-stead and one which she had kept since her early married days. Lilian was still warm and just alive when Ken found her and called the ambulance. She never really regained consciousness and died the following day, peacefully in Russell's Hall Hospital in her ninety-third year. Lilian would have been quite satisfied with the way she had departed this life as she had always been proud to boast that she had never needed the services of a Doctor and, after a full and happy life, she slipped quietly away.

Ron arranged her funeral service with Hartland's Funeral Directors of Hurst Hill, and Lilian was cremated at Lower Gornal and her ashes scattered where those of her husband had been years before.

In September, Diane took up a new position in Ashton-Saint-Peter, Dunstable where, as well as her normal teaching duties, she was responsible for the music taught in the school, and for playing the piano for assemblies and school concerts. She and Daniel had aquired a new dog as the old one (Charlie), had died. The new one was a pedigree Bearded Collie and they chose to call it 'Purdey'.

Ron had a particular friend who shared his interest in antiques and, like Ron was something of a collector. Ray Hindmarsh had worked as Sales Director for Brierley Hill Glass, and would often drop round to 'Rivoli' for a visit, nearly always managing to choose a day when Vi had been baking. He enjoyed her cakes and, when he and Ron went on one of their trips to an antique fair, would often bring her a small piece of cut-glass as a 'thank-you' for her hospitality.

In November 1987 Ray died and Ron had lost yet another of his close friends and companions. Ray was only sixty-three years old when he died and Ron fondly remembered the sight of his brown trilby hat and the familiar smell of his briar pipe which were his trademarks, and missed his quiet companionship as they had travelled around the countryside on their expeditions.

At the start of 1989, Ron and Vi took delivery of a new car and they decided to give it a good run by visiting their daughter and spend a few days with her. They set out on a Wednesday morning, calling in at Milton Keynes Shopping Centre to break their journey and to give Vi a chance to do some shopping. The park was fairly full, and they drove slowly around trying to find an empty space. Eventually Ron saw a car backing out of a parking space and as soon as the car had left it, he drove straight in with the rain pouring down. They got out of the car and hurried in to the Centre, spending an hour or so looking round before returning to the car. When they arrived back at their vehicle, Ron saw a notice attached to his windscreen informing them that they had parked in a restricted area and were fined £20. The space was reserved for disabled drivers, a fact which they had both missed in their haste to park in the pouring rain.

They continued their journey and enjoyed their visit with Diane and Daniel, but their troubles were far from over. On returning home on Sunday 22nd January, Vi noticed, as they turned into the drive, that all the curtains both upstairs and downstairs were drawn and commented that she was sure she had not left them like that. As they entered the house they knew something was seriously wrong, the house was freezing cold, the central heating wasn't working, the rear doors were wide open as was the bathroom window. A quick look round confirmed their fears that they had been burgled and Ron immediately called the police who arrived very quickly.

Ron and Vi had to go from room to room to try to establish what items had been stolen. Cash and jewelry was missing from the main bedroom, eight oil paintings and Ron's Masonic regalia had been taken from the spare bedroom over the garage and water colours had been removed from the other two bedrooms. Some of these water colours had been left strewn on the bed in the fourth bedroom which Ron used as his studio and gallery. Pictures had been taken from the walls on the landing and down the stairs, and oil-paintings had been stolen from the lounge and dining room. Several paintings were still stacked against the wall in the verandah, obviously waiting to be loaded onto the getaway lorry which had been driven round to the back of the house. The vehicle had been driven through the gates at the side of the house which led to the nearby school and alongside the six foot high wire fencing which had been cut to allow the pictures to be passed through to someone waiting on the other side.

The police checked out the whole of the house and when they eventually left, gave Ron and Vi a device by which they could contact the Police Station directly if they were in trouble or if the thieves returned to collect the rest of their haul.

During the course of the discussion with the police, Ron told them about his parking ticket, saying that he'd had quite enough trouble over these last few days. He was told that he would have to pay the fine but that it wouldn't hurt to send a covering letter in mitigation for his error. This he did, explaining that it had been pouring with rain, he was a stranger to the area and had not realised that he had parked in a restricted space. He enclosed a cheque to cover the fine and also added the information about his burglary, hoping to attract the sympathy vote! It worked, and some time later his £20 was refunded in full!

The trauma and the temperature of the house on the evening of their return, left the pair in a state of numb shock. The heating had somehow got broken during the burglary and Ron now had to get that mended and re-establish the security of his home as quickly as possible. The total value of what had been taken amounted to £22,500. Ron eventually recouped this from his insurance, but it in no way made up for the loss of his precious art collection or the personal items which both he and Vi had prized. They both felt vulnerable for a long time afterwards, even when they had fitted security alarms and lights and replaced door and window locks all round the house.

During the next few months, the police took in various people to interview in connection with the theft. One of those questioned was an art dealer whom Ron had considered to be a friend and who had called on him at home on the Monday before the burglary. In the course of the conversation, Vi had said that she was taking delivery of a new car and said they would be away for a few days. The man was known to the police, as were some of his aquaintances, particularly one who went by the name of 'The Fox' and who had been to prison for similar offences in the past. His home was searched by the police but none of Ron and Vi's possessions were found there.

They heard nothing more about this until much later in the year, when late one evening they were returned home, from their usual Thursday night dance. As they opened the door, the phone was ringing. Ron was pleased and surprised to hear the voice of an old pal who had moved away from the Black Country and was living in Conway in North Wales. Eric was very excited and related to his old friend what he had seen on the television earlier that evening. At that time there was a programme called 'Police Five' which asked for the public's help in solving different crimes. At the end of each programme, recovered stolen goods were displayed in the hope that the owners would recognise them and so be able to reclaim their property. Eric had recognised four of the pictures displayed as being owned by Ron and he had taken down the contact number for him to ring. Ron contacted the police immediately, and arrangements were made for him to go to Leominster to identify the pictures. He and Vi went together and were able to confirm that the pictures were indeed part of their collection which had been stolen.

The police told them that they would have to wait and see if it was possible to charge the person in whose possession the pictures had been found. There was an obvious connection to the art dealer originally suspected and at first, the man caught in possession of the pictures, named him as the person who had sold them to him, but unfortunately, before the case came to court, he changed his story and denied even knowing the man and the case collapsed for lack of evidence.

Ron had already been paid by his insurance company for the loss of the pictures, so the recovered items were returned to the company, and they approached Ron inviting him to buy them back. Ron had noticed that, of the four pictures, two of the oil paintings and one of the water colours had been damaged and so agreed to buy them back at a reduced price. Mr Baker, the loss adjuster from the company said that he would take this offer back to the company and let him know their response. Two days later he phoned Ron to say that the company would agree to the figures discussed, on the proviso that the money was paid immediately. Ron readily agreed to this and told them that if the pictures were brought to his house next day, the money would be waiting for collection. So it was that the following day, just two days before Christmas, four of the stolen pictures were returned to their rightful owners and put back in their original places on the walls. To this day, these are the only ones of the twenty-two stolen pictures that have ever been recovered.

Ron restored the damaged pictures; a small watercolour by David Cox, 'A Farm Yard' in Bettys-y-Coed, North Wales, two of Patrick Nasmith's Scottish landscapes dated 1815 and another oil whose subjects were three Cavaliers sitting at a table, entitled 'Tales of Spain.'

This whole episode had quite unnerved Ron, and he now began discussions with his neighbours with a view to establishing a 'Neighbourhood Watch' scheme. A meeting was called, to be held in the nearby Cotwall End Primary School. It was well attended and it began with a representative from the Dudley Constabulary giving them advice on home security. Ron and his neighbour, Roy, were chosen as the co-ordinators for the area and all correspondence would go through them. 'Neighbourhood Watch' signs were obtained and displayed on lamp-posts all around the area and everyone resolved to be far more vigilant in order to protect themselves and their property.

His brother, Ken, died of throat cancer at the age of seventy four and Ron realised that he had been wise to abstain from the habit of smoking. He was losing so many of his family and friends as the years went by, that he resolved to pack as much into his life as he could.

On October 16th 1991, James Richard Baker was born to Carys and Tony in Wrexham Hospital. This was their first child born after Carys had suffered a series of miscarriages and they were now living in Stretton near Malpass in Cheshire. Ron and Vi were thrilled at the birth of their second grandson and relieved that he had been delivered safely after so much heartache and disappointment for his parents.

Ron had been working on a collection of watercolour drawings of buildings in the Sedgley Manor for many years and by October 1991, there were one hundred and twenty of them. He was now ready to produce his second book, entitled: 'Sedgley Manor - A Pictorial

History'. It contained some written information concerning the area, but the majority of the work consisted of the drawings which illustrated more clearly than any words could have done, how Sedgley had changed and developed.

Ron produced just five hundred signed, limited editions of his book and they were sold for fourteen pounds and ninety-five pence each. The book which had taken over twenty years to produce was sold within eight months and demand surpassed all expectation. Nine years later, copies were changing hands for a price in excess of sixty pounds, so keen were the local people to have this record of their history.

Ron wanted to think of something that he and Vi could do to celebrate the success of his second book. He thought long and hard about it and finally came to a decision. He had travelled quite broadly by this time - Africa, America, Mediterranean Countries and seen a fair bit of the British Isles too, but one place that appealed to him was Norway and its unique scenery. Vi agreed that after twenty years of working on his book this was just what he needed; a complete change from anything they had done before. Ron started in the New Year to look for something suitable and, after much research, came up with the solution; a fifteen day cruise on 'The Black Prince' to the Norwegian Fjords, leaving Tilbury Docks on 7th July, 1992.

On a bright summer's day, Vi and Ron boarded the ship and were shown to their cabin on the main deck. They began their journey, sailing up the North Sea for two days before reaching their first destination of Jondal where they went ashore. A coach was waiting for the party and drove them up into the hills where they saw their first snow of the holiday. The depth of the snow was, in parts, up to eight feet deep and much of it never melted. They continued next day to Gravdal in the Lofoten Islands and saw the famous 18th century Flakstad Church. The ship continued its journey next day to Honningsvag, where Ron and Vi had the opportunity to visit the North Cape, and there they stood at midnight, in bright sunshine watching the reindeer grazing all around them. It was an awe-inspiring experience. In front of them lay nothing but hundreds of miles of ocean and then ice between them and the North Pole.

It was cold now even though the sun shone through the ship's portholes into the cabins throughout the night and they found it difficult to adjust to new sleeping habits. The cruise took them even further north to Longyearben in Spitzbergen. The land and the high peaks which surrounded it were continually covered in snow and ice, beneath which were glaciers. Ron missed the sight of vegetation and he scanned

Two drawings from Norway cruise.

Tromso.

Spitzbergen.

the scenery as they went ashore. They wished that they had brought a few more woolly sweaters and gloves and began to wonder what the temperature must be like in winter as this was their summer period.

Spitzbergen means 'high pointed mountains' and here was the land of Polar Bear, Walrus, Whales and Seals, which were the main inhabitants of the area.

They sailed out of the bay and around some of the islands, passed a Russian mining village and on to the mighty Von Post Glacier. Their voyage took them then to the most awe inspiring sight Ron had ever experienced at the city of Tromso. It was the oldest city in northern Norway and often referred to as the 'gateway to the Arctic.' Here Ron gazed on the exquisite ultra-modern architecture of the 'Arctic Cathedral' and, after inspecting its interior, took a trip to the summit of nearby Mount Storsteinen to view the city laid out beneath them in its impressive surroundings. Ron stored these images, as he had grown used to doing, to commit them to paper at his leisure, later.

The next stage of the cruise was equally inspiring, as they entered the Hellesylt and Geirange Fjord. Their passage was bordered on either side with the sights of glorious waterfalls, tiny farms perched on the rocky hillsides, and narrow, winding mountain roads weaving their way between them. Few of the passengers spoke as they took in the views around them and were reluctant to break the spell of the magical images which surrounded them. The ship took them to the head of the Fjord where a coach awaited them to transport the party up the twisting Strynefjell road, negotiating nineteen stomach churning, hair-pin bends before crossing the Jolbrua Bridge and on to the thundering Buldrefossen Waterfall. They returned via Geiraner Village where they stopped to look down on the harbour beneath. From their position, Ron felt like a bird floating in the sky looking down upon the earth below and was pleased that he had thought of this exact holiday as a way of recharging his batteries and renewing his artistic spirits. It had given him so many new ideas that he began to put into practice.

As usual, Ron had tucked his sketch pad into his luggage, and, as the ship approached each harbour or bay, he could be seen sitting in the window of the ship's lounge, where it was nice and warm, recording the views. Passengers had grown accustomed to seeing Ron in this position and many of them had passed by and commented on his work.

"I wish I could do that, it's much better than taking photographs," was the general concensus of those who saw his drawings.

Towards the end of the cruise, the Entertainments Officer approached Ron and asked if he would be agreeable to allowing them to use some of the drawings for a novel way of making money for a couple of charities. Ron, naturally, was pleased and delighted at the suggestion and readily agreed. The suggestion was for Ron to select eight of his drawings and the officer would print off sets of these as momentos for the other passengers to purchase. Each set was priced at ten pounds and all the proceeds were to be divided between the Life Boat Association, the Sailor's Association and Cancer Research. The Captain announced the sale once the sets were prepared and they were snapped up by the passengers. They were pleased with their novel momento, Ron was happy to see his efforts appreciated, and the various charities benefitted to the tune of nearly four-hundred pounds.

Ron and Vi still had the original drawings to remind them of their happy time on board ship, as well as a Diploma, signed by the Norwegian ship's Captain, presented by the Fred Olsen line to commemorate their crossing the Arctic circle.

On Sunday 19th July they sailed into Bergen harbour and disembarked for their last look around a Norwegian town, with its wooden buildings and harbour shops. They returned to the ship with their head full of wonderful sights and memories and sailed slowly back home.

Ron and Vi were happy to see that Diane had at last met a new man after her unhappy break from Andy almost eight years previously. Diane told them that she and Charles Mendes had decided to marry. Ron and Vi went to look after Daniel for the time his mother was away on her honeymoon, in February 1993.

Their one regret was that, as Charles had been offered a job in America, the marriage would mean that Diane and Daniel would be much farther away.

Soon after Diane and Charles had returned from their honeymoon in Antigua, they packed up and moved across the Atlantic to their new home in Princetown, New Jersey. In May of that same year Ron and Vi paid them a visit and were delighted to see how well they had settled into their new life.

This was proving to be a year of new beginnings for all the family as, in July, Ron and Vi went to see Tony receive his Master's Degree from The University of Science and Technology in Manchester. A month later Tony started a new job as the Practice Manager of Liverpool City Architects Department. He was later promoted to Head of Architecture within the department, a position he held for several years, before moving to work for a private firm which specialised in developing health-care homes.

On March 19th 1995, Ron and Vi were delighted to receive the news that Diane had given birth to a little girl. Charlotte Francesca Mendes was born in America, but was brought, with her brother and parents to be christened at Sedgley Parish Church on July 16th of that same year.

The following year, Tony and Carys added another granddaughter to the Baker family, with the birth of their baby, Emma on 2nd April 1996.

Ron was approaching two important milestones in his life. On 18th November 1998, he would be eighty years old, and on 26th December 1997, he and Vi would celebrate their Golden Wedding. He fully intended that the whole family would mark the occasions in memorable fashion and planned to take them all on a Caribbean Cruise.

He and his wife, with Tony, Carys, James and Emma flew from Birmingham to Newark in the States, where they joined Diane, Charles, and Charlotte at their home in Princetown.

The contingent from England made themselves comfortable in Diane's beautiful large home for a few days while they adjusted to the five hour time difference.

Ron had really decided to do things in style, and on Saturday, 23rd May, the morning of their departure, a large white stretch limousine glided up to the front door to transport the happy gang to the airport for the first stage of their holiday.

At Newark Airport the family group boarded a plane for the flight to Puerto Rico and on landing, they travelled by taxis to the harbour at San Juan where they boarded their cruise ship - the M.S. Norwegian Sea, a 42,000 ton vessel with the capacity to carry over fifteen hundred passengers and more than six hundred crew on its ten decks. They found their cabins which were situated close to each other along the promenade deck across which they could look out over the sea.

When they had settled into their respective cabins, the family reassembled and made their way to the dining area for their first meal on board ship. To accommodate the children, Ron had arranged for them to be in the first sitting for meals, and a large round table was set for the use of the family, who happily took their places together. The table was set with two more places and a young couple from West Virginia was allocated to these seats and they very soon made everyone's aquaintance and got on well with all the Baker 'Clan,' - especially the grandchildren. In fact the children were favourites with many of those on board, not least of all their head waiter, a man from Trinidad, who took it upon himself to pander to their every whim and request, and became quite a father-figure to the young ones, adding in no small measure to the enjoyment of their trip.

After dinner on the first night, the family joined in with the entertainment arranged for the evening, before retiring to their cabins for the night, knowing that there was much to look forward to in successive days.

True enough, next day, Sunday saw the ship call in at the port of Santa Domingo in the Dominican Republic, on Monday they cruised the southern Caribbean and on Tuesday they arrived at St. Lucia. Here the family took a boat trip on a small catamaran to a secluded sandy bay, where they could swim and sun-bathe before visiting a rain forest arboretum. Here they were caught in a tropical rainstorm and got soaked to the skin. Not to be put off, they continued their exploration of the island, as the rains had stopped, and took a ride in a delapidated old taxi up a narrow mountain pass towards the summit of the smoking volcanic crater. They were steaming as much as their surroundings as they approached the peak and had quite dried off by the time they climbed out of the taxi. The smell was atrocious with the stench of sulphur fumes and very soon the family were surrounded by young native boys keen to sell their wares to the tourists. They were shrewd and soon 'sussed' that Ron was the leader of his little party, directing their attention to him and attempting to sell him some of their beaded necklaces.

"You from England?" one asked.

When Ron confirmed his assumption, the youngster chatted on, "English people very rich," he said.

Ron looked down at the little chap, who by that time had been joined by several other boys, he shook his head despondantly and kept a solemn expression on his face while he began his tale.

"No, I'm not rich, I'm very poor," he said shaking his head sadly to give his words effect. "When I buy a loaf of bread I have to cut off a slice and go round to someone in the next street who is better off than me and ask for some butter to spread on it. They know how poor I am and they will give me some butter for my bread. I then go round to the next street, where they are richer, and knock on a door there to ask for some jam to spread on my bread and they will give me some because they know how poor I am too. Then I can eat my slice of jam and bread." The lads were looking up into Ron's face, with their huge dark eyes, as he told his woeful tale, and he continued, "So you see not all English people are rich."

Ron and the family were making their way back into the taxi by the time the boys realised he had been having them on and not one bead had been sold. His own grandchildren chuckled and Vi nudged him,

"Ronnie, you are the end!" she said as they made their way back to their large luxury liner.

Charles had informed the crew of his wife's parent's anniversary, and one evening, at dinner, a group of the waiters came towards their table. One of the waiters was carrying a cake on his head. The cake, with candles burning on top of it, was ceremoniously placed in front of the couple. The waiters then gathered around and began to serenade them with Caribbean songs and music, much to their delight. Everyone on board joined in with the spirit of the evening and it turned into a very special night.

On Wednesday the ship docked again, this time in the small harbour of St. Johns in Antigua. By now the temperature was rising and Ron had to acquire a large peaked cap to protect his fair skin. Antigua is one of the largest of the British Leeward Islands and possesses a beautiful cathedral dedicated to St John the Divine, which the family visited during their day ashore.

The next day they arrived at Philipsburg, St Maarten (the north side of the island is French and referred to as St Martin, the south side is Dutch and has the Dutch spelling to its name.) The party went ashore and had a marvellous trip on a glass-bottomed boat, viewing the fantastic array of colourful fish that inhabited those waters, in and around the reef.

That day was special for another reason too, as they were invited up onto the bridge while the ship was sailing out of the harbour, and in the evening the Captain held a cocktail party when everyone had the opportunity to meet him and the ship's officers. Vi and Ron, along with four other couples were then invited to join the captain, for dinner in his private dining room which was next to the bridge. They were treated royally, and after a splendid meal were escorted to the main theatre for the evening's entertainment. Each couple was given a group photograph and an embossed menu as momentos of their evening. Ron and his family were given front seats near the stage as the captain had been informed of the celebratory nature of this cruise for Vi and Ron. Drinks were laid on for them to toast their Golden Wedding anniversary. As the evening progressed Ron was drawn up onto the stage by one of the beautiful female singers. She sat him on a chair and then positioned herself on his lap while she sang her song, seductively to him. Ron was somewhat bemused by this, and didn't realise that her short skirt rose even higher as she sat on his knee to sing. She stroked his face and hair as she sang and he realised afterwards that he had been stroking her bare thigh in full view of the whole audience including his wife, children and grandchildren. They took it in good part, however, and many of the male passengers met Ron in the days that followed to comment on what a lucky chap he was to have had such a privelege!

The cruise continued to St Thomas in the Virgin Islands and then they returned to their starting point of Puerto Rico, where they now disembarked after bidding farewell to the waiters and cabin staff.

Ron and his family then took a taxi from the dockside to the Hilton Hotel in San Juan for the next stage of their holiday together. Here they stayed for a few days, enjoying the facilities of the hotel, bathing in one of the swimming pools or in the private lagoon nearby, or looking around the city and its surroundings. Eventually, very reluctantly, they had to pack up and return to the airport for their flight back to Newark, to Diane and Charles' home. They remained there for a few more days before another flight took them back to Birmingham and then a car ride back to Sedgley. They all had some splendid memories to look back on and knew that it was very unlikely that they would be repeating this experience all together again.

Ron and Vi's actual special anniversary date was in December and the celebrations continued a little longer with another holiday the following summer, this time just with Diane, Charles and Charlotte to Williamsburge. They arranged to meet up with the couple who had shared their table on the previous trip, at their home and, after renewing their aquaintance met their family and friends and were able to add to their growing list of friends abroad.

Ron and Vi continued to pay regular visits to their daughter in America, crossing the Atlantic at least twice a year to spend time with Diane, her husband and Charlotte, their adorable little daughter. Daniel, as he grew older, yearned for the 'old country' and returned to live and work in the south of England near his father.

They often took the road north to Tony's home and enjoyed the company of his children when they baby-sat to allow the busy parents the odd night off. Just as they delighted in seeing the achievements of Tony and Diane, Ron and Vi now had the satisfaction of watching the progress of their grandchildren too.

Towards the end of the twentieth century they both realised that they were approaching their eighties and were quite prepared to drop everything if their son asked them to go up to Cheshire for a couple of days. Both Tony and Carys worked long hours and at times knew that neither of them could be home to greet their two children when they returned from school, it was then that the willing grandparents would stand in. They knew that the children were growing up fast and wanted to spend as much time with them as possible, and make the most of the time they had with them.

The ritual was always the same when they arrived at the front door. Emma and James would greet them with hugs and kisses and then James would lug their suitcase up to their bedroom. The youngsters always had a lot to tell Ron and Vi and would begin their tales as soon as they stepped in the door. James would be filling his grandparents in on his latest exploits at the same time as little Emma was pulling at her grandfather's sleeve and asking for him to play their favourite game of 'Hide and Seek'. "Ronnie, Ronnie" she would twitter at him until he succumbed and they would begin their fun together while James would be left to tell Vi about his own news.

Tony and Carys lived in a large country house set in about three acres of gardens with a number of sturdy trees and a paddock for the lucky children to play in. Tony had built a tree-house for his son and his friends to play in and even to sleep in if the weather permitted. It was an idyllic place for the youngsters to grow up in, with lots of rooms and places for them to run and play and for Emma to hide in her games with her grandad, 'Ronnie.'

When they could sit down for a few minutes with a cup of tea, Ron had some good memories to look back on and enjoyed regailing his grandchildren with stories of his exploits when he was their age. He had drawn pictures of many of the places he had known as a child, so could illustrate his tales for them. They particularly liked to hear stories of 'Grandad's' naughty little escapades and Ron was quite happy to oblige.

One story concerned The Toll House on the Sedgley road which in the 20's, could be reached by following the village brook which ran under the main road and came out in the back garden of the house itself. Ron, and his childhood friends, would scramble under the tunnel until they could clamber out at the other end where they emerged in the garden. They would stop just before they reached the opening to listen carefully in case anyone from the house was in their garden. If all was quiet, the boys would climb up the bank and crawl gingerly to their intended destination which, depending on the time of year, was either the apple trees or the rhubarb patch. Pockets were filled and jumpers were stuffed with the produce which the lads had 'scrumped' and they would then carefully retrace their steps taking the fruit home to be devoured at their leisure. A particular favourite was the thin, tender, pink sticks of young rhubarb. The boys would make a cone out of paper and fill it with sugar. The stick of rhubarb was then dipped into the sugar and munched until all the sugar was sucked off it and the rhubarb was then plunged back into the sugar again. This continued until either all the sugar had been used up or the stick of rhubarb was devoured.

The lads usually got away with their little tricks, but occasionally they were not so alert and the owner, Mrs Hutchinson would be wise to them and lie in wait as they crept out of the tunnel. She would then come out from her hiding place behind a bush, wielding a broom or a mop threatening the youngsters and yelling "I'll catch you little vandals if it's the last thing I do." Luckily for the lads, Mrs Hutchinson was a very old lady and could not move as fast as they could, so she never fulfilled her prophecy.

James and Emma would chortle with glee at the thought of their prim and proper grandfather being mischievous and they too could entertain their grandparents in return. James grew up with a natural knack for acting and would wake Vi and Ron up at some ungodly hour when they were staying up in Cheshire with the family. They would then be treated to a scene from his latest play or a sample of his mimicry of some charactor or other, and the little one would join in with an offering of her own to amuse them.

Ron could explain how times had changed and recall how theatres used to be run in the days before microphones and amplifying equipment. He told James about a friend of his from Sedgley who ran the Clifton Cinema from 1946 onwards, but who had been in the theatre for many years before that. Ron had made Fred Pitt a dress-suit and had done the measuring and fitting in his office there. While Ron worked, Fred related tales of 'the old days' when he had started out. On one occasion, when he was being interviewed for a job, the proprietor of the theatre took Fred up onto the stage and then he himself marched off down the aisle of the theatre and out through the front door after giving the bemused man the signal to begin his audition piece. The owner gave Fred a job on the strength of having heard every word of what he had said and sung out on the pavement. In those days every member of the audience expected to hear the performance clearly from all over the theatre and the owner was keen to ensure that they would get their money's worth!

Fred was an artist too, and although not in the same way as himself, Ron was quick to acknowledge his talents. Ron recalled for his grandchildren, how Fred's office was stacked with wonderful models including his speciality of sailing ships in full rig, mounted in narrow-necked bottles. The youngsters were keen to discover how this feat could be accomplished, and Ron did his best to explain the clever technique.

The morning ritual at Tony's home began rather sooner than Ron would have liked, as, since his retirement, he had not been an early riser, often painting late into the early hours of the morning and then staying in bed until almost midday. The children, however had other ideas and wanted to make the most of their time with Ron and Vi. At first light, a knock would be heard on the bedroom door and at the sound of "Come in," Emma's eager little face would appear and she would climb into the bed between her grandparents. It wouldn't be long before her brother put in an appearance and attempt to snuggle in the bed too. Ron would find himself holding on to the bedclothes in an effort to stop himself from falling out and landing on the floor. It was just when he had almost given up the struggle that James would decide to entertain them all with one of his 'party-pieces'. His actions and voice variations were a credit to his training at the 'Stagecoach' school he attended each Saturday, for lessons in drama, dance and elocution.

The children would be sent back to their rooms when their father brought in a tray of tea and biscuits for his parents and then Tony and Carys would leave for their respective places of work while Ron and Vi supervised the children's day and looked after the family pets.

Ron and Vi were very aware that their grandchildren's ideas about money were very different to what theirs had been at the same age and had always put away one pound a week for each of them. No matter how long it was between visits, they always went furnished with the relevant number of pound coins for each child and you can be sure that the children had kept a careful tally for every week that passed between visits. On one occasion, when four weeks had elapsed, Vi went with the eight pounds for James and Emma. Emma was not at home when they arrived and Vi gave James the coins for himself and his little sister. She was astonished to see, a little while later, the boy putting the money into piles. However, one pile was considerably taller than the other and James was studying the money with a look of contemplation. "I don't think that's quite right," she said to her grandson. One pile held six coins, the other two!

"Oh yes, I think so," said the wily lad, "Emma's only four and I'm nine so I should have more than her."

Vi retrieved four pounds." I think I'll give this to Emma myself," she said, and went to tell Ron of James' financial logic.

They chuckled together and recalled how tight money had been for both of them when they had been growing up in the 'twenties.'

They told the children the story that evening of Ron's annual Sunday-school treat, when he would come away with the odd ha'penny or two, if he was very lucky.

The Sunday school party would be held in a field opposite West Coseley school and close to the old Parish Hall near to what was originally West Coseley Bull-Ring. The day chosen would be a Saturday during the summer holidays, and the children would assemble in the Parish Hall to be given a brown paper bag containing their tea. A large buttered roll, a sticky iced bun, a piece of fruit and a handful of assorted boiled fruit sweets made up each allocation and the children tucked into the contents before being ushered into the field for their organised games and sports. The winners of each event would be awarded a shiny silver thre'penny bit as their prize, but they all looked forward to the climax of the afternoon when the curate would appear. He would be carrying a bag containing five shilling's worth of ha'pennies. The children had to form a circle and when they were all in place, the Vicar would dip his hand into the bag and throw a handful of the coins into the middle of the circle. The children then made a mad scramble to pick up as many of them as they could and, this time, the smaller children had the advantage. When the Vicar thought that all the coins had been found, the circle was reformed and the same thing was repeated until he had used up all one hundred and twenty of the ha'penny pieces.

All the children would then break off into groups to make their way home and compare notes about their 'winnings.' Ron remembered one occasion when Harry Cartwright, a friend of his had managed to collect the grand total of thirteen coins - which amounted to sixpence ha'penny. "I can go to the cinema six times and buy two giant gob-stoppers with this." Harry told his envious friends.

James wanted to know what 'sixpence ha'penny' meant in present day money and his Grandparents explained, remembering the hardships which they had endured at his age.

Ron has achieved much in his life despite the set-backs which had thwarted his early attempts at self-advancement. He made a good living from his profession and has left behind, for his own children and the people of Sedgley, a permanent record of what their village was like during the twentieth century. The legacy which he has left for this part of the Black Country is invaluable as so many of the buildings, which he drew over the years, have now been demolished and replaced. His accurate and intricate, black ink drawings are, in many cases, all that are left to remind people of what this area was like.

But the Black Country is more than mere buildings. It is a miscellany of stalwart people, like Ron and his wife, who have been confronted from time to time with problems, hardship and heart-ache, and overcome it all. The buildings may change, the scenery may change, some occupations most certainly have completely disappeared but the character of the folk remains the same.